Peta Mathias

A COOK'S TOUR OF NEW ZEALAND

Peta Mathias

A COOK'S TOUR OF NEW ZEALAND

Photography Laurence Belcher

VIKING
An imprint of PENGUIN BOOKS

INTRODUCTION

Food professionals are lucky to be part of the oldest profession on earth — the making of good food and wine.

THE first thing we do when we enter this world, after screaming our heads off in fright, is eat. Babies are born with only one innate taste preference – sweetness – and as the mother's milk is sweet rather than bitter, the baby knows it is safe to drink. From then on, we never stop eating or thinking about food, and we also never stop talking. So producing food, cooking and eating become another form of communicating, if you like, a 'mother tongue'. Our food mother tongue in New Zealand is all about meat, vegetables, fruit, fish and dairy products.

I feel I'm so lucky to be involved with food and wine because both things make you feel good and are the best way for anybody to express welcome, affection and respect for friends and colleagues.

New Zealand food and cooking have moved from being the embarrassing cousin to the glamorous aunt in the space of half a generation. We still love our meat pies, fish and chips, roast dinners and beer, but despite being an island – separated from the rest of the world by oceans of delicious fish and seafood – we have finally made a huge effort to bring the outside world in. New Zealanders have one of the most adventurous national palates I know of – we will try anything, and because we have such good growing conditions we understand and respect the meaning of the word 'flavour'. It's hard to impress us when we travel.

We love the land, have a pride in craftsmanship and a strong sense of integrity. Think about the Pacific Rose apple. We invented this apple – one of the most delicious in the world. We care about taste in New Zealand, and we want to preserve the fabulous sensation of that first bite as the sweet juice runs down the chin and the crunchiness is just right.

The privilege of writing and broadcasting about food for the last ten years in New Zealand means that I know first-hand what's going on in the local food industry and, better still, what the people are like who are producing the food. I know that our southern clams are harvested by hand; Speights beer is still made from spring water in traditional copper vessels; and that Lisa's hummus was started in a small kitchen by a woman on a family benefit. Her initial investment was $75 for a sack of chickpeas – the company now turns over millions.

I know about New Zealand Hothouse Tomatoes – they don't use herbicides, instead they use insects for pest control and bees to pollinate the flowers. They are the largest and most technically advanced hothouse facility in the southern hemisphere. And avocado oil – how incredible is that story? We are the first people in the world to produce avocado oil for consumption. I know about our olive oil – all virgin, cold pressings – fruity, peppery, slightly bitter and often lemony. There's still a lot to learn but if New Zealand olive oil progresses the way our wine industry has, I'm not too worried about oil.

New Zealand is not trapped in the grip of tradition. We're inventive, we don't like rules and we always try to think outside the square. In 1984 New Zealand farmers were shorn of government subsidies and, through sheer skill and hard work, have made their farms thrive. New uses of technology, cost cutting, efficiency gains and economies of scale have all helped. So has the development of niche products like kiwifruit, merino wool, clove- or chicory-fed lamb, wine and even animal embryos. New Zealand farmers are among the least subsidised and the most productive in the world. New Zealand food producers describe the secrets of their success as follows: decide what your principles are and never compromise them, treat others as you would like to be treated and operate with integrity.

The big trend in food today is that the privileged world now lives to eat, rather than eats to live. People are living longer, are more affluent and are more frequently eating for pleasure and demanding upmarket, sophisticated products – resulting in the creation of lots of niche markets. People want the ultimate experience – they want to die with the memories of the great meals they have eaten. Who would have thought that boring old salt would become a designer product? We of course have our own sea salt made by Grassmere. In a tasting at *Cuisine* magazine, it came out on top against international salts.

Consumers also want to know exactly what they are eating and what's in it. They want it to be safe, to promote long life and health, and not harm the environment. But most of all, what New Zealanders want is taste and this is what they get, as well as food that is good for you.

The Slow Food movement is starting to catch on in New Zealand. It is about eating good food slowly, enjoying it, while laughing and talking with your family and friends. Gastronomes and food enthusiasts are sensitive to utilising local cuisines, animal breeds and vegetable species. Slow Food works to counter the degrading effects of industrial and fast-food culture that are endeavouring to standardise taste. By eating fast food that is high in fat and sugar, we are not only eating rubbish, we are being disrespectful of what it means to be a New Zealander and to be unique.

The message is clear – eat seasonal and buy local. Local growers are our life-blood, and if we don't support them, agri-food will take over and we'll be eating hormone-poisoned beef before we know it. I challenge you to deliberately go forth and stuff yourselves with as much fresh, nutritious food made with love as you can. If we lose the myriad tastes of regional New Zealand produce and don't eat food at its optimal ripeness, then we lose the spectacular food culture we inherited.

Bon appetit.

Peta Mathias, July 2005
www.petamathias.com

AÏOLI This fabulous glistening sauce from Venus is the new mayonnaise, and has replaced our salad dressings of old. Tui Flower, the doyenne of New Zealand cooking whose method instructions always started with 'Do this', told us many years ago that to make a salad dressing we must mix together condensed milk, malt vinegar, English mustard, sugar, salt and pepper. To make a dressing that keeps well, we were told to boil together eggs, sugar, flour, water, malt vinegar, mustard, salt and pepper. Tui also had an interesting recipe that combined boiled dressing with sour milk.

Then, in the 1970s, we travelled and were so entranced with what we saw that we brought the food ideas home. What the French had been making for centuries was a new and miraculous thing to us. In the old days only Italian, Greek and Chinese immigrants ate garlic; by the 1980s we were shoving it into our roast lamb and grinding it on to innocent lumps of bread, and by the 1990s we were whipping it into home-made olive-oil mayonnaise and prancing off to dinner parties with a bowl of it surrounded by fresh vegetables. 'It's aïoli, darling,' we said. 'We learnt it in the south of France when we were picking grapes.'

You can fold all sorts of scrumptious things into basic aïoli, such as chopped sun-dried tomatoes, roasted garlic instead of fresh garlic, diced beetroot, saffron, smoked paprika, or chopped preserved limes. In France it is eaten as 'grande aïoli', wherein the mayonnaise is placed in the centre of a huge platter surrounded by boiled vegetables served at room temperature such as baby artichokes, potatoes, fennel, carrots, green beans and asparagus, along with salt cod, snails, baby octopus, langoustines, olives, hard-boiled eggs and vine tomatoes.

Aïoli

3 CLOVES GARLIC, CHOPPED

1/2 TEASPOON SEA SALT

2 EGG YOLKS

1 TEASPOON DIJON MUSTARD

500ML EXTRA VIRGIN OLIVE OIL
OR 250ML OLIVE OIL AND 250ML
VEGETABLE OIL

LEMON JUICE

1. Mash the garlic and sea salt together with a mortar and pestle.

2. Stir in the egg yolks and mustard with the pestle, then gradually add the oil drop by drop.

3. When half the oil is in, add a little lemon juice and warm water and continue adding oil in a thin stream, stirring with the pestle until all is incorporated. Aïoli can also be made with an electric beater or food processor. You may add more salt or lemon juice to taste.

makes about 2 cups

Note: If the aïoli curdles, throw in an ice cube and beat like mad. If that doesn't work, take a clean bowl and crack an egg yolk into it. With a hand beater, gradually add in the turned mayonnaise.

APHRODISIAC

There is no such thing, which is a pity as New Zealanders need all the help they can get. We are probably the least sexy people in the world after Asian businessmen, Finnish poets and Bolivian politicians. People have talked of the powers of truffles, paua, oysters, crabs, crab-apples, skink (a reptile), the blood of a snake and its still beating heart, and a variety of endangered animals. Some people believe the boundless enthusiasm for aphrodisiacs through the ages ultimately represents mankind's search for life's essence, for a divine substance that, like gods and goddesses, has the power to beget and prolong life and that, like the foods those gods eat, will provide ecstasy, energy and immortality. The belief that some foods are aphrodisiacs is irrational, metaphysical and arbitrary, like sacred or forbidden foods, vegetarianism and allergies. Very few humans suffer from genuine food allergies, and there is not one skerrick of scientific proof that any food enhances sexual arousal or performance. The belief that certain foods are magical or linked to sexuality is ancient and happens in cultures of every level of sophistication. The only possible explanation for these beliefs is that they make one feel part of a group, give one identity, mark one's position in society and permit one to make outrageous culinary demands in restaurants. I don't agree with chefs who pander to this irrational neuroticism. A chef spends hours composing and testing a balanced menu for diners and it is extremely impolite to ask for changes to satisfy your ego.

In the *Kama Sutra* it suggests you crush sweet potatoes in cow's milk, together with swayamgupta seeds, sugar, honey and clarified butter, and use it to make biscuits with wheat flour. By constantly eating these biscuits, one's sperm acquires such force that it is possible to sleep with thousands of women, who, in the end, will ask for pity … Ahem.

However, I would say, just as you can tell what a man is like in bed by the way he dances, you can make similar deductions by the way he eats asparagus. The only connection between food and sex I can think of is that they are both very sensual experiences. You only have to break a fig open to get a sexual message. Could anyone miss the metaphor of an oyster? The truth is all food is aphrodisiac; all food cooked for a lover is sensual. Food has the power to transport you with happiness and love, and we all know that eating and dancing lead to sex.

APPLES

The apple is the symbol of temptation. When Adam and Eve tasted the forbidden fruit of the tree of knowledge of good and evil, it was their downfall. How times have changed! Now an apple's only purpose in life is to be eaten. The original apples in the garden of Eden were tiny, sour little things, a bit like crab apples, consisting mostly of core and very little flesh. Subsequent breeding and grafting have persuaded them, against their natural inclination, to grow a lot more flesh. In New Zealand we love apples so much we invent new ones to keep ourselves happy. New apple varieties such as Braeburn, Royal Gala and Pacific Rose have been introduced to the national and international markets during the past 20 years and now represent over 75 per cent of export sales. Pacific Rose is one of a series of apples: Pacific Rose was the first, then came Pacific Beauty and then Pacific Queen. Pacific Rose is now the most

A

popular eating apple in New Zealand; the epitome of the *Sleeping Beauty* story, it is rose-pink and has a gorgeous round shape. This apple is the art piece of the apple world, created as much for its aesthetic appeal as its flavour, its ability to keep and its crunch when bitten.

Money does grow on trees in New Zealand – apple trees. Picking starts around Valentine's Day every year and by the time it has finished somewhere near the end of April, 19 million cartons of apples have been dispatched to the four corners of the earth. This amounts to $339 million worth of apples to 66 countries. Hawke's Bay is New Zealand's main apple-growing region, and the principal varieties are Braeburn, Royal Gala, Pacific Rose, Fuji, Cox's Orange, Granny Smith and Pink Lady. The Red Delicious apple I grew up with is a variety that has almost disappeared from New Zealand apple orchards. A recent shining light for New Zealand is the Jazz variety, which in its first two years of sales has been well received by markets. Napier/Hastings has been dubbed New Zealand's fruit bowl. The soil is some of the richest in the country and the hot, dry Mediterranean climate makes the Hawke's Bay a natural for pastoral farming. The locals say there's no such thing as a bad apple in their neck of the woods. Each variety has a definite harvesting season of four weeks, and all the fruit of that variety has to be picked during that period. The Cox's Oranges ripen first, then come the Galas, and by late March it's the turn of the Braeburns, then the Fujis and Granny Smiths.

Even though we throw our most perfect apples at every overseas market we can think of, we still manage to save a few for ourselves. They are second grade, but still smashing. The thing I most long for when travelling is a hard, crisp, sweet New Zealand apple. I spent many gloomy winters in Paris longing for the light of a New Zealand summer, the frenzied taste of apple sugar, of acid, of eyes watering, of teeth sharp and shining. An apple will taste awful if it has been stored for too long, especially when refrigerated – so to enjoy the perfect apple eat one in season

Cheese and apple gougères

250ML (1 CUP) WATER
100G BUTTER, CHOPPED
1/2 TEASPOON SALT
130G FLOUR
4 SMALL EGGS
100G GRUYÈRE CHEESE, FINELY DICED
100G TART APPLE, FINELY DICED
PINCH FRESHLY GROUND BLACK PEPPER OR CAYENNE
PINCH FRESHLY GRATED NUTMEG
STAMS GUSTO APPLE SYRUP FOR DRIZZLING

1. Preheat the oven to 220°C. In a medium-sized saucepan bring the water, butter and salt to the boil.

2. When the water has boiled and the butter melted, remove the saucepan from the heat and immediately add all the flour. Beat enthusiastically with a wooden spoon until the paste is smooth and pulls away from the saucepan to form a ball.

3. Put the saucepan back on a low heat and continue beating for five minutes to dry the paste out.

4. Remove pan from heat and beat in the eggs, one by one, incorporating each egg thoroughly before moving onto the next one. The dough should be shiny and just able to drop from the spoon.

5. Stir in the diced cheese, diced apple, black pepper or cayenne and nutmeg.

6. Grease a baking sheet or cover with baking paper and drop the gougères onto it with a teaspoon so that they look like little rock cakes. Leave plenty of room for them to puff out.

7. Bake gougères for 10 minutes. Turn the oven down to 180°C, then bake for another 10 minutes or until golden and crisp.

8. Turn the oven off, open the door and let the gougères sit there for 5 minutes to dry out. Drizzle apple syrup over them or have a bowl of apple syrup for dipping, and serve immediately.

makes about 30 gougères

A

when ripe and bursting with sweetness. They're good for you too. Scientific research into the cancer-beating qualities of apples has proved the old adage 'an apple a day keeps the doctor away', and it's also true that it is the skin that matters. The antioxidant in apple peel is strong enough to stop cancer cells growing, and apparently Granny Smith is one of the best.

Apples have always been paired with fatty meats and fish, such as pork and herrings. They are also good sautéed with black pudding. From apples you can make your own apple syrup. The best brand to buy in New Zealand is Stams Gusto – divine drizzled over cheese fritters. You can also make apple-blossom water, apple butter, cider and calvados, and in the old days verjuice was sometimes made from apples.

STAMS GUSTO APPLE SYRUP

This is a groovy new product on the market, exploding with the taste and aroma of crunchy, juicy apples and the promise of sunshine. To make the syrup, Jill and Robert Stam have developed a careful process. The apples are washed, milled and pressed to capture the fresh apple juice, which is stored in large insulated holding tanks and allowed to settle. The resultant clear juice is gently heated in large closed vats, and the aroma-rich steam is captured to save the volatile oils. The process continues until the desired brix (sugar) level is reached, about 70 per cent. The captured aroma is added back in once the dark-red syrup is cool, and it is then bottled ready for delivery.

Gusto has an unbelievable 16.5kg of apples per 250ml bottle, comes in tart, sweet and organic, and is incredibly versatile. I first tasted it at a cocktail party, drizzled over deep-fried cheese balls and fell in love with it instantly. I became a social embarrassment over apple syrup. You can use it in place of sugar, caramel, golden syrup or maple syrup. Drizzle it on fried black pudding, ice-cream, sorbet, yoghurt, blue cheese, porridge, or French toast. Glaze ham on the bone with it or pour some over your fresh fruit and nuts in the morning with a squeeze of lime juice. Use it in citrus/olive oil cakes instead of honey or sugar. And stick it into Brazilian cocktails where sugar syrup is called for. Put some in a glass with sparkling water, a sprig of Vietnamese mint and a lemon wedge. Is it too obvious to mention roast pork? Stams Gusto website is: www.stams.co.nz.

CAMLA FARM APPLE JUICE

There she is, the lovely Annabel Graham, entirely spiffing in fitting jeans, blue cardie, dottie scarf tight around the neck and flowers in her buttonhole. She sports a BBC accent and a smile, and wears her dark hair cropped. Watching her process of extracting sunshine in the guise of juice from apples is a fascinating and heart-warming pastime. It's all very hands on. First you pluck your apples from the trees on her beautiful property – Braeburn, Granny Smith, Cox, Fiesta, Pacific Rose, Royal Gala and Fuji. All the juices are single variety with completely different tastes, so if you have a hankering for Pacific Rose juice, that's what you buy. No preservatives, no concentrate, no added sugar or water.

The milling is very traditional. Once the apples have been picked, within 24 hours they are chopped, wrapped in muslin and pressed between acacia boards, producing a pulp called 'cheese'. The juice that emerges is pasteurised on a low heat, which enables it to last for 18 months. A charmingly low-tech machine puts the tops on. Annabel is secretly experimenting with lots of other old and forgotten varieties like Golden Russet, Tyderman's Orange and Mother-in-law (which has a bitter taste). She and her husband Peter also grow cider apples like Kingston Black and Sweet Alfred to make their traditional still cider. Most people don't like still cider – they expect it to be sparkling. Annabel admits it's an acquired taste, but Peter loves it.

While all this is going on, the peacocks are performing their mating rituals. The males have dating zones, where they shimmer and shiver their fabulous multicoloured tails to attract the blasé peahens in their dowdy beige frocks. Talk about boring and talk about disinterested. How could you refuse a man making such an effort and putting on such a show-stopping display? Yet the girls act like they'd rather have a cup of tea any day. There are also ducks, chickens and guinea fowl wandering around in a bucolic haze.

If you're lucky enough to be invited into Annabel's wonderful big farmhouse kitchen, on the way you will walk past the curing shed where her salamis and prosciuttos, made from her own pigs, are hanging or lying in beds of salt. She gave me some to take home and it was fabulous – sweet and succulent with a lovely layer of fat. She also makes her own sausages and black puddings, and grows vegetables and fruit in her Italian-style country garden. The brick courtyard is divided into ordered but not obsessive herb gardens. The peacocks eat the veggies, but Annabel doesn't care. All this is competing with fragrant and blowsy delphiniums, poppies, granny's bonnets, lavender, undies on the line and apples on transverse vines. Around the side is an old tennis court surrounded by pale pink roses.

If you can't find Camla Farm Apple Juice in a shop near

Annabel Graham from the Dunsandel Store

you, you will just have to go to Annabel's store in Dunsandel, Canterbury.

DUNSANDEL STORE

Everything Annabel Graham touches, does well. She's one of these capable women who just have the knack. Four years ago she and Peter bought the 80-year-old Dunsandel store and restored it to its former glory of weatherboards, veranda, pitched roof and courtyard garden out back. The store was always the hub of the community where people bought basic food supplies, dropped off the dry cleaning, picked up the post and hung out for the latest gossip. You can still do all these things, but it's now also a café, restaurant and deli. The courtyard wooden tables are graced with bunches of voluptuous peonies, roses climb up the walls and plane trees grow alongside the herb garden, strawberry patch and hollyhocks.

The airy, country interior is very pretty, with rose-laden wooden tables, couches, wooden floors, logs stacked up on either side of the fireplace and a piano. On one side you can find basics like baking powder and washing-up liquid, and on the other side Canterbury products like olive oil and saffron. The restaurant food is particularly good and has gained a reputation all over Canterbury. Annabel calls it sophisticated home cooking. I ate the most glamorous *choucroute garni* (sauerkraut with potatoes and sausages) I'd ever eaten and then dived into the kitchen full of apple cakes and pies. The food reminded me of the sort you eat at Ballymaloe House in Cork, Ireland – fresh, good produce cooked simply but well. And sure enough, there in the steam was the Irish chef Sinead who had worked at Ballymaloe.

QUALITY TREE COMPANY

If you fancy some old-fashioned apples, you can buy your very own trees and grow them yourself. Linda Gardner propagates about 50 heritage varieties with poetic names like Egremont Russet, Lord Nelson, Black Prince, Fairbelle, Tydeman's Late Orange and Reinette de Thorn. Not only does Linda sell her trees, she will graft and save your favourite old tree on to vigorous rootstock. A lot of Linda's trees came from the orchard at Lincoln University and also from an elderly lady whose great-grandfather brought heritage apples out with him from England. Linda encourages buyers to plant a selection of apples that will provide different taste treats and early and late ripenings. She also suggests making the trees an integral part of the garden rather than hiding them away. Linda's website is: www.qtc.co.nz.

This is a meal in itself. It takes a long time to cook and a long time to eat, and once you've finished, your thoughts will surely turn to seduction.

6 LARGE GLOBE ARTICHOKES
6 CUPS FRESH BREADCRUMBS
1 HEAD GARLIC, PEELED
BUNCH OF PARSLEY
SEA SALT AND FRESHLY GROUND
BLACK PEPPER
EXTRA VIRGIN OLIVE OIL

1. Preheat the oven to 180°C. Chop the stalks off the artichokes close to the base so they can sit flat. Trim tips off the outer leaves with scissors so they look neat.

2. In a food processor, roughly blend the breadcrumbs, garlic, parsley, salt and pepper. You'll have to do it in several lots.

3. Stuff this mixture down in between as many leaves of the artichoke as possible. You won't be able to get to the inside ones. The artichoke will end up with its leaves sticking out, bursting with the stuffing.

4. Place the artichokes in a roasting tray. Drizzle them copiously with olive oil and bake for at least an hour or until tender, when a skewer can be easily passed through the base. Baste frequently with the oil.

5. To eat, arrange a large napkin or small tablecloth around yourself and have plenty of finger bowls. Eat the tender base of the leaves with the stuffing and keep pulling them off until you get to the centre. Discard the furry choke and get to the heart of the matter, which is the point of the whole exercise.

serves 6

ARTICHOKES

Artichokes are the edible, immature flowers of a cultivated thistle. They produce two crops a year, in spring and in autumn. You should buy them as fresh as possible with tightly closed leaves. If the leaves are open, they're too old and will be bitter rather than mild and nutty. Artichokes are rather sexy because they are best eaten with the fingers and you have to slowly undress them leaf by leaf until you have revealed the hidden, inner heart. It is said of a person who goes from love affair to love affair that he or she has a 'heart like an artichoke', scattering leaves right and left. Artichokes contain an acid called cynarin. This affects the taste of other things eaten with them, or particularly straight after them, making them taste sweet – which is why water tastes sweet and wine tastes awful when consumed in conjunction with this vegetable. In New Zealand they are mainly available from October to December, but you can find them on either side of those months.

ASIAN FOOD

Chinese restaurants have been around in New Zealand since the days of Chinese settlement on the gold fields of Central Otago. After the gold fields dried

Artichoke, fennel and blood-orange salad with apple aïoli

for the salad:

500G FENNEL BULBS
LEMONS
4 BLOOD ORANGES
8 BABY ARTICHOKES OR 1 X 390G TIN ARTICHOKE HEARTS IN BRINE
100G BLACK OLIVES
EXTRA VIRGIN OLIVE OIL
SEA SALT AND FRESHLY GROUND BLACK PEPPER
1 CUP FRESH MINT, TORN BUT NOT CHOPPED

for the aïoli:

4 CLOVES GARLIC, CHOPPED
1/2 TEASPOON SEA SALT
2 EGG YOLKS
1 TEASPOON DIJON MUSTARD
500ML EXTRA VIRGIN OLIVE OIL OR 250ML OLIVE OIL AND 250ML VEGETABLE OIL
LEMON JUICE
1 SMALL TART APPLE, PEELED AND DICED

1. Trim the ends off the fennel bulbs. Cut in half and cut tough hearts out in a V and discard. Slice bulbs finely and immediately place in lemon water to prevent browning.

2. Take one orange and zest half of it. Peel the rest of this orange and the others, removing all the pith, then slice.

3. Cut the baby artichokes in half, scrape out the hairy choke with your finger, and boil for 10 minutes in salted, lemon water. If using tinned artichokes, drain well and cut in half.

4. Remove the olive stones with an olive stoner and sauté the olives in hot oil for 5 minutes.

5. Drain the fennel well and toss gently with the oranges, zest, artichokes, olives, salt, pepper and mint. Pile up on a platter and squeeze lemon juice all over. Serve the apple aïoli on the side.

1. Mash the garlic and sea salt together with a mortar and pestle.

2. Stir in the egg yolks and mustard with the pestle, then gradually add the oil drop by drop.

3. When half the oil is in, add a little lemon juice and warm water and continue adding the oil in a thin stream, stirring with the pestle until all is incorporated. This can also be done with a food processor or hand beater.

4. Taste for seasoning and stir in the diced apple.

serves 4

up the Chinese settlers dispersed to low-rent areas of the cities, setting up cheap restaurants, boarding houses, gambling rooms and opium dens. These restaurants served an exclusively Chinese clientele up to the 1950s, when more adventurous New Zealand eaters gradually started trying them out.

New Zealand's relationship with Japan dates from the 19th century when Kiwi entrepreneurs maintained a range of business interests there, including running stage coaches. In the 1970s trade became well established when New Zealand had to find new markets in Asia as a result of the United Kingdom joining the European Economic Community (EEC), today known as the European Union (EU). These days we earn around $4 billion mostly from exporting chilled beef, cheese and curd, fish, shellfish, vegetables, fruit, wood, pulp and aluminium.

When Asian communities started emigrating to New Zealand they brought sophisticated cooking skills with them. With their healthy, low-fat diet, high standards and artistic attitude to food, they raised the level of seafood/fish shops to unimaginable heights. The Japanese consider food to be art, and fish must not only be desperately fresh but also a carefully orchestrated symphony of flavour, colour, texture and seasonal appropriateness. In spite of our high-quality fish, Japanese chefs still consider our relatively warm-water varieties to be not as tasty as fish from the freezing waters off Japan.

Today we can enjoy the sweet aromas of lime leaves and coconut milk in Thai cuisine, star anise and soy sauce from Hong Kong, the fermented, chillied kimch'i from Korea, mouth-searing wasabi and raw fish from Japan, and fresh coriander and fish sauce from Vietnam. We have many Asian supermarkets, so we can now buy tofu, seaweed paper, glass noodles, five-spice powder and dried shrimps to make Asian dishes at home. We have outdoor markets such as Avondale in Auckland, bursting with freshly grown greens, banana flowers, lemongrass and exotic fruit. Fish sauce, rice paper and Thai sweet chilli sauce are now ingredients ordinary New Zealanders have in their cupboards alongside the ubiquitous tomato sauce and Vegemite.

ASPARAGUS

Asparagus is a perennial member of the lily family, which also includes onions, leeks and garlic. Asparagus spears, like sweetcorn, taste completely different eaten raw, straight out of the ground, before the sugar has converted to starch. They taste sweet, like fresh peas. Even cooked, they should be eaten with the fingers, paying homage to their sensuality. Asparagus is one of the sexiest of vegetables – think dripping butter, intolerably fabulous taste, guaranteed satisfaction and decadently expensive in the high season. Most of the country's crop comes from Waikato and Hawke's Bay, where the tender asparagus shoots up, literally growing in front of your eyes. It is harvested daily when the spears emerge in the spring and is available from September to January. Asparagus is a great source of vitamins and minerals. But most importantly, if you wish to stay young and beautiful forever, eat lots of them, as they have higher levels of antioxidant compounds than almost any other vegetable.

White asparagus confit

Confit means cooked slowly in oil. In this recipe the asparagus and oil seem to melt together in an alchemy of sweetness and harmony.

32 FAT WHITE ASPARAGUS SPEARS
PARCHMENT OR BAKING PAPER
1/4 CUP EXTRA VIRGIN OLIVE OIL
SEA SALT AND FRESHLY GROUND BLACK PEPPER
SUGAR
2 SPRIGS OF MINT OR TARRAGON

1. Preheat the oven to 120°C. Break ends off asparagus and wash.

2. Tear off a 90cm strip of parchment and lay it across a shallow roasting tray. Place asparagus on it, neatly lined up, and pour oil over. Sprinkle with salt, pepper and a little sugar and top with herbs. Fold the parchment over, folding the edges three times to make it secure.

3. Bake for 1 hour.

4. To serve, slide parchment packet on to platter and slit open at the table.

serves 8

A

The most common asparagus grown in New Zealand is green, but you can also get purple, pink, red and white asparagus. In country farmers' markets you can sometimes buy wild asparagus, and Sabato in Auckland stock frozen ones from France – they are actually wild hop-shoots, but they look and taste like very skinny asparagus. Elizabeth David says these should be briefly boiled in water with lemon juice then served with vinaigrette or melted butter. They are also very good in an omelette or in risotto.

A good way to cook asparagus is to steam it in salted water, preferably in an upright steamer designed for the purpose, until al dente, or you can brush with avocado oil, sprinkle with salt and pepper and grill. There is a Frenchman in Hawke's Bay called Pierre who produces very good *Délices d'Asperges* under his label Pierre sur le Quai. This is a moreish bottled paste made from asparagus and preserved lemon pesto. He suggests you spread it on fish prior to cooking, add it to risotto, and put it on toast with fresh tomatoes. I can't stop myself from eating the stuff straight out of the jar with a silver spoon.

Recently I found unbelievably sweet white asparagus in my local vegetable shop. It was around only for a few weeks then agonisingly disappeared, but not before I had gorged myself on it. Subsequently I found a grower in Cambridge and discovered his secret plan for keeping the spears white. John Snodgrass of Ridgevale Farm began experimenting with white asparagus four years ago when he found some of his green asparagus growing upside down in the ground so the sun couldn't develop the chlorophyll and turn them green. *Quelle idée*! thought he, I should grow some white ones right side up. He's very passionate about the colour and describes it as creamy, just like white chocolate.

White asparagus is exactly the same plant as green asparagus except you grow it in the dark, and you have to grow the right variety. Not all varieties taste good white and John would have had to kill me if I had got that information out of him. In northern Europe, where white asparagus is very common, the plants are grown deep in the dirt like potatoes and if the tips show they are quickly covered up with soil until it's time to harvest. John thought there had to be a better way, so he built a long, black, polythene tent and grows his asparagus in there. It works like a charm and he picks the asparagus wearing a little miner's hat with a light attached to it. So why would you eat white asparagus? Because it seems more tender, and is sweet and nutty rather than pea-like in flavour. Some spears need peeling, but John's ones don't.

AVOCADO OIL

Avocado gets its name from the South American word *ahuacatl*, meaning testicle. (I didn't make that up.) We grow lots of avocados in New Zealand but it's avocado oil that is the 'in' ingredient on the food scene. The oil is cold-pressed, extra virgin, 100 per cent pure and natural. The harvest starts in September and continues for seven months. For health-conscious food lovers, avocado oil is acknowledged as one of the healthiest of all food oils, with a high level of monounsaturates, the 'good' fat that helps to lower harmful cholesterol levels in the bloodstream. Cold pressing ensures no damage to nutrients occurs and the goodness of the avocado is preserved. The acidity reading of the oil is less than one per cent. The oil is packaged in green glass bottles to protect it from the negative influences of light and oxygen. Completely unrefined, with a vibrant green colour, a soft nutty taste and a mild avocado aroma, this oil enhances the natural flavours of other ingredients rather than overpowering them. What is more, it leaves no greasy aftertaste. Use in the same recipes in which you would use the very finest extra virgin olive oils. As a general rule you need to use less avocado oil than olive oil. It's viscosity makes the oil more economical because it coats food so finely and delicately. As well as being easy to use, it's also good for cooking and baking because of its high smoke point of 255°C. It keeps fresh because there is no contact with air or light. As a result less oil is absorbed into the food, therefore less is required. Avocado oil is also used in cosmetics and as a body oil. If you don't like the taste, just rub it all over your significant other and use it as a massage oil. I don't advise using it in your mashed potatoes unless it's St Patrick's Day. There are two major producers of avocado oil in New Zealand: Olivado in Kerikeri and The Grove in Tauranga.

OLIVADO

Olivado comes as pure avocado oil, and also infused with lemon, rosemary, basil, chilli and bell pepper. Olivado avocado oil is also produced in an aerosol spray can. The company also makes Olivado Omega Plus, a combination of avocado oil, olive oil and flaxseed oil.

THE GROVE

The Grove oil comes pure and in three infused flavours: horopito pepper, garlic and lime. They also do an organic avocado oil and make AvoHealth capsules.

A

BALSAMIC VINEGAR

Balsamic production is tiny in New Zealand but there are a few brave and noble souls giving it a go. Anna-Barbara and Bruce Helliwell of Unison Vineyard in Hastings not only make very good red wine but also have a loft impregnated with the sweet aroma of ageing balsamic. They use the traditional process, making it in barrels they brought back from Modena in Italy. Five barrels – a batteria – are required and these are made of chestnut, cherry, mulberry, ash and oak, each one getting progressively smaller. Strictly speaking, balsamic is not a vinegar because it is not made by adding a mother bug to wine. It was originally a medicine made only for the family's use, and consumed as a cure-all and sometimes as a digestive after the meal. It is made by slow simmering the must of white grapes to reduce it to a half or third of its volume. Then it begins its long journey through a process of acetification and fermentation to become the intensely complex liquid we all adore.

Unison Vineyard started making their balsamic in Italy from several types of white grape and they continued the process in New Zealand, putting the vinegar in the first and largest barrel. A year later some of the vinegar is siphoned off into the next barrel down and new syrup is added to the first barrel. This process is repeated in further years filling the third, fourth and fifth barrels, always adding new syrup to the first. After six years the balsamic can be harvested, but it can also be left there to age even more – sometimes for 50 years. The reason the barrels are in the loft is that the roof provides the extremes of temperature required for the

maturing process – the balsamic concentrates by evaporation in the hot summer, and rests and matures in the cold winter. Unison's balsamic is available for purchase every year in November and can only be bought at the cellar door or by mail order. I ordered some from Anna-Barbara while writing this and I am eagerly waiting for it to arrive, full of the smell of molasses and the taste of deep caramel, wood and slight acid.

BARBECUE
The barbecue is a game the whole family can play in summer. The New Zealand male does absolutely nothing except stand by the barbie and burn the food while drinking large amounts of cheap beer and wearing a stupid apron. The female does everything else – the shopping, the prep, the salads, the spuds in tinfoil, the cleanup and stopping the kids from falling in the pool. However, despite all this it is the male who takes all the credit. The children do nothing but stuff lamb chops into their mouths and eat potato salad with their hands. When it comes time to clean up, the male turns into an ornamental tree. Australians do a barbie very well, and they think they invented it. They didn't – the caveman did, soon after discovering fire.

My childhood barbecue was a sheet of aluminium placed across bricks – and it worked perfectly. Barbecues have got more sophisticated lately and even us inner-city-pad chicks can experience the outdoor feel of burning bangers on our designer table grills and boat barbies attached to our balcony railing. This way we can access our inner cavewoman and still wear Issy Miyake frocks. Added sand and mosquitoes are optional. Be careful cooking barbecues in your city pad, however, as the fire alarm will probably go off, which will irritate the neighbours.

SIMPLE RULES TO KEEP IN MIND FOR BARBECUES
- Lock the male in the toilet.
- Let the wood or coals burn down to embers – never cook food over a naked flame.
- Use marinades if you must, but sparingly.
- Don't chuck everything on at once. Put the longest-cooking foods on first. They might go on in this order: lamb chops, chicken, pork, sausages, steak, fish, then vegetables. A barbecue should be a long degustation symphony with delicacies coming off the grill for hours.
- Let the male out of the toilet just as the first foods are coming off the grill.

BEEF

We claim to produce the very best pasture-fed beef cattle in the world – all nine million of them. The Scottish also say they grow the best beef in the world, and the Argentineans say the same. But here the light is clear, the air is pure, the water is clean and we are attached to and respect the land. We are most famous for our lamb, but the quality of our outdoor, grass-fed cattle is our best-kept secret. New Zealand is one of the least crowded places on earth, and with its gentle climate and ample rainfall, it's the perfect environment for pastoral farming. Far and away the safest place to raise beef, our island isolation gives animal-health advantages that are carefully guarded.

The essential thing is that the animals can range freely to feed on grass rather than grain. New Zealand farmers set high standards, taking enormous pride in the way they care for their animals and manage their land. Rich, fertile pasture is the essential ingredient in flavoursome, tender beef. New Zealand's experts have developed new, nutritious pasture species that maximise beef production in a sustainable way. Only on New Zealand pastures can beef animals grow to premium condition at a young and tender age.

Fine-textured and naturally nutritious, our beef is a product of rare quality and distinctive flavour. It is tender and lean, a healthy food with fresh-tasting appeal. Beef from animals raised on grass has been found to be lower in saturated fats but higher in the 'good fats' including monounsaturated fats, omega 3 and conjugated linoleic acid (CLA). It is also higher in beta-carotene, a precursor to vitamin A, and in vitamin E than beef from cattle raised on grain diets.

Some butchers say New Zealand meat is properly hung on the bone, then matured in vacuum packs. I don't consider maturing meat in vacuum packs proper curing, and it shows in the taste. You can tell good beef in the butcher's shop because it's quite a dark red colour, marbled and surrounded by creamy yellow-coloured fat. I prefer cheaper cuts of beef like oxtail and shin because of the intense flavour and glutinous consistency, and I'm mad about beef marrow.

I once made the mistake of suggesting on television that we never saw our top-quality beef and lamb in New Zealand because it was all exported. I had the Beef and Lamb Marketing Bureau and Richmond Meats in Hastings both down on me like a ton of bricks. The true story is we can buy export-quality beef here but we pay more for it. If cost is a factor, I'd prefer to buy top-quality beef, preferably organic, and eat less of it. If you buy organic the butcher knows the farm the animal came from, and you the buyer know the animal has had a good life and is not full of foreign additives. If you can develop a good friendship with your butcher, ask him to hang your meat for at least 14 to 17 days and you'll see the difference in taste.

BERRIES

In New Zealand we grow strawberries, raspberries, boysenberries, blackcurrants and redcurrants, gooseberries, tayberries (a cross between a raspberry and a blackberry),

Salmon barbecued in grape leaves

20 LARGE, FRESH GRAPE LEAVES OR 40 SMALL
1KG FRESH SALMON FILLET
EXTRA VIRGIN OLIVE OIL
SEA SALT AND FRESHLY GROUND BLACK PEPPER
SHREDDED ZEST OF 2 LEMONS
20 VIETNAMESE MINT LEAVES
LEMON QUARTERS FOR SQUEEZING

1. Remove stems from grape leaves and blanch for 5 minutes. Dry on kitchen paper.

2. Cut salmon into 5cm squares, taking care to remove the bones.

3. Brush each grape leaf, stem side up, with oil. If using small leaves, overlap 2 to make a bigger surface. Place fish squares in the middle, sprinkle with salt and pepper, then top with a good pinch of lemon zest and a torn-up mint leaf. Fold the grape leaf around the fish like a little parcel.

4. Brush the packets all over with oil and barbecue for 3 minutes on each side, then leave to rest for a few minutes.

5. To serve, display the salmon packets as they are and squeeze lemon juice over them. They may be eaten with or without the grape leaves.

serves 6

loganberries, elderberries and blueberries, and we often spent our childhoods eating berries off bushes as we walked home from school. We love to pick our own berries at berry farms and run home to make pies, sorbets and summer puddings. There is absolutely nothing better than a plump summer pudding oozing with red and purple berries.

STRAWBERRIES

We're mad about strawberries in New Zealand, to the extent that we grow 6600 tonnes of them every season and consider them, along with cherries, an essential part of Christmas feasts. As kids, some of us spent from October onwards picking them, eating four kilos in one sitting and spending the rest of the week enjoying hives. By the end of January,

the heart-shaped mouthfuls of red fragrance are but a drooling memory, to last on only in our dreams and as jam. Their botanical name *Fragaria* actually means fragrant and they belong to the rose family. And if you take a glance at my entry on roses, you'll never be able to watch a middle-aged man eating strawberries again. The business of strawberry production is very labour intensive, as everything has to be done by hand – planting, picking, grading and packing. Strawberries are sensitive to root disease, and hate rain, which makes it perplexing that most of them are grown in Auckland, a region that has plenty of rain.

Strawberries grown in New Zealand are American cultivars, chosen for their shininess, roundness and colour. They don't get any riper after picking, so it's important to

Summer pudding

800G MIXED BERRIES: BLACKBERRIES, RASPBERRIES, REDCURRANTS, BLUEBERRIES
1 TABLESPOON LEMON JUICE
100G CASTOR SUGAR
1 LOAF SLICED WHITE SANDWICH BREAD, 2 DAYS OLD
EXTRA BERRIES AND LEAVES FOR GARNISH
WHIPPED CREAM

1. Place the berries, lemon juice and sugar in a saucepan and gently bring to the boil. Remove from heat immediately and drain the berries, allowing the juice to drip into a saucepan. Leave the berries to cool and reduce the juice by hard boiling to one cup. Cool.

2. Cut the crusts off the bread and trim the slices to fit the shape of a pudding bowl plus a round one for the base. Dip the slices into the berry syrup and line the bowl, beginning with the base and making sure the edges overlap. Spoon the berries and syrup into the bowl and put a lid of bread on top.

3. Cover the bowl with plastic wrap, place a lid on top and a weight on top of that. Refrigerate overnight or for at least 8 hours.

4. To serve, remove the weight, lid and wrap, and invert the pudding on to a plate large enough to accommodate the syrup that will ooze out. Garnish with fresh berries and serve with whipped cream.

serves 6

Gooseberry fool

1KG FRESH GOOSEBERRIES
1 SMALL PIECE FRESH GINGER
250G SUGAR
500ML CREAM
COOKED BLACKCURRANTS AND RASPBERRIES TO SERVE

1. Place gooseberries, ginger and sugar in a saucepan with 2 tablespoons water. Cover and cook gently for 20 minutes.

2. Remove ginger and purée fruit in a food processor. Allow to cool.

3. Whip the cream, then fold in the gooseberries. Serve with blackcurrants and raspberries cooked with sugar, and place some lemon peel on the side.

serves 8

Roast chicken

1 ORGANIC CHICKEN WEIGHING 1.5 TO 2KG
4 CLOVES GARLIC
SHORT SPRIG OF ROSEMARY
GOOD SPRIG OF MARJORAM
SEVERAL BRANCHES OF PARSLEY
FEW SPRIGS OF THYME
SEA SALT AND FRESHLY GROUND BLACK PEPPER
EXTRA VIRGIN OLIVE OIL
2 ONIONS IN THEIR SKINS, QUARTERED
1 CARROT, QUARTERED
1/2 CUP WHITE WINE
1/2 CUP FRESH CHICKEN OR VEGETABLE STOCK

1. Preheat the oven to 230°C. Place the chicken, untied, on a roasting tray. Smash the garlic, herbs, salt, pepper and olive oil together in a mortar and pestle and rub this mixture all over the chicken, inside and out. Place the onion and carrot around the chicken – this will give the gravy extra flavour.

2. Roast the chicken for 30 minutes, remove from the oven and pour in the wine and stock. Turn the oven down to 180°C and return the chicken to the oven. Roast for another hour.

3. Meat always has to be rested for 15 minutes, so remove it from the roasting dish to a serving platter, cover with a tea-towel and leave in a warm place. Alternatively you can turn the oven off, open the door and leave the chicken sitting for 15 minutes.

4. I never add flour to the roasting juices, and chicken produces such good juice you don't need to add much else. If you really feel the sauce needs a lift, sprinkle in a few drops of good balsamic vinegar. Remove the vegetables and place the roasting pan of juices on a hot element. Bring to the boil, scraping up the bits stuck on the bottom.

5. To serve, pour the hot sauce into a jug and bring the chicken to the table where it will be carved. To carve well you need a sharp knife. Cut off the legs, then cut them into smaller portions. Next, slice off the wings, then cut thick slices off the breast. Serve with Agria potatoes that have been roasted in duck fat, and a crisp green salad.

serves 4

pick only the bright red ones. The deeper the colour, the sweeter the berry. If buying them from a shop, try to buy the day you're going to eat them, because putting them in the fridge deadens the flavour – as it does with most fruit, including tomatoes. You must eat as many strawberries as possible, because they make you happy with their high levels of depression-fighting vitamin B and keep you young forever with their antioxidants. They're best eaten with clotted cream, icing sugar and pink champagne.

BLUEBERRIES

Purple, blue and black berries are particularly good for you. They contain four times the vitamin C of oranges and are powerful antioxidants because of the anthocyanins in them. And you know what antioxidants do – they keep you young and beautiful forever. Blueberries have a stupendous taste and are grown in New Zealand between November and March. Growing perfect blueberries is very labour intensive – requiring hand weeding, hand picking and high quality control. They are more expensive than other berries, but according to one source they are one of a dozen super foods we shouldn't live without. They are full of fibre, are antibacterial, contain folic acid, are beneficial during pregnancy and might be anticancer agents also.

There is an organic blueberry orchard at Omaha in the north of the North Island. Robert and Shannon Auton of Omaha Blueberries also make blueberry sorbet and pasteurised blueberry juice.

BIRDS

CHICKEN

When I was a child, chicken tasted of something. It was a treat, usually eaten for special occasions like Christmas and birthdays. The only chooks available for eating were the ones in your backyard or the ones you went to the farm to buy. Needless to say they were free range and meltingly delicious. My father couldn't bring himself to kill one of his chooks when the time came, so he got the neighbour to do it. In return, Dad killed the neighbour's chooks when their time came, while we kids stood nearby shrieking at the headless chook as it ran around in its death dash. Later I went through a period of darkness, eating battery birds because I didn't know better. I forgot the taste of real healthy chicken and closed my mind to the

Double duck

for the brine:

1 DUCK
1 CUP SALT
1/2 CUP SUGAR
1/2 TEASPOON CRUSHED PEPPERCORNS
CINNAMON STICK
BOUQUET GARNI
6 CARDAMOM SEEDS, CRUSHED

for the poaching stock:

4 LITRES DUCK OR CHICKEN STOCK
1 CARROT, HALVED
1 LEEK, WASHED AND HALVED
1 ONION, HALVED
6 CLOVES GARLIC
BOUQUET GARNI

Note: When every last morsel has been cut off the duck, put the carcass back into the stock and cook for half an hour. Strain stock and leave in the fridge overnight for the fat to rise. Next morning skim the fat off and use it to fry potatoes. You can freeze the delicious stock and use it to cook your next bird.

1. Take a pot large enough to hold the duck plus brine. To make sure, put the duck in the saucepan and cover with water – you will need about 4 litres. Remove the duck and bring the water to the boil with the salt and sugar.

2. Take brine off the heat. Add spices, let the brine cool and put the duck back in. Cover and refrigerate for 24 hours. When you brine a duck the salt draws water out of the duck and the brine itself seeps into the duck flesh. This magical process of osmosis adds flavour, juiciness and tenderness.

1. Remove duck from fridge, discard brine and let bird sit for 20 minutes. Chop off wing tips and remove neck and innards, keeping them for the stock.

2. Pour stock into a large pot, add the vegetables, herbs and duck bits and bring to the boil.

3. Prick the duck skin all over with the sharp point of a small knife, being careful not to pierce the skin. Carefully lower it into the hot stock neck end first, allowing the cavity to fill so the duck sinks to the bottom of the pot where you want it to be. Add water if necessary to cover the duck.

4. Bring stock to the boil and reduce to a simmer. Cover and simmer for 45 minutes.

5. Remove duck carefully, draining liquid from the cavity, and place it on a cake rack or similar strainer over a pan. Keep the stock.

to roast the duck:

1. Preheat the oven to the highest it will go.

2. Dry the duck skin with a hair dryer, gently pressing the skin with paper towels to get the fat out. It takes about 10 minutes to dry both sides. This, along with the short, high-heat roasting, is essential to get a skin which is a paragon of crispness, crunch and deliciousness. Sprinkle with sea salt and freshly ground black pepper and place in a roasting dish, breast side up.

3. Place the dish in the oven on the second rung from the bottom and roast for 30 minutes.

4. Allow to rest for 10 minutes, then cut it up as best you can.

serves 4

horrors that battery birds are subjected to in their short lives.

Chickens reared in intensive gulags are usually fed chemicals, additives and antibiotics to facilitate their unnatural lifestyle of accelerated growth and overcrowding. They have an area about the size of a foolscap sheet of paper to move around in, and their beaks are cut off to prevent them fighting to the death. After slaughter they are injected with protein and water in an effort to maximise the weight and give the meat some kind of taste. In intensive farming it is acceptable to lose up to 30 per cent of your chickens to premature death. Premature death is caused by tumours, broken legs, aggressive behaviour, heart attack, infection, fighting and a form of suicide called 'smothering'. In a smother, thousands of cramped birds in a shed will suddenly and spontaneously rush into a huge pile in which most of them will die of suffocation. These are the chickens you don't eat under any circumstances.

If it's not stated on a restaurant menu that the chicken is organic, or free-range and corn-fed, you can assume it isn't. The reason organic and free-range chickens taste better is because they grow at a natural rate (20 weeks), which is three times slower than battery birds (six weeks), they eat corn, grass, grain and grubs, have plenty of exercise, enjoy the sunshine and are happy. After slaughter they are dry-plucked, hung properly and clearly labelled. Good chicken costs at least twice as much as cheap chicken. So what? We eat far too much meat anyway, so halve your consumption of meat and eat good quality.

When was the last time you slow-roasted a whole chicken and carved it up at the table, smiling happily as your guests gasped with the smell of crisp skin and tender flesh? Chicken tastes better cooked on the bone, and it feels hospitable and civilised to indulge in this heart-warming way of eating and sharing. When roasting chicken I don't stuff it – partly because I don't like stuffing (too many memories of uncooked onions and medicinal amounts of sage) and partly because the bird cooks better and is juicier without it. Sometimes, however, I will poke a cut lemon and a few sprigs of lemon thyme into the cavity.

CANTER VALLEY FARM IN RANGIORA

This is a bird farm. They don't use antibiotics or growth promoters here and the first thing you notice about a bird farm, and this is a scrupulously clean one, is the smell. The second thing you notice are the picturesque surroundings, which help you ignore the smell of hundreds of birdies doing doodoo. There is a huge shed full of creamy white ducks with white beaks and black eyes. For the camera, they all waddled out of the shed in a shimmering, fluffy sea of feathers, chattering incessantly among themselves. We were greeted by a scintillating tidal wave of little, lemon-curd coloured four-day-old chicks with tiny, black eyes. Laurence the photographer, crouched very still to photograph them and within minutes they were climbing all over his boots and hands.

We walked past large tables spread with drying feathers to be shipped to Australia for duvets and, continuing back through the life cycle, squeezed ourselves into the egg-incubating chamber, where rows and rows of turkey, duck, pheasant and quail eggs sat in temperature-controlled closets. They also have brown ducks that lay blue eggs specially for the Chinese market (how they know they are laying them for the Chinese I can't imagine). Every so often, John takes the eggs out and looks at them with a little light held right against the shell to check they are still alive. You can actually see the little critters moving about inside the shell.

The photo shoot finished up on the terrace of John and Mary's house, where we sipped tea and ate her home-made fruit cake.

DUCKS AND GEESE

Ducks, unlike chickens, are water birds and thus have a larger carcass and less meat, but for a luxury meat the price is not too bad. Canter Valley ducks are really ducklings, being only six weeks old, which is an extraordinary growth rate when you consider the size of them. Duck is delicious roasted whole but is one of the most difficult roasts to get right. Personally I think duckling needs to be cooked in separate bits. The breast is rich in taste and tender, so it should be eaten pink in the middle. On the other hand the legs, which have a deliciously intense flavour, need much longer cooking. There is an exception to this in the recipe given on the previous page for Double Duck.

Goose is quite hard to come by in New Zealand but I developed a taste for it after living in France for ten years. Try using the Double Duck recipe with goose, if you can lay your hands on one.

QUAILS AND POUSSINS

Quails are fat little birds, speckled with brown, pale lemon and cream feathers, and the chicks look exactly like those little things you put on cakes and Easter eggs. It is one of

Shredded quail with mint & lemon

6 PINCHES OF SAFFRON
3 QUAILS OR 3 POUSSINS
2 LEMONS, QUARTERED
1 ½ CUPS FRESH MINT LEAVES
2 TEASPOONS PAPRIKA
SEA SALT
4 TABLESPOONS FENNEL LIQUEUR
(PASTIS IS A GOOD SUBSTITUTE)
2 CUPS CHICKEN STOCK
SPRIGS OF MINT TO GARNISH

1. Prepare the saffron by soaking it in a little boiling water for at least 15 minutes.

2. Place all the ingredients in a pot, bring to the boil and simmer covered for an hour, turning the birds occasionally. Allow to cool in the sauce.

3. Take all the flesh off the bones and shred. Discard the lemons and mix the reduced sauce in with the quail meat.

4. Serve at room temperature with grilled fennel and ricotta ravioli. Garnish with sprigs of mint.

serves 6

my favourite birds as it is surprisingly meaty and the texture is silky smooth and slightly gamy. Quail eggs are lovely to eat and very pretty to look at, speckled just like they are when they hatch into birdies. Quail is good spatchcocked (split down the backbone and spread out), marinated for half an hour in rose water, lemon juice and olive oil, then barbecued on a high heat for ten minutes on each side. When cooked, rest them in a dish and pour the marinade over.

Poussin is simply baby chicken – very tender and wonderful spatchcocked, squirted with lemon juice and grilled or barbecued with feta cheese on top.

TURKEY

Turkey is a thoroughly underused and underappreciated meat in New Zealand. It has the highest meat-to-bone ratio of any edible meat and it has less than half of the calories of a T-bone steak, 28 per cent more protein and 75 per cent less fat. A turkey leg makes a great roast, and the breast meat is very good if not overcooked. You can also eat turkey as a rolled roast, in kebabs, as schnitzel, smoked and in stir-fry strips.

PHEASANT

Pheasants are pretty when babies and the adult males turn into very fine specimens with red heads, purple and green necks with white bands, sweeping down to brown, grey, orange and purple-feathered bodies, ending in a long tail. If I was a boring old brown female pheasant, I would be terribly impressed. A really simple way to cook pheasant is to roast it in a hot oven for 15 minutes, cut it in half lengthways, then place the halves on generously buttered papillotes of tinfoil or baking paper. Pour over the roasting juices, salt and pepper and a slug of Madeira, topping the pheasant halves with a slice of smoked bacon. Fold over the edges of the papillotes three times, place them back in a very hot oven for ten minutes at which point they will have blown up. This method is like an oven within an oven and produces unimaginable succulence. Serve the whole sarcophagus to your grateful guests so they can open it themselves and not lose one drop of the sauce.

All game birds are best cooked on their side, not breast side up. If you are given game, don't refuse it whatever you do because you will be missing out on a great treat. If you get desperate and can't come up with a recipe on the spot, put it in the freezer, as freezers are kinder to game than to vegetables, meat and fish. Incidentally, one of the best solutions for using game is to make it into pâtés and terrines – absolutely divine with pickled figs and walnuts.

BREAD
Throughout history bread has always been hugely important and symbolic. Muslims were once forbidden to sell bread, only trade or give it away, so much was it considered a gift from Allah. Christians use bread to represent the body of Christ and believe it symbolises the nourishment of the soul. The workers who built the pyramids were paid in bread, and we still use the words 'bread', 'earn a crust' and 'dough' to mean money. Bread provides us with more energy value, more protein, more iron, more nicotinic acid and more vitamin B1 than any other basic food. Bread is one of the finest foods it is possible to get and it is not an exaggeration to say we cannot do without it. New

B

Zealanders eat nearly a million loaves of it every day, seven days a week. That costs us $340 million a year, which breaks down to an average weekly spend per household of around $6.

According to *The New Zealand Bread Book* by Mary Browne, Helen Leach and Nancy Tichborne (Godwit, 1994), bread-making techniques were brought to New Zealand in the early 1800s by our first missionary settlers, who transported sacks of wheat and a steel hand-mill for grinding that they picked up in Australia en route. These stalwart women, who had little idea of the hardship they were facing, set themselves to baking in camp ovens set over the glowing embers in the fireplace or in upturned cauldrons placed directly on the hearth. A camp oven is an iron pot with three stumpy legs and an iron lid, similar to the ones used in Ireland. By the 1840s we were growing our own wheat and milling it with water mills and windmills, hence the invention of the bigger 'colonial' ovens in which you could bake many loaves. These were essentially iron boxes set into a brick fireplace with the fire burning above and below them. If you were out digging gold or felling trees, you cooked unleavened damper on the camp fire, thanked God you were alive and never dreamed that your descendants would later write about how romantic it all was.

In 1850 the first brick-and-stone commercial oven to be built in Canterbury was built behind a shop in Lyttelton. To heat it they burned wood on the floor or 'sole' of the oven until it reached a certain temperature, raked out the ashes and put in the bread.

Where did the yeast come from? Well it was commonly made from scalded malt and boiled hops, which fermented together for a few days then mashed potatoes were added. If you had a bakery near a brewery, you not only had two major food groups provided for you, you could use the brewer's yeast. Home cooks mixed mashed potatoes, brewer's yeast and water together to make a ferment. They let it sit around for 30 minutes then added some flour, making a thick spongy mixture, which was left overnight to grow. When I was a child my mother bought compressed bakers' yeast in a little block, and put it in glasses of water in the fridge overnight, where magic occurred and we drank it in the morning before school. It was the most delicious frothy, creamy, malty drink – far more appetising than the vile cod-liver oil mothers were obsessed with in those days. And while I'm on that topic, some women also gave their children a medicinal tablespoon of olive oil, which you bought from the chemist. Who would have thought we'd end up living on the stuff and thinking we were Mediterraneans?

Mechanisation changed everything but not necessarily for the better, resulting in my childhood breakfasts of appalling white or brown bread, made to last forever and survive another world war. Some small cake and bread shops did survive though, and so did farm baking. Remote high-country sheep stations and rugged coastal farms continued to bake bread in large wood ranges. Bread and cake competitions are still going strong today at country shows. Hippies rescued and revived bread-making at home, as they rescued lots of other basic skills like the making of yoghurt, butter and cheese, and the revival of whole-grain cereals and oils in the diet. Why, the world would have run out of alfalfa sprouts were it not for the counter-revolution.

These days in New Zealand there are quite a few very good bread-makers, and we have developed a pronounced taste for artisan and ethnic breads. Sourdough bread is the biggest single growth area now. Vogels bread, invented by Dutchman Hans Klisser, and fabulously dense and nutty, was the first of the boutique breads and it was an instant and lasting hit. Although he sold the company to Quality Bakers, the original Vogels is still exactly the same; subsequent variations invented by Quality Bakers are not as good but they're still pretty delicious. If there are two things New Zealanders really miss when they are overseas, they are Vogels and Vegemite.

There are only four main ingredients required to make good bread – strong flour, salt, yeast and water. The rest is down to skill. Two of the best books you can buy on New Zealand baking are *New Zealand Baker* and *Baker – The Best of International Baking from Australia and New Zealand* by Dean Brettschneider and Lauraine Jacobs, published by Tandem Press. Their latest book, *Taste: The Flavours of Baking*, is more rustic, and takes a global approach to baking and pastry making. Dean is also looking at opening a bakery in Auckland. A bread and pastry expert and consultant, he says to be a successful baker you have to have commitment, dedication and passion combined with a little fun. When I interviewed him on 'Taste New Zealand' he made me the most delicious fig, almond and aniseed bread, the recipe for which is on page 37, with his kind permission. His website is: www.nzbaker.co.nz.

A delightful New Zealand novel called *By Bread Alone* by Sarah-Kate Lynch tells in great detail of a woman's love affair with sourdough (and a sexy Frenchman). Here's an extract:

'The sweet, sharp scent of sourdough bread cooking in an oak-fired oven whirled around her unsuspecting senses and unleashed a hunger she had not known existed. It hit her so hard she could barely breathe. The air was hot and thick with the promise of life's simple and not-so-simple pleasures. She could feel it. She could smell it. She could taste it on the tip of her tongue. Bread. Yes, bread. Pain au levain, to be precise, the speciality of the house. Never mind the baguettes, the croissants, the pastries after which she had so recently hankered. Compared to just one crumb from the sourdough loaves they were nothing, nothing but sand, dry and gritty, in the memory of her taste-buds. No other paltry pretender could ever hope to measure up to the beauty of the fat round boules with their thick crunchy crusts and soft, shining flesh.'

WILD WHEAT BREAD IN AUCKLAND

Andrew Fearnside is another person absolutely dedicated to great bread made with care and integrity. He makes all sorts of breads in his factory in East Tamaki, Auckland, but the speciality, for which I would walk quite a few miles, is his sourdough. Sourdough bread is bread raised with a leaven of flour and water (and often other things like potato, sugar and fruit) in which wild yeast has been encouraged to grow by keeping it warm and allowing it to ferment over a period of days. During this time the dough develops its characteristic sour flavour so appreciated by aficionados. Each loaf has some of the previous loaves in it because you keep a bit of the 'starter' yeast and feed it with warm water and flour to keep it going. Then you add that to make the next batch of bread.

Andrew fermented some apple back in 1997 and produced a bug that he still uses as his starter dough today. He keeps pots of the starter at home as well as at work in case one lot dies. Andrew hand-makes rolls and shapes rosemary and olive sourdough, potato sourdough, country sourdough (wholemeal, rye and apple cider) and Puglia – a white crusty bread made with durum flour in an old dough base. He also makes a huge, flat Turkish pide which looks very dramatic placed in the centre of the table. He supplies the trade, and you can buy his bread at Sabato, Kapiti Cheese Shop and The Italian Grocer in Auckland. You can also buy it at his new, buttercup-coloured shop on Mt Eden Rd, Auckland. Alongside the bread he also does sandwiches, apple doughnuts and, at Christmas, beautiful Dutch stollen – that hard-to-make, dense, fine-grained, fragrant bread full of butter, dried fruit and almond paste. Because of its low-moisture content stollen keeps really well, so you can eat a slice every afternoon with a glass of sherry. (Please don't ask me how I know this.)

Andrew's website is: wildwheat@slingshot.co.nz.

LE MOULIN IN WELLINGTON

I was at the irrepressible Rex Morgan's Citron restaurant on Willis Street one morning and felt the pressing need for a croissant to go with the flat white he had just made me. 'Of course you know about Le Moulin down the road, don't you?' said he. One minute later I was munching on the best croissant I have eaten in New Zealand and gossiping with sprightly French baker Paul Pioch. To say his Cambodian wife Setha's bakery/patisserie is nothing special to look at is an understatement. Honestly, you would walk right past if you didn't know. Paul rises at about 4 a.m. and sets to making what he feels like making. Today it is croissants full of butter and light enough to dance out the door. By the way, if you ever eat a croissant and it just doesn't taste right, it is because the butter has been supplemented with something else, or the mix is industrial, or some sort of short cut has been taken. An infinite amount of knowledge and time goes into making a good croissant.

Every day, twice a day, Paul makes perfect baguettes. The day I was there his brother Michel was visiting from France and, as is typical in France, if you arrive when the brother is busy, you just put on an apron and help. Michel is very proud of his brother. With a big smile he grabbed a tray of baguettes and said, 'Smell how beautiful this is. Put your nose in this. My brother makes bread and pastries *à la lettre*, exactly the way he did in Paris. His work is truly artisinal and he will work like this until he dies.'

They all kept giving me things to try and smell, chatting constantly with excitement. There were the bread rolls for Citron, *chaussons aux pommes* (apple turnovers), conversations (puff pastry stuffed with almond paste and rum-marinated raisins, topped with royal icing), *la pêche* (peach-shaped pastry), *canelés* (a Bordeaux speciality), and *baguette aux marrons* (chestnut cakes). That's just what I tasted out the back, but the shop has lots of other pastries like *pains aux raisins*, fruit tarts, *palmiers* and other breads. Paul's wife Setha assured me he may be hitting 70 but he was *un jeune coq* in every way. Just as well, as everything in the shop almost sells out every day. They are open all week except Monday, and Paul says it is a *métier merveilleuse* – a wonderful profession.

B

BORDEAUX BAKERY IN WELLINGTON

Jean-Louis Macadré is from Bordeaux, and thank God he fell in love with a New Zealand girl or we wouldn't be able to eat his beautifully made French breads and pastries. He can't stand the industrial baguettes you find in Paris and in an explosion of indignation he says you couldn't even call them bread. He talks a lot about respecting the process, slow-rising times, and resting bread near the oven after it is baked. Jean-Louis aims to have GE-free ingredients and no preservatives or additives in his products, and certainly no premix, but loads of fresh unsalted butter and the best products he can lay his hands on. I was particularly happy to find an unusual pastry and one of my favourites in the world – *canelé*, a Bordeaux speciality. It's hard to make, cooked in special moulds and has a dark, sticky exterior with a soft, custardy interior. He has a huge Bongard bread oven from France that releases steam during cooking and he goes spare over uneven New Zealand flour, saying you can't trust the gluten levels. It's true there are problems with the protein quality and strength of our flour; it has a high water content, and also, we are not producing enough to satisfy the need. Somehow Jean-Louis has managed though, because the Bordeaux Bakery on Thorndon Quay has now expanded to twice the size with a brasserie, and there is now also a Petit Bordeaux branch on Featherston Street.

DOVEDALE BREAD IN NELSON

The man who started Dovedale bread in Nelson is Roland Dallas. He had been making bread almost all his life and says he started making his Dallas bread, later called Dovedale bread, in 1992 because he wanted to bake bread that was wholesome and vital, as organic as possible and didn't contain preservatives. He originally used flour from traditional varieties of wheat that were hardier and didn't require spraying, and then sourced all the organic grains from New Zealand Biograins in Christchurch. He decided to specialise in gluten-free and wheat-free breads and uses only wild yeast (yeast that is naturally floating around in the air). Roland says his breads are special, not only because of this but also because of the lactobacilli the leavens attract, which produce lactic acid and contribute to the piquant flavour. Wild yeast and lactobacilli produce different flavours depending on the area. In Dovedale they were close to beech and pine forests and hedgerows of hawthorn and barberry, so these dictated the flavour of the ferments. He makes rice bread, rice and oat bread,

Moïse Cerson from Le Pommier, Wairarapa

Rachel Scott, Rachel Scott Bread in Canterbury

rice and fruit bread, bannock, Easter buns, and rye and linseed bread – all manna from heaven for coeliacs. The breads are all hand moulded in the European style of wet-ferment.

Last year Roland sold the business to Greg Tzinavos; he consults and helps Greg from time to time and the bread is still as good. He is now building a brick wood-fired bread oven in his garden and teaches bread-making classes in Nelson. Roland can be contacted at: crdallas@xtra.co.nz. You can buy Dovedale bread in health-food shops and supermarkets all over New Zealand and by mail order, and their email address is: dovedale@ts.co.nz.

THE FRENCH BAKER IN GREYTOWN

When French pâtissier Moïse Cerson founded his French bakery, Le Pommier, in the Wairarapa in 2000, the local food scene was somewhat limited. With a small budget, a tiny kitchen and barely adequate equipment, his own resources were limited too. Undaunted, Cerson focused on producing artisan French breads, viennoiserie and pâtisserie. And right from the outset his customers were in love – we heard about Le Pommier all the way up in Auckland. With recognition came expansion. Cerson now has a larger shop on Main Street with the name changed to The French Baker, a larger kitchen, better equipment and lots more staff. The bakery is very light and airy, with lots of room for sitting and munching on a tuna-filled bun and flat white. In the new shop he maintains his perfectionism and exacting professional standards. Never compromising on ingredients, he hates 'baker's butter' and egg and milk powders, instead using real ingredients. Moïse is a gifted baker and his skills have been honed by his experience in fine dining kitchens and bakeries all over the world. He is renowned for his refined, pure touch with pastries like *tarte au citron*, *tart au chocolat*, *chausson aux pommes* or apple turnover, berry tart, and French breads like *pain au chocolat*, and *brioche framboise*. On the sunny day when I visited at lunchtime the filled breads were walking out the door and I could just glimpse scraps of terrine and salad. His wife Andrea told me they will soon start doing *plats du jour* like lentils with sausage, which will change daily. Can't wait.

RACHEL SCOTT BREAD IN CANTERBURY

Rachel Scott Bread produces artisanal hand-moulded breads using the highest quality unadulterated ingredients. As Rachel puts it: 'Keeping it simple means finding balance

Dean Brettschneider's fig, almond & aniseed puffette

This action-packed mini loaf is 'chock full' of delicious small, sweet figs, toasted almonds and is elegantly scented with whole aniseeds. Slice thinly and enjoy with a mild full-cream blue cheese.

2/3 CUP WHOLE ALMONDS

3/4 CUP DRIED FIGS

3 TABLESPOONS WHOLE ANISEEDS

2 CUPS STRONG FLOUR
(OR HIGH GRADE)

2 TEASPOONS SALT

2 TEASPOONS OLIVE OIL

14G (2 SACHETS) DRIED YEAST

310ML WARM WATER
(approximately blood temperature)

1. Preheat the oven to 150°C. On an oven tray lightly toast the almonds until light brown in colour, then cool and roughly chop.

2. To prepare the figs, remove the hard stem and cut each fig into 5 or 6 pieces.

3. Place the whole aniseeds in a mortar and very gently bruise by rotating the pestle around the mortar 2–3 times. Alternatively, place the aniseeds on a solid bench and lightly roll with a rolling pin to bruise.

4. Place flour, salt, olive oil and yeast in a large mixing bowl and mix together. Add the warm water and using a wooden spoon combine these ingredients until a dough mass has formed. Tip the dough out on to a lightly floured surface and knead for 10–15 minutes (taking a rest period of 30 seconds every 3–4 minutes) until the dough is smooth and elastic in feel.

5. Add the figs, almonds and aniseeds and gently knead to incorporate evenly into the dough, taking care not to smash up the figs too much. Place in a lightly oiled bowl, cover with cling film and leave in a warm place to almost double in size (approximately 45 minutes).

6. Remove the cling film and tip the dough out on to the bench. Gently deflate the gassed dough by folding it on to itself 3–4 times. Return dough to the lightly oiled bowl and cover with cling film. Leave for a further 30 minutes in a warm place.

7. Tip the dough out on to the bench and divide into 4 equal pieces. Flatten each piece of dough into a small rectangle and roll up into a tight 'Swiss roll' with tapered ends. Place the roll on an oven tray lined with baking paper. Cover with a sheet of plastic wrap and allow to prove (rise) for approximately 45 minutes.

8. Preheat your oven to 230°C and place a small ovenproof dish in the bottom. Using a sharp knife, slash 3 times diagonally across the top of the roll. Brush with water and place in the preheated oven on the middle shelf. Quickly throw 3–4 ice cubes into the small ovenproof dish to create steam in the oven.

9. Bake for 15 minutes and then turn the tray around. Reduce the oven temperature to 200°C and bake for a further 10 minutes or until a dark golden-brown colour. When the bottom is tapped it should sound hollow. Remove from the oven and place on a cooling rack to cool.

makes 1 small loaf

within this elemental process; allowing food to taste of itself through recognising inherent flavours and aiming to enhance, not cloud them. In my experience, a loaf of bread made with passion is not only sustenance for the body, it is also fuel for the spirit.' Rachel lives in the small town of Amberley in North Canterbury, is beautiful and esoteric, and talks of the poetry and free-flowing spirit of bread. Eating her bread makes you feel you are doing something good and sensual for yourself. The bread is made from organic, stone-ground wheat flour from Ashburton and is slowly fermented in cool temperatures. My favourite is her soft, perfumed ciabatta. This is raised with an Italian *biga* starter – a fermentation of flour, water and a little yeast. It is kneaded with extra virgin olive oil and is pulled into the true ciabatta or 'slipper' shape. Rachel also makes sourdough, baguettes, fougasse, rye boule and seasonally, thyme bread, walnut bread and brioche. A recent innovation is a uniquely New Zealand bread made with karengo seaweed, rye flour and purple wheat. This loaf, very good with seafood, is probably the closest New Zealand has come to producing a true indigenous bread. Because she makes every single loaf with her own hands and refuses to do otherwise, Rachel's bread is mostly found near where she lives, in places such as the Nor'Wester Café in Amberley, but it can also be found at the Epicurean Workshop and The Italian Grocer in Auckland, Kapiti Fine Foods and Merivale Fresh Choice in Christchurch. Demand far exceeds her supply, but she doesn't wish to expand because bread-making is a labour of love.

Rachel is also well regarded for her chocolates made from Belgian Callebaut chocolate which she considers has a clear base taste on which to impose other flavours, as in her *truffes au chocolats noir* (dark chocolate truffles with a voluptuous centre and thin crisp chocolate shell rolled in cocoa powder) and her almond biscotti, which she calls *ossi dei morti* (bones of the dead), and her caramels. For Rachel, chocolate is as much about texture as about taste. Her astounding salted caramels were inspired by the ones she ate in Normandy but she dips hers in sweet, dark chocolate. I have never eaten anything like them anywhere. You can find her website through: www.canterburyfare.co.nz.

BROAD BEANS
How did those horrible cardboard bullets we were served at boarding school turn into the sweet summer treat we are now gasping over? I'll tell you how. Our betters never took the trouble to shell them. Tiny broad beans can be eaten raw or cooked with the pod but larger, older ones should be shelled. I think the easiest way to do this is to blanch the beans in their pods, shell them, blanch the beans again and serve. They are a lot of work but really worth it. Pale green, slightly chestnutty and unbearably sweet when young, they now find their way on to the best menus in town. They're very good in risotto with sweet peas and asparagus tips or dressed warm with vinaigrette and finely chopped shallots.

BROCCOLINI
This absolutely delicious vegetable is a new hybrid cross between broccoli and Chinese kale, and Leader Brand have the sole rights to it in New Zealand. It has a long, slender stem, reminiscent of asparagus, and is topped with small flower buds that resemble a cross between broccoli florets and an asparagus

---

Broad-bean salad

1.5KG FRESH BROAD BEANS OR 500G FROZEN

2 TABLESPOONS OLIVE OIL

1 SMALL ONION, FINELY CHOPPED

2 CLOVES GARLIC, FINELY CHOPPED

1/2 TEASPOON CUMIN SEEDS

1/2 TEASPOON SEA SALT

JUICE OF ONE LIME

2 TABLESPOONS CHOPPED FRESH MINT OR FLAT-LEAF PARSLEY

1. If the beans are fresh, remove from the pods and plunge them into salted, boiling water for 3 minutes. Drain and run cold water over them to keep the green colour. Remove the outer skins. Follow the same process for frozen beans.

2. Heat the oil in a frying pan and sauté the onion, garlic and cumin for a few minutes until golden, then add the beans and salt. Cook gently for another 3 minutes.

3. Place bean mixture in a bowl, pour over lime juice and toss in the mint or parsley.

serves 4

tip. Broccolini is picked, trimmed, bunched and labelled in the field all in one motion, preventing handling damage to this delicate vegetable. It has a perfumed flavour, the stems reminiscent of sweet peas, while the florets are milder and sweeter than traditional broccoli. It's better than broccoli and steamed until al dente and served with a slash of farm butter and a dash of sea salt it provides exquisite moments of gastronomic pleasure.

BUTCHERS
To be a good butcher is an art that needs to be supported. A good butcher has to buy good meat, treat it with respect, cut it into joints that are attractive and useful, and waste nothing. A good butcher doesn't pre-package the meat, doesn't cover it in plastic and doesn't disguise it in ghastly sauces and terrifying marinades. He hangs his meat properly, is helpful when you ask for something different and labels the product carefully with as much information as possible. He also has to have a fabulous personality, love his job and call you every time something special comes in.

BUTTER
Matatoki farm near Thames in the Waikato make organic cheeses and yoghurt so thick and luscious you could cut it with a knife. They also make farm-style, handmade butter, which is slightly salty, a pale creamy colour and has a faintly nutty flavour. Kelvin and Christine Haigh's butter is in such demand they have a backlog. They only make it when there is cream available, and customers can't get enough of it. It can be purchased from Harvest Wholefoods, Sabato, East West and selected organic food stores in Auckland.

At Rangiuru farm in Norsewood, Simon and Marianne Domper not only make great cheese but also other milk products, including buttermilk, yoghurt, quark and butter. The product that is on my mind as I march purposefully toward their cheese stand at the Hawke's Bay market is always their sweet and fresh-tasting butter. It is unsalted and slightly sour because it's made from sour cream.

Karikaas at Loburn in Rangiora make Dutch-style cheese and a cultured, unsalted butter. Martin at Canterbury Cheesemongers raves about it and, like the other handmade butters, he can never get enough of it. He describes it as smelling like fresh cream and loves slapping dollops of it on to bread and eating it like cheese.

Ridge Processing Ltd in Te Rapa, Hamilton, make organic butter. It is salted, creamy and sweet, the taste altering slightly depending on the season.

Aalt Verkerk of Verkerk's, Christchurch

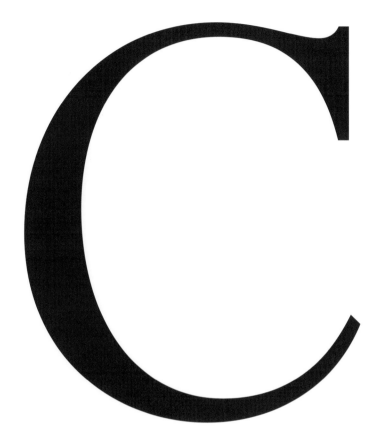

CAKES

We in New Zealand are cake-makers from way back. The first cake I was taught to make at cooking classes in primary school was a sponge, which is quite hard to get right. The best cake-recipe writer in New Zealand in my opinion is Julie Le Clerc, who lives in Auckland. She writes lots of other cookbooks, but people seem to be addicted to her cakes. I am under orders to send my mother Julie's newspaper recipes every Wednesday. There is something deeply reassuring about beating butter and sugar together, then adding eggs and flour – it works in every sense, every time. The smell of good cake-making, like the sound of flowing water, is indescribable in its evocation of innocence and happiness. Cake-making is mysterious, loving and uniquely associated with pleasure – there are no illusions of it being good for you.

It is very therapeutic to depart from reality now and then and go right through the looking glass to indulge in the fantasy world of cake-making. It may only be a trifle (so-called because it was meant to be trifling and easy) or it may be a chocolate and almond cake, but it will clear the kitchen and your mind of any lurking boredom and stagnation. Then, of course, there are the 'unapproachables' – the haute-cuisine, fabled, near-quixotic cakes like Paris-Brest or Black Forest cake. My personal nemesis is to make a real apple strudel from real pulled strudel pastry, which bears no resemblance to the filo pastry it normally replaces. Cake-making is a kind of minuet of graceful movements where no conversation is needed. The room is warm, the spirit of your grandmother is close by and the old rituals lead to serenity.

If you want to experience the happiness of traditional, plain cake-making in New Zealand, you have no further to

Goat's cheese & fig cake

3 TABLESPOONS CASTOR SUGAR

5 FRESH RIPE FIGS, CUT IN HALF CROSSWISE

175G (1½ CUPS) PLAIN FLOUR

1 TABLESPOON BAKING POWDER

175G BUTTER, SOFTENED

175G CASTOR SUGAR

200G CREAMY SOFT GOAT'S CHEESE

3 EGGS

2 TABLESPOONS APRICOT JAM

1. Preheat the oven to 180°C. Butter a 24cm springform cake tin and line the base with buttered baking paper. Sprinkle the paper with the first measure of castor sugar and arrange the figs, cut side down, on top.

2. Sift the flour and baking powder together. In a separate bowl, beat the butter, sugar and goat's cheese together until white and fluffy. Beat in the eggs one by one. Add the dry ingredients and fold in. Spread the cake mixture evenly over the figs.

3. Bake cake for about 50 minutes or until the sides of the cake have pulled away from the tin. Transfer to a wire rack and allow to cool completely. Run a knife around the sides of the tin to loosen the cake, then invert on to a serving dish.

4. Melt the apricot jam in a small saucepan, then push through a sieve. Brush the top of the cake with the jam, and top with fresh berries, if you feel so inclined.

5. To serve, dust lavishly with icing sugar and cut into wedges.

serves 8

go than a good, old-fashioned A&P show. There are women who enter cakes in these shows, at the cost of 20c per entry, whose mothers did the same, as did their grandmothers and their great-grandmothers. And the cakes haven't changed much. The usual suspects are all there – sponges, rich fruit cakes, chocolate cakes, loaves, banana cakes. Believe it or not, most of the recipes come from the *Edmonds Cookbook.*

There are speciality cake shops all round New Zealand now, one of the best being the City Cake Company in Mt Eden, Auckland. They are artisan bakers, and the cakes are baked daily. They use the best ingredients, no premix, and bake in small batches to preserve the authentic flavour. It is physically impossible to walk past their shop while all the beautifully decorated temptations are sitting in the window with your name written all over them. They are a display of such deliciousness as summer-fruit tarts, dark-chocolate Parisian (rich and moist and topped with chocolate rosettes and sparkling silver balls), gin and lemon-syrup Madeira cake and passionfruit cheesecake.

The Goat's cheese and fig cake recipe on this page is kindly reproduced courtesy of Books for Cooks bookshop in London.

CHEESE

New Zealand has picked up on the worldwide renaissance in cheese making. We're not up there with the French but we're not bad, our main problem being forced pasteurisation of our milk. A boiled-milk cheese will never develop the complexity and character of a raw-milk cheese. Having said that, cheese is still one of the most varied and subtle foods in the world, with taste and aroma characteristics so unique that humans have adored eating it for centuries. In New Zealand we make the seven varieties – fresh, fresh-ripened, soft-ripened, washed-rind, semi-soft, semi-firm and hard. We always made good Cheddar, and now seem to be in love with goat's- and sheep's-milk cheeses, having passed through the bland faux-Camembert stage.

At the 2004 cheese awards, 30 of the 450 entries came from sheep. Bob Berry of Whitestone Cheese was the first to experiment with 1000 litres of sheep's milk six years ago and now produces 12 tonnes of the stuff a year, increasing at the rate of 25 per cent yearly.

Europeans have, of course, used sheep's milk for centuries. The Greeks have their briny feta and stretchy haloumi; the French have salty Roquefort, all the Brebis cheeses and the Pyrenees cheeses; the Italians have all their different pecorinos, a myriad ricottas, scamorza and lots of mixed milk cheeses; and then there is the nutty, caramely manchego from Spain. Bob says it's great milk to work with – it's rich, high in protein, high-yielding and produces interesting flavours like parsley, saltiness and lanolin. Sheep's milk cheese is satisfying and rather elegant, and you can age it in the bottom of your wardrobe for a long time.

There's nothing I like better than a lump of sheep curd slathered in Waiheke olive oil, Grassmere sea salt and freshly ground black pepper, with a very flinty sauvignon blanc. There is also nothing wrong with a lump of five-year-old Barry's Bay Cheddar and a glass of Irish whisky while you're waiting for the toenail polish to dry. One of the great wine and food match myths is that red wines work well with cheese. This mix rarely works because most cheeses have a high fat content

and red wines suffer incredibly when drunk with them. Botrytised wines go well with blue cheeses – the sweet and the salty together are sublime. Don't eat cheese with biscuits or crackers, as their crunchy texture detracts from the cheese. Best to use rustic breads, baguettes or walnut and raisin bread with no butter. Serve it simply on a wooden board, refraining from complicated schizophrenic chutney and fruit displays. Maybe just a few slices of quince paste would be sufficient.

Cheese should be kept in the plastic crisper drawer in the bottom of the fridge, wrapped in wax paper. Putting plastic wrap on cheese is the same as putting a plastic bag over a baby's head. Take it out of the fridge an hour before you wish to eat it, to bring it up to room temperature. Never eat cheese cold from the fridge – it tastes bitter.

There are too many good cheese-makers in New Zealand to mention them all, but these are some of my favourites.

MY FAVOURITE CHEESE-MAKERS
- Mahoe in Kerikeri
- Puhoi Valley
- Crescent Dairy Goats in Auckland
- Kapiti Cheeses in Kapiti Coast
- Meyer in Hamilton
- Matatoki Farm in Waikato
- Rangiuru Farm in Norsewood
- Gladstone goat's cheeses in Masterton
- Barry's Bay Cheese in Akaroa
- Whitestone at Waitaki in Oamaru
- Evansdale in Otago
- Hohepa Farms in Clive, Hawke's Bay

ZANY ZEUS CHEESE
This is a boutique cheese-making operation that specialises in handcrafted cheeses. It is a small family business which uses traditional open-vat techniques for cheese manufacture. Mike Matsis and his Greek Cypriot mother, Lefki, make some of the best cheese in New Zealand, but try getting your hands on his ricotta. This guy is a complete natural – he won gold in the 2000 New Zealand Cheese Awards with his Cypriot-style haloumi cheese, just five days after starting commercial production. In 2004 he managed the astonishing feat of beating 432 entries in the awards and scooping the supreme award for his heavenly, fresh, handmade ricotta. As well as haloumi and ricotta, Mike makes feta, mozzarella, Greek yoghurt and is soon to start an organic line of cheese called … guess what? Zorganic.

Haloumi is an unusual semi-hard cheese, characterised by its squeakiness on the teeth. It is made by the usual method of separating the curds from the whey, but then the pressed curd is put back into the hot whey. The curd pieces sink and then rise again to the surface when they are properly textured. The cheese is then removed and cooled, folded with fresh mint, salted and kept in brine. The best way to eat it is to slice it thickly and fry it quickly until golden on both sides. Drizzle the haloumi with lemon juice, open a bottle of retsina and dream on. Lefki lives in Wanganui but pops in from time to time to keep an eye on Mike, and she is a fantastic cook. The day I was there she made a Greek feast worthy of the gods. You can buy the cheese from Mike's shop in Moera, Wellington, or he will deliver anywhere in New Zealand, door to door. His website is: www.zanyzeus.co.nz.

Martin Aspinwall, Canterbury Cheesemongers, Christchurch

CANTERBURY CHEESEMONGERS
Sarah and Martin Aspinwall are the best cheese-maturers and -sellers in New Zealand and they reside in Christchurch. She runs the joint, and he is mad about cheese to the point that he reads cheese-science books for fun. She is a New Zealander and he's English, but no one's perfect, and they are entirely delightful with their two children. Martin is, however, almost perfect, on account of his eccles cakes and bread-making skills. They buy cheeses direct from small cheese-makers then mollycoddle, wash, turn, lard and watch

C

them until they are of perfect maturity when they are sold in the shop and at the market. Buying cheese from Martin is like buying knowledge, beauty and history. Hard cheeses like Cheshire, Gouda, maasdam and Cheddar are kept at 12–14°C, blue cheeses at 5°C and brick and white-moulded cheeses at 8°C. At the shop, the cheeses are in a glass room so everyone can see them maturing, but each week they take an exciting ride to the market in the bright yellow 1970s Simca Fourgenette. This van has been adapted so that the rear doors open revealing a refrigerated cheese display, a door-mounted wash basin and a blackboard listing their wares. The cheeses are cut to order and customers are encouraged to taste before they buy.

In Martin's opinion there are about a dozen really good cheese-makers in New Zealand and a third of those are making good sheep cheeses. Martin says he's hard-pressed to think of something he wouldn't eat with cheese, and one mustn't be all posh about matching cheese and wine. For example, he likes a good espresso or Turkish coffee slightly sweetened with something like baklava or ginger biscuits and a piece of Lancashire cheese that has lactic sourness. Then there's bread, jam and cheese; pasta and pecorino; bittersweet chocolate and hard Cheddar; intense Gouda or Parmesan. Fruit with cheese is gorgeous – try pecorino with pears. Eating fatty sheep cheese with a piece of tart fruit balances the fat.

CHEESE-MAKING WORKSHOPS:

KATHERINE MOBRAY

As soon as I saw tiny Katherine lugging her heavy cheese-making equipment into my apartment kitchen, I knew I wanted to make cheese. As with bread, vinegar, jam and I suppose home beer-making, there's something very romantic and *je ne sais quoi* about concocting your very own cheese. There's a bit of effort involved and special equipment to buy, but it's worth it. I told Katherine my kitchen was small, but she said, 'Don't worry, so's mine, don't let that put you off.' Soon a bucket, a water bath for heating milk, gas burner, trays, cheese press, mould and assorted thermometers, measuring cups and whisks were decorating my flat. Katherine is the size of a toothpick, with long blonde hair in a thick plait. She has huge blue eyes and looks just like a milkmaid from an old painting. I imagine all her life people have treated her like a doll and touched her beautiful hair, marvelling at the honey colour.

Don't be mistaken by her appearance though. Katherine

is a very disciplined woman, meticulous in her method and teaching, and doesn't suffer fools gladly. She's there to teach cheese-making, not to be treated like a delicate fairy.

Katherine showed me how to make Cheddar. All the equipment plus your hands must be sterilised in sodium hypochloride, used for baby's bottles. The first thing you must have is the right milk. The best milk is if you live on a farm and can get fresh, raw milk straight from the cow, sheep or goat. Next to that the best is A2 milk, Naturalea organic whole milk and Meadow Fresh farmhouse full-cream milk. Homogenised types of milk are not suitable as the rennet does not coagulate sufficiently well. We went through the whole magical process, right through until the cheese was sitting in the press. Ten litres of milk was reduced to 1kg of cheese! Now I have to wait two months for it to age, at which point I will feel like a real woman, able to make bread, vinegar, jam and cheese. Katherine also teaches how to make feta, haloumi, ricotta, Gouda, mozzarella, quark, yoghurt and other milk products. The easiest is mascarpone, but you will have to do her class to find out how.

Katherine teaches all over New Zealand, usually at community centres like Epsom Community House in Auckland. The course lasts from 10 a.m. until 3 p.m. and costs $80. Her phone number is 09 276 8411. She has also written a booklet called *Cheese-making at Home*.

You can buy cheese-making equipment from a very nice lady and colleague of Katherine's called Anna Rolfe at Cuisine Accessory Company. Her e-mail address is: anchar@icr.net.nz.

JEAN MANSFIELD

Jean Mansfield teaches cheese-making classes in Waihi. Her e-mail is: jeanmansfield58@hotmail.com.

CHEESELINKS

The people everyone seems to have learned from are Neil and Carole Willman in Victoria, Australia. They manage CheeseLinks, a business supplying ingredients, accessories and cheese-making training at Little River for commercial and farmhouse cheese-makers. Neil is a senior lecturer in cheese-making at Gilbert Chandler College, Australia's only dedicated dairy college. They have written a very good book called *Home Cheese Making*. Their website is: www.cheeselinks.com.au.

The New Zealand representative of CheeseLinks is Cryn Russell who teaches home cheese-making in Hawke's Bay. Her classes are from 9.30 a.m. to 3.30 p.m. and cost $110. Her website is: www.cheeselinksnz.co.nz.

CHERRIES

Bowls of blushing, plump cherries, along with strawberries, are synonymous with Christmas in New Zealand. My childhood memories of cherries are of little flavour bites, like lollies, of pink, red or white fruit. These days we have fallen prey to the 'bigger is better' slogan and expect the 'two-bite' cherry – crisp, flavourful and juicy. Cherries are now so big they are almost little nectarines. These are great for a clafoutis (cherry flan), as there are fewer stones to spit out, but they are somehow uncherry-like. Cherries are grown in Central Otago, Marlborough and Hawke's Bay. I also like bitter, wild cherries found in the subtropical north of New Zealand. Of course, humans are not the only creatures that adore cherries – we have declared all-out war on the birds, who have a tendency to get to the cherries first and can wipe out an entire crop before anyone can do anything about it. We are also at war with the rain, which makes the flesh soft, expanding it and cracking the skin. To combat these enemies, cherry-growers use nets, calcium sprays and raincoats. Like strawberries, cherries don't continue to ripen once picked, so you have to pick them ripe. The whole cherry business is, by its nature, very labour intensive. Everything is done by hand, and as cherries retain the heat of the sun, they have to be immediately hydro-cooled to 2°C after picking to prevent over-ripening in the packing shed.

CHOCOLATE

Chocolate – that heart of darkness, that dangerously addictive drug, that corrupter of cocoa virgins. Few foods inspire passion and loyalty as chocolate does. My siblings and I had our chocolate and lollies rationed as children, which created a culture of chocolate longing for us. Sweet-toothed Dad brought plain dark chocolate home on Friday nights after work; our wealthy and doting grandparents brought us expensive chocolates in boxes with beautiful ladies on the cover at Christmas time; even a Topsy – a chocolate-coated ice-cream on a stick – was a special treat. But it wasn't until I went to live in France that I became a genuine chocophile, seduced by the blatantly pornographic displays in behind those precious plate-glass windows of the Paris shops called *chocolatiers*. It took me a while to get used to quality chocolate with its high cocoa content and to appreciate the slight bitterness, because I had been educated to sugar- and milk-polluted confectionery, clearly the work of the devil.

Ligurian Focaccia

In Recco, Liguria, where I learnt this recipe, the restaurant used a local soft cheese called formaggetta. You can also use stracchino or crescenza. These delightful cheeses are runny and soft but we don't have access to them in New Zealand as they have to be eaten fresh. Possible substitutes are cream cheese or soft goat's cheese. In Liguria they use a large, flat, copper pan about 50cm in diameter to cook the focaccia, but you could also use a cookie tray or roasting pan – the biggest one you have that will fit into your oven. The bread is normally cooked in a wood-fired oven with heather branches thrown in, so it smells heavenly when it emerges. This recipe serves 6 or 12, depending on how much you love it.

200G WHITE FLOUR
4 TABLESPOONS EXTRA VIRGIN OLIVE OIL
4 TABLESPOONS COLD WATER
250G SOFT, FRESH CHEESE
EXTRA OLIVE OIL FOR BRUSHING
SEA SALT

1. Make a circle of flour on the work bench, then pour the oil and water into the middle. Mix together with your hands, adding more water if necessary and knead until you have a soft ball. Allow to rest for an hour.

2. Preheat the oven to the hottest it will go. Knead dough again for a few minutes, let rest for 5 minutes, then divide in 2.

3. Roll out 1 ball of dough very thin, then put your fists under the dough and try to widen it and make it thinner and thinner. It should be almost transparent.

4. Oil a baking pan well and cover it with the dough. Dollop lumps of cheese on top.

5. Roll out the other ball of dough and lay it on top. Brush copiously with oil and sprinkle with sea salt.

6. Bake for 6 minutes. Cut into squares or triangles and eat immediately.

serves 6

Clafoutis with cherry compote

500G CHERRIES
30G FLOUR
PINCH OF SALT
60G SUGAR (OR HONEY)
4 EGGS
600ML MILK
4 TABLESPOONS KIRSCH

1. Preheat the oven to 180°C. Put the washed, unpitted cherries in a shallow, buttered baking dish.

2. Make a batter by sifting the flour and salt into a bowl. Add the sugar or honey. Beat in the eggs, one by one, along with the milk.

3. Strain this mixture over the cherries and drizzle the kirsch over the top. Bake the clafoutis for 45 minutes or until golden and puffy.

4. Sprinkle with sugar and eat warm or at room temperature.

Cherry compote

500G CHERRIES
100G SUGAR (OR HONEY)
JUICE OF HALF A LEMON
1 VANILLA POD
1 TABLESPOON KIRSCH

1. Remove the stalks and wash the cherries. Place them in a saucepan with the sugar, lemon juice and vanilla pod. Gently bring to the boil, then turn down to a simmer.

2. When the fruit is tender, lift it out with a slotted spoon. Reduce the juice for a few minutes, stir in the kirsch and pour over the cherries.

serves 6

The secret to choosing good chocolate is to read the information on the label carefully. Ideally chocolate should contain nothing more than cocoa paste, cane sugar, cocoa butter, maybe a little cream and natural vanilla. With a cocoa content of 60–70 per cent, which is a very good-quality chocolate, there is little room for other ingredients such as sugar. Too much sugar and a low cocoa content means that any chocolate flavour will be masked by sweetness. Good chocolate can be recognised by its uniform dark, glossy surface, silky smooth to the touch. It will make a clean break in your fingers and when you bite into it, it will break with a crisp snap. As you eat the chocolate it will melt in your mouth and you will be aware of its silky, non-cloying texture, smooth but not fatty, and its intense, rich flavour with a pleasant bitterness and a lingering, fruity finish. Chocolate contains everything you need to make you happy – uppers, endorphins, seratonin, anti-depressives and phenols, which are good for coronary arteries. As you can see from this impressive research, you would ruin your health if you did not eat chocolate.

And guess what? Chocolate really does grow on trees. When I was in Oaxaca, Mexico, I saw with my very own eyes the large cocoa pods that had fallen from the trees. If you shook the pods you could hear the cocoa beans inside rattling around. In Mexico they drink chocolate rather than eat it and in the country it is still prepared in the home. The brownish-red beans are roasted to develop flavour, reduce moisture content and remove the skins, then they are ground on a flat stone called a metate until they become a thick, sticky paste. Sugar is then ground in, along with any other additives the family might like such as vanilla, coffee, cinnamon or almonds. The smell is intoxicating. Chocolate produced for sale in bulk to chocolate-makers is a much more complicated process. Grinding is done by temperature-controlled metal mills, then the paste is refined by passing through steel rollers. It is then conched – a process of kneading the mass intensively with heated rotary conches. This is how the chocolate ends up smooth, rather than with a biscuity texture like the Mexican stuff.

The best chocolate in the world is the French Valrhona, which you can buy in specialty shops in New Zealand. But we also have some very good chocolate-makers here buying their chocolate couverture (with a very high cocoa-butter content) from honourable sources like Belgian Callebaut.

WALTER BAIER OF CHOCOLATE TEMPTATIONS

One bleak day in Austria, a 22-year-old pastry chef looked at a brochure about that exotic, faraway, Pacific paradise – New Zealand. There were girls in grass skirts and the sun apparently shone the whole time. So he jumped on a boat, as one did in those days. Imagine Walter's shock when he arrived in stolid 1960s New Zealand with its beastly Wellington weather and not a dusky maiden in sight. Undeterred, he set to making cakes and pastries, opened a shop in Wellington called Konditorei Aida and ran it successfully for 27 years. Wishing to concentrate solely on chocolate-making, which he had always loved, Walter then bought a small existing chocolate shop in Hataitai called Chocolate Temptations, where today he is a one-man band.

Out the back of the shop, Walter fashions completely by hand wondrous things from Belgian Callebaut chocolate. It could be a decorative piece of marzipan fruit or a four-tier wedding cake that can take up to 20 hours to decorate. He is a true

C

artist in his approach to making traditional chocolates, tempering the liquid by hand, inventing new fillings, using top-quality ingredients and making only as much as he can sell. Tempering or stabilising is a process of melting chocolate down to the perfect temperature to make it set shiny and silky. Walter will take a 4kg slab of dark chocolate and melt it at 48°C, then transfer two-thirds of it to a marble slab where he lets it cool. He then gradually adds the rest of the warm chocolate until the mixture reaches 32°C, which is the perfect consistency to start working with it. Working with it means using a spatula to mix and move it around. He can tell by feel and appearance when the chocolate is exactly right. The object of this exercise is to 'seed' the mixture with cocoa butter crystals of a uniform and stable type that will keep well during storage. If dried fruits or nuts are added, they go in at this stage. Walter makes a range of truffles, moulded chocolates with tiny little hand-piped Queen Marys on top and seasonal specialities. At Christmas he will make special things like *lebkuchen* (gingerbread) figures and trees. He teaches culinary students at WelTec and adult-education classes at Wellington High School and Newlands College. The night classes are more for fun than anything else – people can make something fabulous quickly and take it home to win friends and influence people.

DE SPA CHOCOLATIER

In 1997 I met a wonderful old gentleman called Jean-Marie Bara. He was Belgian, spoke better French than English, and had been talked into coming to New Zealand to make chocolates by John de Spa. Jean-Marie had done the seven-year apprenticeship, as is required in Belgium, had worked for the Belgian royal family, and had been making fabulous pastries and chocolates for 30 years. It is really due to his flair and expertise that de Spa chocolates have been a success story.

The chocolates are made with Callebaut, butter, sugar, fresh cream and milk, with no additives, dyes, preservatives or vegetable fat added. The lack of preservatives mean de Spa chocolates have a shelf life of only six weeks – they are a fresh product handmade to order and are never stored. These chocolates are absolutely succulent with intense flavour and smoothness and a rich, lingering aftertaste. Jean-Marie and his staff make over 75 crème-filled chocolates and chocolate truffles. De Spa Chocolatier also produces dairy-free and sugar-free chocolates for those sensitive souls who are intolerant. I prefer the dark chocolates; these come in flavours like champagne truffles, dipped candied orange, marzipan frangelico cream, orange ganache and kirsch cherries, which literally explode in your mouth. Their list of products is endless and includes chocolate bars, cooking chocolate so you can make your own hot drink, Grand Marnier truffles and speciality wedding and Easter chocolates.

De Spa has always been synonymous with European elegance and style – even their shops are sophisticated temples to the cocoa bean, with glamorous green marble counters and temperature-controlled rooms. Their chocolates are delicate creations and staff in de Spa shops wear gloves and treat them like rubies. Visitors to the de Spa factory at Ferrymead, Christchurch, can observe the *chocolatiers* at work through a glass-walled kitchen and can also do a tour of the factory. The fastest-growing part of the business is now its Internet store. You can buy the product all over New Zealand, and their website is: www.despa.co.nz.

Fig & chocolate panforte

110G HAZELNUTS
100G ALMONDS
3 TEASPOONS SESAME SEEDS
100G CANDIED ORANGE RIND, CHOPPED
125G DRIED FIGS, CHOPPED
80G FLOUR
1 TEASPOON CINNAMON
150G SUGAR
4 TABLESPOONS HONEY
50G BUTTER
1 TABLESPOON ANISEED BRANDY
100G CHOPPED CHOCOLATE
ICING SUGAR FOR DUSTING

1. Grease and line a 23cm springform tin with baking paper. Preheat the oven to 150°C.

2. Grill or fry the nuts and seeds until brown. Leave to cool.

3. Mix the nuts in a bowl with the orange rind, figs, flour and cinnamon.

4. Put sugar, honey, butter and brandy in a saucepan and melt them together. Cook the syrup until it reaches 120°C on a sugar thermometer, or a little of it dropped into cold water forms a soft ball when moulded between your fingers and thumb.

5. Pour the syrup into the nut mixture and mix well. Add the chocolate and immediately pour into the tin. Smooth the surface and bake for 35 minutes.

6. Cool in the tin until the cake firms up enough to remove from the tin. Peel off the paper and cool completely. Dust liberally with icing sugar to serve.

serves 6

Chocolate baklava

Chef Amanda Laird helped me put together this recipe. It makes approximately 50 little 'cigars'.

for the filling:
200G HAZELNUTS, CHOPPED
1/2 CUP DRIED BREADCRUMBS
1/4 CUP SUGAR
1/2 TEASPOON GROUND CINNAMON
1/2 TEASPOON GROUND CLOVES
1/2 CUP CURRANTS
70G DARK VALRHONA CHOCOLATE
1 PACKET FILO PASTRY
3/4 CUP MELTED BUTTER

for the syrup:
2 CUPS SUGAR
1 CUP WATER
1/2 CUP MUSCAT WINE

1. To make the syrup, boil the sugar and water together for 15 minutes or until syrupy. Remove from the heat and add the Muscat, then cool.

2. Mix the filling ingredients together in a bowl.

3. On a dry surface lay one sheet of filo and brush with butter. Lay another sheet on top of that and brush with butter. Sprinkle 2 tablespoons of filling along the short edge, fold long edges in by a centimetre, then tightly roll filo up to the end. Continue with the other sheets until all the filling is used up.

4. Preheat the oven to 180°C. Place the rolls in a greased, shallow roasting pan and bake for 30 minutes or until golden.

5. Remove the pan from the oven and pour over the syrup. Leave for at least an hour or overnight, then cut into short cigar lengths.

SCHOC CHOCOLATES IN GREYTOWN

Talk about Schoc therapy! You walk into this deceptively quaint chocolate shop in deceptively quaint Greytown and the place is a den of iniquity, a haven of good vibrations, a sex shop of pre-traumatic chocolate syndrome. Schoc chocolates are the best and the most unusual chocolates I've tasted recently, and the experience is not superficial. Thanks to Murray Langham and Roger Simpson, you get to find out that you are what you love in chocolate terms. They're into the whole chocolate psychology thing. Murray asks, 'When we choose a chocolate filling we like, what is it that attracts us? Is it the smell, the texture on our tongue and teeth, the colour, the taste? These centres link into our subconscious minds or the inner part that guides our emotions, our moods, our inner thoughts, our self-esteem. By understanding the meanings of the centres we can begin to see what is guiding us through the complexities of life.' So, despite the fact that the road is littered with the corpses of men who have tried to analyse my taste, Murray and Roger came up with this: because I like almond chocolates I am successful, quick-minded and love change. The downside is people think I am flippant if they don't know me, I am impatient and I want to bend people to my will.

The trick in terms of romance is to find someone who adequately complements an almond personality. They told me not to go anywhere near a Turkish delight person, because they just aren't there for you when you need them – they're too busy finding themselves. A good match might be the chocolate-centre person, who has a sense of humour and is forward-looking. But it doesn't end there. What about post-chocolate behaviour? The person who smoothes out the chocolate wrapper loves to massage and is very sensual, so they probably shouldn't go for the person who shapes the wrapper into a ball – they are bored and jealous. Murray writes books on chocolate therapy and conducts workshops. They are both stars of the New York and Perugia chocolate festivals, where they stun people with their chocology theories and urge the faithful to get in touch with their 'inner centres'.

Murray and Roger bring in couverture from different sources – Belgium, Venezuela, Madagascar and Java – and match different flavours with different strengths of chocolate. For example: lime and chilli is matched with dark chocolate made from 53 per cent cocoa; cardamom with white or dark chocolate; sea salt (which is astonishingly delicious and goes well with champagne) with white chocolate; frankincense, myrrh and gold with dark chocolate. Other ingredients include lemon and cracked pepper, toasted sesame, and lemongrass. There were 47 different flavours at last count. They make a milk chocolate at 32 per cent cocoa mass, a bittersweet at 74 per cent and a 100 per cent, which I thought would be inedible, but was strangely fruity. Schoc chocolates not only taste extremely good but they also feel good in the mouth because there is no milk, fat or preservatives and the couverture is meticulously tempered.

OTHER GOOD CHOCOLATE-MAKERS ARE:
● Bennetts of Mangawhai Ltd in North Auckland
● Devonport Chocolates in Auckland
● Rachel Scott Chocolates – see Bread, page 36
● The Seriously Good Chocolate Company in Invercargill

C

Murray Langham, Schoc Chocolates, Greytown

Peta Mathias, on board the Moana, *off the coast of Stewart Island*

COD
Blue cod, found only in the south, is a bottom-dwelling, tropical fish and not related to true cod. It has tender flesh and a sweet, mild flavour. One day while on Stewart Island I went on a blue-cod fishing trip in a 12-metre, carval-planked launch called *Moana*. A storm was brewing that was one out of the meteorological box, a depression to beat all depressions. On Tuesday 21 November the most ferocious storm on the planet, with its associated winds and rain, crossed New Zealand with a low atmospheric pressure of 950 hectopascals. Roofs were lifted, trees were felled, power was cut and on the Wairarapa coast hurricane-force winds of 156km/h were reported. And what did I do on this day? Why, I went to sea of course. The captain had a sure hand on the wheel and a great sound system with a huge speaker called 'The Eliminator'. He had a selection of CDs that included The Cruel Sea, Pink Floyd, Talking Heads and Mike Oldfield. My fellow fisherpersons were in their element and there were lots of male-bonding rituals, guy stuff, 'heave-ho me hearties, arh arh' and fish-catching going on. I, of course, couldn't catch a fish; everyone else caught multiple fish. The blue cod are famous for leaping on to the line, but mine just ate the bait and swam away. No class of a fisherwoman am I. The boylies caught lots of fish (they really are blue), which were gutted there and then on the spot in two flashes of the knife. The captain also had to measure them.

'Yeah, well, it's just in,' he said.

'I didn't know fish had names,' said my friend.

'I told you not to call me Justin,' said my other friend. From then on in all blue cod were called Justin.

On the way back we amused ourselves thinking up all the expressions we could that had a nautical root: 'Freeze the balls off a brass monkey'; 'the sun's over the yard arm' and 'posh' – an expression that came from 'port out, starboard home', the most desirable location for a cabin in British ships sailing to and from the East, being the north-facing or shaded side. There was also 'two sheets to the wind' (drunk); 'to come on board' (with a project); 'get alongside'; 'on the rocks'; 'all washed up'; 'rats leaving a sinking ship'; 'chunder – watch under!' and 'sailing close to the wind'.

COFFEE
We make good espresso coffee in New Zealand cafés. We learnt it from the Australians who learnt it from the Italians. Thank God we didn't learn it from the French because they haven't a clue. Many of us have replaced beer with coffee in cultural and social terms, and we take it just as seriously. Now we're all experts in grind, crema and length of flavour. God, what we don't know about length of flavour … We give our children fluffies in tiny coffee cups and they ask for a set of coffee-making equipment when they turn five. If you ask me, there are far too many babies and children in adult cafés. Do we gate-crash their day-care centres and demand coffee? No. So they have no place in our cafés, breaking the sound barrier and grinding porridge into the floor. Mark my words, next thing they will be expecting us to talk to them.

ALLPRESS COFFEE
Coffee is the second-most traded commodity in the world after oil. While supermarket sales of instant coffee are still about five times those of fresh coffee in New Zealand, there is no doubt our preference for the fresh stuff is on the rise. There are some very good coffee roasters in New Zealand – Atlas in Auckland, Hawthorns in Havelock North, Café L'affare in Wellington, Bravo in Dunedin and others – but for my money the best is Allpress in Auckland. Michael Allpress and his delightful wife Carolyn got into coffee in 1986, starting humbly with a coffee cart in Aotea Square then in Victoria Park Market. Then the chic Allpress Café

C

opened in Victoria Street and beans were roasted out the back. Last year they opened Caffetteria – a stylish espresso- and latté-coloured café behind Victoria Park Market in the Brown's Mill building, where they also do the cupping, roasting and processing. Michael is the kind of guy who does everything well; if he had chosen to go into jellybeans, we would have the best jellybeans in the country and you'd better believe they'd have length of flavour.

Michael is a coffee roaster and espresso specialist, supplying the wholesale market with the best arabica beans he can find. Ninety per cent of his business is supplying hospitality and cafés, and about ten per cent is select retail (including Caffetteria). They mostly get what he calls his 'Ponsonby' blend. He is the New Zealand agent for La Marozza espresso machines, which he considers the best in the world. At his café you can buy ten single-origin coffees and seven blends. These change periodically depending on what's available – as coffee is an agricultural product, it's susceptible to changes in climate, harvesting and processing. A coffee bean is a living, wonderful thing to Michael and he treats it like caviar.

The arabica beans are bought only from plantations grown at high altitudes, which deliver a more intense flavour. The selection process is controlled, and Allpress encourage sustainable cultivation by trading equitably with each farmer. The true secret to the taste and quality of the final product, however, is down to the roasting process. Allpress roast in small batches using a new Sivetz fluidised bed hot- air roaster. This method achieves a cleaner tasting, more aromatic coffee with a smooth finish. If you want the thrill of your life, go and stand on the roaster platform and get the vibe – the whole floor trembles and the noise is incredible – they all wear earmuffs. Allpress also have a training room where they run weekly barista sessions for professionals; and once a month you, the amateur, can go to a class and find out the secrets to crema, milk steaming, pouring and presentation. No latté art is tolerated.

In what is called the 'cupping' process, Michael analyses the beans he has bought, mostly from Kenya, Guatemala, Columbia and Sumatra. He makes up three black shots of each sample (in case one is flawed), using not espresso but filter, then he and his team of experts sip each one loudly and quickly (a bit like olive-oil tasting). They are looking for body, length of flavour and, most of all, acidity. Acidity is the most important because it carries the flavour. When I did this with Michael, we went through about a dozen samples. Honestly, they all tasted more or less the same to

moi. Then it all changed. I slurped a divine coffee that tasted like Christmas cake, like the best Valrhona chocolate, like black treacle. It was from Ethiopia and is the best in the world. I instructed Michael to buy up a whole lot immediately, damn the price. He smiled indulgently and said, 'Yes, of course, Peta.'

The food at Allpress is also really good, especially the grilled sandwiches designed by Michael's friend Tony Papas, with whom he is in partnership in a café in Rosebury, Sydney. My favourite is country bread filled with tuna, eggs, olives, parsley and artichokes then grilled. My taste-buds start wanting it as I walk down the street towards the Brown's Mill building. This helps counteract the bitter taste in my mouth from walking past the Les Mills gym. I find the sight of people exercising deeply offensive.

To be king or queen of coffee in your very own home, Michael suggests you buy whole beans, keep them in a sealed container in the fridge, not the freezer, and grind in a high- quality grinder like a Petra, then brew with a filter apparatus, using bleached filters. In terms of strength, if a coffee is of high quality you can drink it stronger than you think without there being any bitterness, so be generous with your amount – 30g for a large cup of coffee is about right. Don't buy more than you need – coffee only stays fresh for about ten days. Michael also says that a little sugar with coffee is a good idea because it enhances the caramels. Because a huge amount of pressure is necessary to produce an espresso with a good crema (top) and to froth milk to the correct velvetiness, it is basically pointless buying a small, domestic espresso machine. The best place to enjoy espresso made with a big, grunty La Marozza is in an espresso bar, with a newspaper, and without babies, thank you.

COOKBOOKS

COOK THE BOOKS IN AUCKLAND
If I could take a bookshop to a desert island it would be Cook the Books in Mt Eden. What more could you want than a little shop full of culinary literature? Their extensive range includes books on food, wine and the culinary arts. They also stock cuisine magazines, including New Zealand's own fabulous and international-award-winning *Cuisine* magazine, and greeting cards and printed stationery such as journals and note-cards, all featuring food images. On the shelves you'll find more than just simple recipe books –

there's food fiction, food and travel, food history and philosophy, health and nutrition, and many other food-related topics. They stock a comprehensive range of New Zealand produced books, all beautifully representing outstanding New Zealand chefs and food writers. The cookbooks are for everyone – professionals, trainee chefs, novice cooks, enthusiastic amateurs or bedtime readers.

Food writers inspire us, inform us, record history for us and reflect our culture to us. We read to lose ourselves and we read to find ourselves. We need food writers to travel for us because, picturesque as it sounds, not many people actually have the constitution for adventure, excitement and romance as a lifestyle. If you can't cure yourself of an obsession, it's best to give in to it and call it a job. If you can't stop collecting, open a junk shop; if you can't stop giving people advice, get a degree and call yourself a psychologist; if you love eating and cooking and can't afford the thousands of dollars worth of cookbooks you want to buy, open a cookbook shop and sit in there all day drooling. That's what Jonathan Rees and Adele Fitzgerald have done.

Food writing and reading is like being in love – you're under the influence. The normal rules don't apply – you're more open, more tolerant, more reckless. You sink into this marvellous world where your table settings are a visual symphony, your meals look like sun-dappled masterpieces, and you are always placid and smiling. You too can be just like Julie Le Clerc and have your verjuice cherry jellies and palm sugar sago puddings lined up in beautiful glasses in a row. The way you cook is influenced by your childhood experiences, your kitchen equipment, the books or magazines you use, where you live, the weather and even the psychological baggage you carry around with you in relation to eating and cooking. Recipe books push you over all the culinary walls and low horizons that habits and defensiveness have set up. The real voyage of discovery with cookbooks is not in using new food but in seeing it with new eyes, and this is what food literature helps us to do.

Gastronomic travel writing is a romantic subject that recalls a vanished world. A travel writer imports and exports dreams, hopefully with tenderness and generosity. Behind every recipe is a story of local traditions and daily life in villages and towns. Recipes are about ancestral memories – looking back and holding on to old cultures. They are profoundly about identity. The *Bible* recalls in Exodus the wistful longings of the Jews for the foods they had left behind in Egypt. Traditional dishes are important because they are a link with the past, a celebration of roots, a symbol

of continuity. They are the part of a culture that survives the longest, preserved even when traditional clothing, music and language have been abandoned. Cooking in a place like Morocco, for example, is passed down through the genes and the fingertips. Like love, it has the capacity for change and for passing on new experiences from one generation to the next.

COOKING SCHOOLS

The contemporary and chic cuisine style of the Pacific rim is taught in the principal cooking schools in New Zealand. There are also international classes from visiting chefs.

The most prestigious cooking schools in the country are Epicurean Workshop in Auckland, Ruth Pretty's school in Te Horo outside Wellington, and the New Zealand School of Food and Wine in Christchurch.

OTHER COOKING SCHOOLS INCLUDE:
- Kimberley Lodge in Russell
- Auckland Cooking Academy at Milly's Kitchen Warehouse
- Sileni Estates in Hawke's Bay
- An Epicurean Affair at the Stone Aerie Estate in Marlborough
- D'Urville Hotel in Marlborough
- Herzog in Marlborough
- Loaves and Fishes in Nelson
- The Small Kitchen School in Christchurch
- Deux Tarts in Christchurch
- Punatapu Lodge in Queenstown
- Judith Cullen Cooking Classes in Dunedin
- Bungalow Cooking School in Invercargill

There is a very comprehensive list of cooking schools in the May 2004 issue of Cuisine magazine.

EPICUREAN WORKSHOP
This cookware shop and cooking school in Newmarket, Auckland is run by Catherine Bell. All the staff are wonderful and knowledgeable, especially Clare Aldous who is also the food editor of Epicurean's new food magazine, *Dish*. *Dish* is full of ideas and, best of all, it will lie flat on the bench while you cook from it and the pages are sealed to allow any spills to be wiped away without damage.

The little café at the front of the Epicurean shop has the best and most chic sandwiches, rolls and cakes in Newmarket. Honestly, I have found myself going out of my way just to get my hands on a little egg-filled focaccia finger, a dainty club sandwich, fresh asparagus rolls, summer berry cake and friands. They absolutely understand who their clientele are – ladies and gentlemen who wish to lunch but not gorge.

The stylish shop is full of high-quality cookware you cannot possibly live without – Le Creuset casseroles, rice paper, geranium water, exotic ingredients like za'atar and sumac, gift boxes, cookbooks, ice-cream machines, copper pots and pans, white porcelain … the list goes on. The cooking school does 'one hour everyday epicurian' classes plus lunchtime and evening classes taught by the elevated likes of myself, Catherine, Clare, Ray McVinnie, Peter Thornley, Ruth Pretty and overseas stars like Stephanie

Alexander and Martin Boetz from Longrain in Sydney.

It is a pleasure to teach there as everything is done properly, professionally and seriously, and students really get their money's worth. There are Epicurean cookbooks available too. Epicurean also have an award-winning website at: www.epicurean.co.nz. A recipe from the school appears below:

RUTH PRETTY COOKING SCHOOL

People from all over New Zealand line up to spend a day with Ruth Pretty at her beautiful country home and cooking school in Te Horo, an hour north of Wellington. Ruth and her husband Paul are an institution in the lower part of the North Island for their top-notch catering of weddings and any huge or tiny event worth going to. They catered for 2000 people at the *Lord of the Rings: Return of the King* wrap party without batting an eyelid.

Mint & chilli chicken on lime & coconut rice

750G CHICKEN THIGH MEAT CUT INTO LARGE DICE

1 BUNCH OF SNAKE BEANS, CUT INTO 15CM PIECES, COOKED AND REFRESHED IN COLD WATER

for the marinade:

½ CUP COARSELY CHOPPED MINT

2 LARGE CLOVES GARLIC, CRUSHED

½ TEASPOON CHILLI FLAKES

2 TABLESPOONS KECAP MANIS (THICK SOY SAUCE)

2 TABLESPOONS LIGHT SOY SAUCE

2 TABLESPOONS PEANUT OIL

ZEST AND JUICE OF 1 LIME

for the rice:

2 CUPS JASMINE RICE, WELL WASHED AND DRAINED

4 KAFFIR LIME LEAVES, SHREDDED

6 SLICES FRESH GINGER

2 CUPS STOCK OR WATER

2 CUPS LIGHT COCONUT MILK

3 EXTRA KAFFIR LIME LEAVES AND MINT TO GARNISH

1. Combine all the marinade ingredients in a food processor and mix together until finely chopped. Place in a bowl and mix through the chicken, cover and refrigerate for up to 2 hours.

2. Remove the chicken from the marinade, drain and thread 3 or 4 pieces on to each of about 12 skewers. Char-grill over medium heat for 3–4 minutes each side until the chicken is cooked through.

1. Place the rice, Kaffir lime leaves, ginger, stock or water and coconut milk in a medium-sized saucepan with a tight-fitting lid. Bring to the boil then turn down to the lowest setting and simmer very gently for 20 minutes without lifting the lid.

2. Remove from heat and allow to stand for 5 minutes.

3. Remove the ginger slices, then fork through 3 finely chopped Kaffir lime leaves and 3 sprigs of chopped mint.

4. To serve, place beans on a long platter and spoon rice down the centre. Top with the chicken skewers.

serves 4—6

RUTH PRETTY
CATERING

RUTH PRETTY
COOKING SCHOOL

RUTH PRETTY
WEDDINGS

RUTH PRETTY
KITCHEN SHOP

At the weekend cooking classes the students arrive at 9.30 a.m., drive down the long, rose-lined entrance road, past the restored 1910 homestead wrapped in covered verandas, past the two-acre garden with sweeping lawns, past the beautiful trees and a stream, and thence to the cooking school. They are plied with cakes and tea, taught many splendoured things by the likes of Julie Le Clerc, Annabel Langbein, moi, Ruth and international stars like Tony Tan and Maggie Beer, plied with more tea and cakes, and told to go for a walk around the lovely property. At about 2 p.m. they are summoned to eat. At a long lunch on the veranda under sun umbrellas, or even at the chefs' benches, the students are encouraged to savour every dish from the class (with matching wines). Ruth's greatest fear is that someone will die of hunger on her shift. There is also a shop on the property where you can splurge on mortar and pestles, Ruth Pretty preserves, Ruth's cookbooks, cast-iron frying pans, gem irons, cookware and the like. A recipe from Ruth's collection is featured on this page.

LOAVES AND FISHES

These cooking classes are quite special and are run by the gorgeous and dynamic Vivienne Fox. They operate under the auspices of a Nelson-based outfit called Creative Tourism (see page 204 for more information). Vivienne and her husband Tom have owned and managed the Craypot in Kaikoura and, more recently, The Smokehouse Café in Mapua. Under Vivienne's leadership and astute business sense, both have won awards and become regional icons.

Food and its preparation have always played a big part in Vivienne's life. She has a particular interest and passion for seafood, which developed through being brought up by the sea and spending time in the kitchens of her seaside cafés. Eating at The Smokehouse Café when Vivienne owned it was always the biggest joy because she treated everyone like royalty and the food was always perfection. People drove for miles to eat there. She would do mad things like crack open champagne just because you had walked in or send a box of freshly smoked fish to the airport for you, which you would only discover when you checked in.

What Vivienne doesn't know about fish ain't worth knowing. This day-long workshop, suitable for foodies, innocent bystanders and tourists, starts with her explaining what characterises fresh seafood and how and where it is harvested. Then, working with a range of whole, fresh fish that are particular to her part of the world, she teaches students to fillet and prepare the fish. At Vivienne's beautiful home, Lavender Hill, and using the fish you have filleted, she will explain and demonstrate a variety of cooking methods. You will also help prepare home-made bread, and then sit down and enjoy a leisurely lunch that will include the food you have helped prepare, other local produce and some of Nelson's best wines. I don't know how anyone gets out of Vivienne's house after the class, because she is such a people lover and so entertaining that why would you want to leave? Their website is: www.creativetourism.co.nz.

NEW ZEALAND SCHOOL OF FOOD AND WINE (NZSFW)

This registered, private cookery school offers full and part-time courses. Its NZQA accredited courses are the only local alternative programmes to those based on the

Pinot noir & summer-berry jelly

This recipe fills 8 x 125ml sundae glasses or makes 24 shot glasses. It's a very refreshing dessert as it is not overly sweet.

350G CASTOR SUGAR
500ML PINOT NOIR
3 STAR ANISE

if you are using fresh berries:
14G (4 TEASPOONS) GELATINE
120G RASPBERRIES
120G BLUEBERRIES
120G BLACKBERRIES

if you are using frozen berries:
20G (6 TEASPOONS) GELATINE
180G RASPBERRIES
180G BLUEBERRIES
180G BLACKBERRIES

1. Place the sugar, pinot noir and star anise in a saucepan over a gentle heat. Stir until the sugar is dissolved. Increase heat and heat syrup to just below boiling.

2. Strain the syrup into a bowl and dissolve gelatine in 125ml ($1/2$ cup) of syrup. Return this to the remaining syrup and stir. Leave to cool.

3. Put layers of fruit in sundae glasses and then cover with pinot noir syrup. Refrigerate for at least 2 hours or until it is set.

serves 8

polytech system. Principal Celia Hay also offers evening demonstration classes, barista workshops and wine-appreciation courses. She has written a book called *How to Grow Your Hospitality Business: A Guide for Owners and Managers* which is used as a textbook for the Certificate in Restaurant and Café Management and as a resource for all the courses offered by the NZSFW. It can be bought from her website: www.foodwine.co.nz.

There is a restaurant, Hay's, downstairs from the school, where students are able to obtain work experience in the kitchen and restaurant. Hay's features modern New Zealand cuisine and specialises in lamb grazed by Celia's husband, Allan Hay, on their family farm in Pigeon Bay. Celia also does casual evening cooking demonstrations for domestic cooks, where you might learn to cook dishes like roast red onion with balsamic vinegar and goat's cheese; roast salmon with sauce tartare; paua with tamari, garlic and ginger; or saffron and semillon panna cotta.

Celia says she finds it interesting that over 25 per cent of her full-time students are international (those from USA, UK, Japan, Germany and Malaysia are the biggest groups). Many students are enrolling for 'culinary tourism' courses so they can spend time here, get to know some Kiwis and enjoy good food. The average age is 32, and many want to set up their own businesses. One of Celia's recipes is featured on the opposite page.

NGA KETE E TORU

The title of this Maori cooking class refers to the three baskets of knowledge – harvesting, cooking and customs. Chef Stan Tawa of Christchurch Polytechnic's Culinary Institute teaches this one-year, full-time accredited course to his chef students so that the custom and culture of Maori cooking won't be lost. The course also includes kapa haka (dance), te reo (language) and tikanga (customs), and the students stay over in marae (meeting houses). Like Charles Royal in Rotorua, Stan says harvesting is all about sustainability – you take what you need from the land and the sea, and no more. There's no standing around chopping up purchased primary ingredients at a sterile bench – if you want the food, you go and catch it. If they are cooking paua, the students have to dive for it, learning about resource control, size and how to get the beast off the rock without damaging it. If they are cooking a hangi, they are taught how to find the right rocks for heating. They learn how to harvest and cook seaweed, catch and smoke eel, harvest and eat kina (sea urchin), and prepare rewana

bread by making the potato starter. Most of all, the students learn to take pride in their culture and how to bring traditional food into the mainstream. The course is evolving and changing every year, with the students wanting more and more field trips.

THE COOKHOUSE

Graham Brown is well known in the New Zealand food industry, mostly because of his Christchurch restaurant, Scarborough Fair, which he has now sold, and his involvement with the New Zealand venison board promoting cervena, the overseas marketing name for venison. Graham and his wife Glenda love venison so much they grow about 60 deer on their 8-hectare property in Loburn, Canterbury. They have hinds only, and when they reach 110kg they go off for processing. Graham says stags are too much trouble and female meat is better than male anyway.

When I visited him, he made a delicious rhubarb clafoutis (flan) where he stuck the rhubarb in upright like the Giant's Causeway in Ireland. It's worth visiting him out in the sticks, especially if you go to his cooking classes. He loves the land, loves teaching and is an endless fund of culinary knowledge. Students get to spend a whole day with Graham sitting around the counter in his large country kitchen. You start off by visiting local growers, cheese-makers or vineyards to buy the day's supplies. Then you come back and learn menu planning, recipes, food and wine or beer matching, and good culinary techniques. You leave with the recipes, a full tummy and lots of new knowledge about food. Graham's recipe is on page 62.

SAVOUR NEW ZEALAND

Savour New Zealand is an international master class of food and wine – an extravagant mouth-watering weekend of wall-to-wall cooking demonstrations, food and wine tastings, and panel discussions. Stars of the gastronomic firmament – chefs, experts, producers and writers of food and wine – come from around the country and the world to teach in Christchurch, tutor the tastings, and talk, talk, talk. It is truly a feasting weekend – a time to taste, sniff, sip and slurp, observe, discuss, listen, learn and party.

The brainchild of Christchurch chef Michael Lee-Richards, Savour New Zealand is the joint enterprise of a committed team of food lovers, with the support of corporate and civic sponsors. It could not hold together,

Lamb shanks with lemongrass & ginger on noodles

These lamb shanks are best eaten the day after cooking them. Ideally, allow them to cool in cooking liquor in shallow trays and refrigerate overnight or until the fat has solidified and can be scraped off. When reheating make sure you do this thoroughly but on a low heat and reduce the cooking liquor to give a rich, flavoursome sauce. It is better to finish seasoning at the end of the cooking process to make sure your sauce doesn't get too salty.

12 SMALL/MEDIUM LAMB SHANKS

2 TABLESPOONS SESAME OIL

3 TABLESPOONS PEANUT OIL

MALDON SALT

FRESHLY GROUND BLACK PEPPER

1 CUP PEANUT OIL

2 RED ONIONS, CUT INTO
2CM DICE

4 STICKS CELERY, CUT INTO
2CM DICE

3 CARROTS, PEELED AND CUT INTO
2CM DICE

6 LEMONGRASS SHOOTS, CUT INTO
4CM LENGTHS

4 MILD CHILLIES, DESEEDED AND
FINELY CHOPPED

4CM CUBE GINGER, PEELED AND
FINELY GRATED

24 CLOVES GARLIC,
ROUGHLY CHOPPED

3 TABLESPOONS GROUND CUMIN

2 TABLESPOONS GROUND
CORIANDER

4 KAFFIR LIME LEAVES

12 TABLESPOONS TURMERIC

2 CUPS SWEET COOKING SHERRY

4 TABLESPOONS THAI FISH SAUCE

1 CUP TERIYAKI SAUCE

2 LITRES LAMB STOCK, OR ENOUGH
TO COVER

1 PACKET RICE NOODLES, SOAKED
FOR AT LEAST 2 HOURS IN
COLD WATER

1. Preheat the oven to 220°C. Coat the shanks in the sesame and first measure of peanut oil. Season with Maldon salt and pepper. Place shanks on a trivet and roast in the hot oven for approximately 45 minutes, until golden brown.

2. Heat a large heavy-bottomed saucepan. Add 1 cup peanut oil and allow to heat until just starting to smoke. Add red onions, celery and carrots, and cook for approximately 5 minutes or until it starts to caramelise. Stir during cooking to prevent the ingredients sticking.

3. Add the lemongrass, chillies, ginger and garlic. Stir thoroughly and cook for approximately 2 minutes longer, until aromatic. Add ground cumin and coriander, Kaffir lime leaves and turmeric. Stir thoroughly and cook for approximately 1 minute longer.

4. Add the sherry and bring to a simmer. Reduce the liquid by half, then put aside until the shanks are ready.

5. Place the roasted shanks in the large saucepan. Add the fish sauce and teriyaki sauce. Cover with stock and bring to a simmer over a medium heat. Skim the surface and turn the heat down very low so that it is just simmering. Cook like this for approximately 3 hours or until the meat is tender. The shanks can be served straight away, but it is preferable to skim off the excess fat and intensify the flavour of the sauce by reducing the cooking liquid as in the next step.

6. Allow sauce to cool in the saucepan for about 1 hour. Tip into a suitable tray and refrigerate once cooled. Remove the fat. Reheat sauce thoroughly on a low heat and reduce the cooking liquid to the consistency desired. Approximately 2 minutes before you are ready to serve add the rice noodles and simmer until tender, plump and succulent.

serves 6

Drunken lime verbena cake with tequila candied peels & sunset sauce

for the cake:
250G UNSALTED BUTTER
1 CUP CASTOR SUGAR
¼ TEASPOON SALT
5 LARGE EGGS
½ TEASPOON VANILLA ESSENCE
½ TEASPOON ALMOND ESSENCE
½ TEASPOON ORANGE ZEST, GRATED
½ TEASPOON LEMON ZEST, GRATED
1 TEASPOON LIME ZEST, GRATED
1 TEASPOON FINELY CHOPPED LIME-VERBENA LEAVES
2 CUPS WELL-SIFTED CAKE FLOUR (SOFT)

for the tequila syrup:
½ CUP CASTOR SUGAR
1 CUP WATER
¼ CUP LIME JUICE
½ CUP TEQUILA

for the sunset sauce (optional):
½ CUP RASPBERRY COULIS
2 CUPS PAW PAW COULIS WITH LIME JUICE ADDED
4 TABLESPOONS JUST-RUNNY CREAM OR CRÈME ANGLAIS

1. To make the cake, grease and line a 23cm springform tin with baking paper. Beat the butter, castor sugar and salt together until creamy.

2. In a separate bowl whisk the eggs, vanilla essence, almond essence, zests and lime verbena leaves together. Add the egg mixture slowly to the creamed butter.

3. Fold in the flour in three parts until a nice smooth batter is formed. Pour into a greased cake tin and bake in a moderate oven (170°C) for approximately 1 hour 10 minutes. Remove cake from tin and cool.

4. To make syrup, bring the castor sugar, water and lime juice to the boil, add the tequila and reduce by a quarter to form a syrup.

5. While the cake is cooling, prick with a roasting fork and pour over the tequila syrup. Allow to cool completely.

6. Mix together the sunset sauce ingredients and serve with the cake if desired.

serves 8

C

however, without the wacky personality of Michael. The others, like Tina Duncan and Astrid Andersen, are excellent organisers, but it is Michael's pulling power that gets the big names all the way over to New Zealand. At the first weekend we had a live radio discussion with Julia Child, and at the most recent, Antonio Carluccio charmed us all with lashings of olive oil and simple good cooking. The most interesting for me was Tetsuya Wakuda from Sydney, with his extraordinarily sophisticated and intelligent Japanese fusion cooking. No one can keep away from this event because it is so professionally organised and so genuinely interesting. And they have a gala dinner with floor show, singing and dancing, and everything.

The other important thing about Savour New Zealand is that visitors listen to our top chefs and food writers, and taste our produce and cuisine. Marieke Brugman and Sarah Stegley of Howqua Dale Gourmet Retreat in Australia said:

'We applaud, congratulate and celebrate Savour New Zealand for an event that shone with vigour, freshness, immense hospitality and the courage to travel new gastronomic roads. The Gala Dinner was utterly uplifting in its harnessing of a community of food and arts, and such a memorable and life-affirming performance. This has cemented New Zealand's important role in the New World Revolution in gastronomy; showcasing its distinctive and exciting produce and wine, cultivating an audience who love food, wine and cooking, and creating a commitment to sustainability. We were honoured to be among you.'

The website is: www.savournewzealand.co.nz.

COOKWARE

2 FISH LTD

2 Fish Ltd is a small New Zealand-based houseware manufacturing company. Their aim is to provide innovative and practical housewares at an affordable price through direct marketing. They make a beautiful oiled platter from untreated New Zealand pine; a traditional cotton overall apron in a variety of colours, stripes and plain white damask; a rimu muffin tray; and my favourite is the Fromager, a pretty cheese box with a wire mesh trap-door. It can be used to store cheese until ripened, at which point it must be consumed or refrigerated at 2–4°C. The shelf can be removed from the Fromager and used as a cheeseboard for serving. Their website is: www.2fish.co.nz.

ST CLAIR

When I was first falling in love with cooking, I made things like béarnaise sauce, pommes dauphinoise, daubes and salads from dandelion leaves. I imagined the pinnacle of success would be to have a collection of shining copper pots hanging in a row like golden geese in my kitchen. Everyone would know then that I was serious. In those days I was a counsellor in Canada and never imagined I would end up with a row of copper pots in the kitchen of my own restaurant in Paris. I still have some of them in my home because they last a lifetime, and I have added to the collection with some New Zealand-made ones.

St Clair is the one and only company in New Zealand making copper pots and pans. Nothing is as strong or resilient as a copper pan, I don't care how much you pay for it. Although a comparatively soft metal, it is not porous and will not pit; it hardens with work and age, and this is the secret of its longevity. Nothing is as dramatic, elegant or beautiful, which is why these pans are passed from mother to daughter in France. It is almost impossible to burn something in a copper pot because it distributes heat evenly and loses heat very quickly after it is taken off the flame. St Clair copperware is spun or pressed from 16-gauge half-hard copper in Auckland. The interior linings are hand-tinned in the traditional manner to provide a non-toxic and stick-resistant cooking surface. The solidly riveted handles are cast from high-tensile manganese bronze and cannot deteriorate through use. All pieces are mop-polished and come unlacquered or lacquered. You can buy them in all good kitchenware shops or from their website: www.stclaircookware.com.

KNIVES

A good knife and sharpener is the only kitchen tool you can't live without. It is an extension of your hand and your self. Professional chefs never go anywhere without their knives and if you borrow another chef's knife in a restaurant kitchen, you will do it only once. The blade changes when a different person uses it, and the personal relationship between the cook and knife is destroyed. Travelling internationally with your knives has become almost impossible due to as a result of increased airport security against terrorism. I used to travel the world with mine but gave up explaining their presence to airport officials. It's worth forking out the money for a good knife because it lasts a lifetime, and makes cooking much easier. Keep knives in a block designed for the purpose or on a magnet – never in the drawer – and when reading your husband the riot act, keep the knife pointed downwards. A good place to buy knives is at House of Knives in Wellington and Auckland: www.houseofknives.co.nz.

RIPI KNIVES

John Worthington makes very good knives and has very eclectic taste – you only have to look at his website www.ripiknives.com, to see what an exciting life he has out there in Wanaka. Not only can you buy knives but you get to be privy to his favourite site links like Exotic Sheer Lingerie, Plus Size Lingerie, and Motor Cycle Parts and Accessories. 'We've been snail-mail marketers of collector-grade knives for over ten years,' says John. 'We DO NOT sell "automatics" or switchblades and would greatly appreciate it if you didn't ask after them because we don't associate with anyone who does sell such items.' Yikes! And they say life is quiet in the provinces. Yet when you visit the man, there he is in his workshop under the house, perfectly dedicated and ordinary, crafting the truly state-of-the-art knives he is famous for. He's not a big talker, but who needs words when you've got a 15cm fire-forged butcher's knife?

John started making knives when a friend gave him a piece of 100-year-old sawmill blade, originally from the old Granite Creek Mill in Waitaha, South Westland. He went down to the shed and simply made it into a knife. Now John makes sailors' deck or work knives and butchers' or chefs' filleting, skinning and gutting knives. Blades can be flexible or stiff and are made in one of the stainless steels or in carbon steel. I reckon the terrifying survivor knife would do just fine for the low-lifes who can't get switchblades.

John selects the steel (mostly bars from the USA), draws the knife pattern on the blade, cuts out the shape, grinds the blade hollow or to a taper depending on the design and drills holes for fitting blades. Next he places the blade in a gas-fired forge, hardening the steel but leaving it brittle, then tempers the blade, keeping it hard but replacing the brittleness with toughness. Finally, the blade is polished, the handle fitted and the knife sharpened to a shaving edge. The handles are made from all sorts of materials – native and exotic timber, bone, merino sheep's horn, greenstone and even wood from old wooden bowling balls called *Lignum vitae*, reputedly one of the hardest timbers in the world. John will make anything you want, within reason, although

he did make a sword for a customer once. Just don't ask for a plus-size bra.

He can be contacted at: information@ripiknives.com.

CRABS

The common New Zealand paddle crab, *Ovalipes catharus*, otherwise known as the swimming crab, has large, paddle-like back legs that enable it to swim and burrow into the sandy bottoms where it loves to be. It is abundant everywhere in the sea, from the surf zone right down to 100m or deeper, and can be found in Northland, Auckland, Bay of Plenty, Hawke's Bay, Kapiti Coast and Golden Bay. Crabs gorge on toheroa and pipi beds by chipping the edges of their shells then opening them, using their claws as wedges. To catch a crab you use baited crab pots with collapsible sides, which prevent the little critters from swimming out sideways.

The exciting bit is that at least once a year a paddle crab moults, losing its hard outside shell. Immediately after moulting it stands up in a defence position with claws up and open, and might stay like this for two weeks; or ideally, it will burrow into the sand. At this point it is very vulnerable because of its soft shell (soft-shell crab is very delicious by the way). The female can only mate when she's soft, and guess what? The male is cannibalistic. But just like human males, the male crab is usually more interested in sex than food, so he will more than likely mate with her than eat her and he will then protect her until the shell hardens. A medium-sized female can carry up to 750,000 eggs. The paddle crab is very sweet and delicate to eat and is a year-round succulent treat. Once caught it must be kept cool – between 1–7°C – and should be cooked and prepared as soon as possible.

CRAYFISH

They say the best crays in New Zealand are caught in Kaikoura, a very pretty seaside village sitting on a peninsula that protrudes from the spectacular coastline. Crays live all around New Zealand of course, but the exceptionally large Kaikoura reef provides the protection they need to moult and breed. Even on a cold, grey day, Kaikoura is lovely. Driving along this road you get the impression that you're going to fall into the sea at any moment, so little room is there between the sea and the mountains. Kaikoura's main industry is marine tourism, and the town is inundated with crayfish – they're in takeaways, restaurants, pubs, Chinese restaurants, pizza joints, on the wharf, in seaside stalls,

Crab packets

for the packets:

6 LIVE PADDLE CRABS
SALTED WATER
APPROXIMATELY 24 SMALL SHEETS OF RICE PAPER
12 SNOW PEAS, FINELY SLICED ON THE CROSS
1 CUCUMBER, FINELY SLICED ON THE CROSS
2 SPRING ONIONS, FINELY SLICED ON THE CROSS
1 MEDIUM CARROT, FINELY SLICED ON THE CROSS
FRESH CORIANDER LEAVES
1/2 CUP CHOPPED PEANUTS AND SESAME SEEDS,
ROASTED FOR 5 MINUTES

for the dipping sauce:

1 SMALL, FRESH RED CHILLI
1/2 CUP RICE VINEGAR
1 TEASPOON CASTOR SUGAR
1 TABLESPOON FISH SAUCE
2 TABLESPOONS LEMON JUICE

1. To kill crabs humanely, put them in the freezer for at least an hour. Bring a large pot of salted water to the boil and submerge the crabs. Boil for 5 minutes, drain and rinse in cold water.

2. Twist off the legs and discard the upper shell. Remove and discard the spongy grey gill tissue from inside the crab. Remove and keep the coral and creamy parts from the shell. Cut the main shell in half and squeeze the flesh out with a rolling pin. Crack the claws and remove the meat. Keep the shells to make a bisque or stock.

3. Soak the rice-paper sheets in hot water for 1 minute until soft. Lay out on paper towels.

4. In the middle of the sheets lay a line of crab meat and top this with a mixture of the vegetables, coriander and nuts. Fold the bottom up then roll. Bits of vegetable should be sticking out the top.

5. Mix together all the ingredients for the dipping sauce and serve with the crab parcels.

serves 6 as a starter or finger food

strolling down the street (just kidding) and eventually I even found one in my motel room, courtesy of an admirer.

Archaeological remains indicate that moa hunters inhabited the Kaikoura Peninsula 900 years ago. To Maori this area is of great historical significance, for Maori legend tells it was from this peninsula that Maui fished up the North Island (Te ika a Maui – the fish Maui caught) from the ocean. The great Polynesian explorer, Tamatea Pokai Whenua gave Kaikoura its name – kai (food) koura (cray). During the mid-19th century European settlers established whaling stations along the coast, using clifftops as lookouts. Just off the peninsula is a complex submarine canyon system with deep water, the reason giant sperm whales can be seen within a few kilometres of the coast. This system provides a rich habitat for numerous marine organisms, both large and small, lots of which end up at the Pacifica Kaikoura Seafest, the three-day seafood festival held on the first Saturday of October every year.

NIN'S BIN

Nin's Bin is a dear little white caravan all on its own near Rakautara. It has a tiny garden around it, bordered by white- painted rocks and a big sign saying crayfish in eight languages. The reason it has to be in eight languages is because people come from all over the world to eat the cooked crays. There's an envelope on the wall addressed thus: Nin's Bin, Lobster, Kaikoura, Neuseeland, with a photo of the caravan on the front. Named after a friend, Nin's Bin opened in 1977. It was owned by Ron and Judith Clark until sadly Ron died last year, just after I had visited him, and it is now run by his son Rodney. Nin's Bin is dedicated to one thing and one thing only – crayfish. In Ron's day you couldn't even get lemon, salt and pepper or any sauces to eat with it. Now, Rodney has gone wild and offers a very popular garlic crayfish. He's also invested in a newer, bigger white caravan.

'I deliberately sell these crays au naturel,' said the loquacious Ron (I could hardly get a word in edgeways). 'I don't believe in disguising the flavour with any condiments whatsoever. There's no point. Why pay that much money and then cover up the taste?' Crayfish will stay alive for 75 hours after they're caught, and when Ron used to cook them he would first drown them in fresh water for ten minutes, then put them in a large pot of cold water, bring it to the boil and boil them for five minutes only. There is no point in putting herbs or salt in the water as crayfish are hermetically sealed. He would then immerse them in

The late Ron Clark, Nin's Bin, Rakautara

cold water to stop the cooking process, snap off the two long antennae and place them upside down to drain off any water. The cooked crays were all laid out on ice trays and covered with white gauze. They were cut in half length-wise, wrapped up for the buyer in newspaper, and that's the end of the story.

The more I talked to Ron, the more I realised I had met a kindred spirit. Although I eat and enjoy crayfish, it is not without guilt. I admire them – they are a very ancient, noble animal, having been around for tens of thousands of years, and they go on incredible journeys around New Zealand. They can live to a very old age, and if you catch a huge one, it could be 90 years old or more. The shell is amazingly complex, having about 135 movable joints. Ron felt ambivalent about eating them, too.

Male crays are about 500mm in length and females 200mm. To reproduce, the male inserts sperm into a receptacle in the female's thorax in the autumn, and after a time of wonder, the eggs are hatched in great numbers in the spring. They become attached to the silk-like hairs under the female's fanned tail by a clear fluid secreted by glands at the base of the swimmerets. They hatch six months after being laid and after a larval stage lasting two years, they reach 75cm in length. From then on in they grow by 25cm a year.

'I've always been fascinated by crayfish and have kept diaries for many years about their life cycle and habitat,' Ron told me. 'Some people catch the females when they are laden with eggs, which is really stupid for fishing. They should be put back, and none under the age of seven should be taken. Fortunately, mother nature looks after crays to a certain extent with inclement weather, but nevertheless there are about 200 good fishing days a year. The moulting process is very interesting and happens twice a year. First they find a safe place, then the body or carapace hinges up. They pull themselves out of that and then wriggle out of the rest of the shell – everything gets shed, even the thin covering over the eyes. At this point they are obviously very vulnerable so they hide for a few weeks until the new shell has grown. If you find a moulted shell it looks exactly like a real crayfish and until you get up real close it's hard to tell the difference.'

'Were crays more plentiful in your childhood?' I asked Ron.

'Crikey yes, and in those days you could catch them during the day easily. When we were kids we used to bike up the coast, get a paua, make a hole in the shell and thread some flax through it. The crays would grab it and we'd haul them up and that was the extent of the operation. We had nothing to put them in so we'd bike home to Mum with all these crays sticking to our jumpers.'

PACIFICA SEAFOODS IN CHRISTCHURCH

When I visited the packing room at Pacifica Seafoods, hundreds of crays were crawling around in big, white, plastic boxes with sea water spraying constantly over them, waiting to be packed by workers wearing white overalls, white caps and white plastic gumboots. The packers grab the snapping crays and unceremoniously pack them tightly in rows in Styrofoam boxes with ice and wood wool. The packers work very quickly, the lid is taped on, then the boxes are stacked on a trolley and driven straight to the airport.

The system for exporting live crayfish seems very simple, but things can go very expensively wrong. The Japanese are meticulous customers, and any shipment that contains dead crays will not be paid for. The crays are slowly reduced to a temperature of 6°C, which makes them very drowsy, then they must get to Japan within 36 hours of leaving Kaikoura. By the time they reach Tokyo and Hong Kong the temperature is back to about 16°C and they're as fresh as the moment they were caught and trying to jump out of the box.

THE CRITICAL FACTORS ARE:
- They have to be carefully fished with no legs or antennae missing.
- A very skilled crayfish expert is required, one who knows which crays are strong enough to survive the journey.
- The temperature when they leave Kaikoura has to be 6°C.
- The timing to Christchurch airport has to be exact, and the planes have to be running on time.

SUNSET POINT SPORTS BAR AND BISTRO

Another hard-case but more sophisticated place to feast on a well-prepared crayfish is at the marvellously named Sunset Point Sports Bar and Bistro at Mahia. Diana and Arthur Symes were introduced to me by Robyn Bickford of Opou Lodge in Gisborne. They are born-and-bred local tangata whenua who are very much part of the swiftly flowing renaissance in Maori food. Arthur's father was a crayfisherman and he has his own crayfish quota. He has been going out every day for 46 years in his custom-built boat to bring the crayfish pots up. The live tanks are at his home just up from the beach, and the crays either get exported to China or disappear down the grateful gullets of the punters in his bar. If he brings up kina, you can buy that too.

Diana serves it plain – her motto is 'keep it simple, stupid'. She drowns the cray in fresh water, boils it for six minutes, sits it in iced water to stop the cooking, halves it then spreads a bit of garlic butter on and gives it a minute under the salamander. The cray is served accompanied by big fat chips and a salad. Sunset Point is the only bar I know where you can go in covered in sand and order a beer and a cray over the counter. They wrap it in newspaper and off you go. It costs $44 for a sit-down lunch and $25 over the bar.

When Arthur said he wanted to open a bar-restaurant, Diana said, 'But darling, you don't even know how to pour piss.' But they did it! The couple started the place five years ago; the locals objected of course, but now they're all drinking there. Arthur and Diana continue to make all their decisions in bed, and he insists her brothers lassoed him and made him marry her.

Crayfish with lemon–wasabi soldiers

3 THIN-SKINNED, UNWAXED LEMONS
BUTTER
12 THIN SLICES BREAD
SEA SALT
WASABI PASTE
600G COOKED CRAYFISH MEAT

1. Pour boiling water over the lemons to cover for 5 minutes.

2. Drain and slice the lemons very thinly.

3. Butter the bread. Arrange lemon slices on half the bread and sprinkle with salt. Spread wasabi paste on the remaining slices, put them together, slice the crusts off and cut into soldiers.

4. Serve with sliced crayfish and apple aïoli – see recipe, page 15.

serves 6

DELICATESSENS AND GOOD FOOD STORES

SABATO IN AUCKLAND

Thanks to the Dixons, we now find we cannot live without real buffalo mozzarella, San Danielle cured ham, marinated baby artichokes, durum wheat pasta ground between the thighs of Ligurian maidens, and grana padano cheese. The best supply place in Auckland is Sabato, owned and run by the sardonic Phil and his wife, the charming and exotic-looking Jacqui Dixon. Where a girl from Auckland got such almond-shaped eyes, rosebud mouth and Roman nose is a mystery to me, but what she doesn't know about her Italian and Spanish produce would probably fit on your fingernail. They started off showing the products they had brought back from Italy in their home kitchen. I can remember going there years ago and sighing over the dried pasta and Puy lentils. Now they have a large shop in Mt Eden and travel twice yearly to Italy, Spain and France to source wines, risotto rices, sweets, chocolates (including Valrhona Grand Cru, the best in the world), single-estate olive oils, balsamic vinegars, El Navarrico white asparagus, white beans and peaches, and sublime canned tuna and sardines. Lately Sabato have been making their own gelato in two flavours – vanilla and Valrhona cocoa. Their gelato is creamier than the Italian version but just as delicious, and not over sweet. There is a walk-in cheese chiller pregnant with Italian, Spanish and New Zealand cheeses, handmade butters, cured meats and salads, and a freezer full of sausages, duck breasts, stocks and naughty things like croissants and puff pastry.

They have glamorous guest chefs like Julie Le Clerc (whose condiments you can also buy there), Ray McVinnie and Gabriele Ferron of the risotto family to teach cooking classes. They even have chocolate Cuban cigars and *foie gras* for God's sake! One of the latest bits of deliciousness Sabato have started bringing in is *fregola* or Sardinian 'couscous', which is actually tiny artisan pasta unique to Sardinia. You can also buy pretty Rachel Carley crockery, bumblebee glasses and assorted cookware like paella pans. Jacqui and Phil are generous, witty, committed to educating the public and tireless in their devotion to good living. When you enter Sabato you feel like you're on holiday and about to eat every favourite thing you ever ate. And they make you coffee … and there are no children in the tiny trolleys. Their website is: www.sabato.co.nz.

THE URBAN FOOD STORE IN HAVELOCK NORTH

Everyone calls this store Boldersons because everyone in Havelock North knows Vicki and Kevin. Vicki should really be in the hero section. A woman with more good looks, vigour, experience and love of good food you would go a long way to meet. When I go to Havelock North to visit my sister Keriann, the first thing she says is, 'Let's go to Boldersons.' Vicki is a renowned, award-winning, local and international chef and teacher who did something that was desperately needed in Havelock North – opened a fabulous but unpretentious food store. She had a small bakery, then got a bigger space and turned it into the friendly, unpretentious, barn-like epicurean heartland we all love to visit. Now Kevin is making the bread and Vicki is running the shop, often with her daughter behind the big, wooden counter. The counter itself is a devil's lair of cookies, chocolates and homemade marshmallows with adult flavours like star anise, lime and ginger, vanilla bean and espresso. Kevin makes all sorts of breads like roasted beetroot loaf, triple-herb flat bread, roast-pumpkin bread, and garlic-and-spelt bread, which disappear early in the day. That just leaves farm fresh eggs, chutneys, pastas, cheeses, pomegranate molasses, olive oils, pulses, St Andrews preserved limes, organic produce, fresh vegetables and fruit, and much more. Vicki believes in keeping everything fresh so there is no stock room as such. Everything she has is arranged in neat piles in the middle of the shop – shoppers just walk around with a white plastic bucket and help themselves.

MOORE WILSON FRESH IN WELLINGTON

Frederick Moore opened the original business in 1918 with a partner called Wilson, as a wholesaler distributing produce via trucks to corner grocery stores around Wellington. Mr Wilson was only in the business for a few years, but the name remains. Graeme Moore, Frederick's great-grandson, is the managing director, and his daughter Julie and son Nick are in the business too.

This is how the Moore Wilson empire works. The traditional side of the business is the wholesale-grocery warehouse, with imported and local bulk supplies and basics. Next to this is the spirits-and-wine shop, which has very competitive prices and special discounts for bulk buyers. Upstairs is the huge homewares department, bursting with linen, glassware, pots and pans, and also the much-loved cooking-class corner where well-known Wellington cooks show you how to do it with bells on. But the best is the Ian Athfield-designed, purpose-built market called Moore Wilson Fresh. Moore Wilson Fresh is a well-known name among food lovers in New Zealand, especially Wellingtonians, and boy, it rocks! It's the sort of place you see friends in, see famous people in, want to move in and live in, and get totally inspired by. Well, you probably wouldn't want to live in there because it's kept very cool to protect the produce.

It's a one-stop foodies' paradise where you can buy practically anything from Special Reserve Spanish balsamic vinegar or wasabi caviar to freshly plucked yellow Hungarian chillies or a bunch of fragrant flowers. If they haven't got it, they'll do their best to get it. They carry a huge range of particularly fresh vegetables – particularly fresh because they buy the produce directly from the farmer, who chills the produce immediately upon picking, and it stays cool from that moment until it arrives in the shop and is snapped up by all the big chefs, drooling foodies, and ordinary mums and dads. This system is called Cool Chain Management. You want broccolini, tomatillos, celeriac? No problem. You want organic meat, wild game and Holly bacon, or bratwurst, pickled mushrooms and temperature-controlled cheese? Still no problem. While you're having an attack of the lazies and buying some chef-designed, ready-to-go gourmet packs, you can sip on a coffee or a fresh orange juice. Like other good food shops in this section, Moore Wilson are generous with tastings. There is always a vast selection of olive oils, breads and pastes, etc for customers to sample.

Mr Johnson, Johnson's Grocers in Christchurch

Phil and Jacquie Dixon, Sabato, Auckland

LA BELLA ITALIA IN WELLINGTON
See page 113.

JOHNSON'S IN CHRISTCHURCH
Walking into this marvellous old grocery shop is like stepping back in time. Ladders take the staff to the precarious item the customer requires, which can be just about anything you could think of – Vegemite, tuatara soup, baking soda, unusual vinegars, extra virgin olive oils, Dutch cocoa, Belgian chocolate, tinned *foie gras*. Provisions are piled up to the ceiling absolutely everywhere in this small shop, and the staff dress like old-fashioned sellers in white dust coats who are very polite and knowledgeable. You can get lollies, liquorice, ham and Stilton cheese cut from the block with a wire. Any sane person would much rather shop there than at a supermarket.

HIGHGATE BRIDGE IN DUNEDIN
Every Friday morning there is a long queue outside a shop in Roslyn Village, Dunedin. When you get to the top of the queue and your nose precedes you into the shop, you are rewarded with the most heart-warming aromas of freshly baked croissants and homemade pies. Highgate Bridge opens at 7.30 a.m. and everything is usually sold out by 10.30 a.m. And when it's sold out, it's sold out. Owner and chef Jim Byars just turns around and starts baking and cooking again 12 hours a day to fill up the larders for the next Friday.

Dunedin is extremely lucky to have a man like Jim Byars in its midst. Jim is a shy man with an illustrious past. He trained at Otago Polytechnic in 1978, went overseas, and eventually ended up working with the famous Roux brothers at Le Gavroche. His wife Rachel also worked as an apprentice chef at Le Gavroche. Jim stayed with the brothers Roux for 10 years working on various ventures with them, including Boucherie le Matin (now Roux Britannia), which sold French cuts of meat, French cheese, cakes, pastries and the pioneering idea of take-home gourmet meals in vac-pacs. Subsequent to that he worked as executive chef at the exclusive New York lodge called The Point, where all the chefs were trained under Albert Roux. Eight years ago Jim and Rachel came home and began teaching at the Otago Polytechnic. Jim also had great success selling his mussel soup out of the boot of his car at school fairs – a bit like selling caviar out of a railway teacup.

This led to the opening of his shop Highgate Bridge, where he bakes and cooks classic European cuisine – apple, lemon and chocolate tarts, croissants, *pains au chocolat*, almond croissants, pies and quiches. He also makes vac-packed meals like lamb navarin and veal stew, and flash things like chicken breast stuffed with chicken mousseline wrapped in puff pastry. When I interviewed him he made me a classic French-apple tart and a coulibiac of salmon, rice and mushroom. Coulibiac is a wonderfully rich French dish involving brioche dough and artery-clogging amounts of melted sweet butter. You will not find fashionable, light, 'Mediterrasian' food here – this is classic *cuisine bourgeois*, with enormous attention to the basics of proper cooking, prepared by a highly trained master who doesn't know the meaning of the words short-cut or cheap ingredients. Needless to say, Jim's customers know what they're talking about too.

DRAMA AND GASTRONOMY

My paternal grandmother, a woman of great grace and finesse, was prostrate on the couch weeping uncontrollably. Everyone else in the room except the children were also weeping, rigid with the effort of faking emotional control. The other children were looking perplexed at me, their artistic director. I was irritated.

'Why is Nana crying, Mum?' I asked, adjusting my blue veil.

'She's not crying, darling,' my mother wailed. 'She's laughing.'

We children furrowed our brows and looked at one another. Dad started helping Nana out of the room.

'But we haven't finished yet, Dad. The play's not over,' I blurted, wounded that a member of the audience could feel free to abandon ship.

'Grandma has to lie down dear. She might have a heart attack.'

Childhood Christmas performances were my earliest connection between food and drama, and one of the only creative outlets left to me, as I had been banned from every birthday party in the parish for insubordination and subversiveness. At ten I had no idea what the words meant. But at least I had three tenured actors in the form of my younger siblings, and there were two more to come. The one other thing in my misunderstood little life that I loved was food, which thankfully wasn't restricted. We all routinely ate huge meals. Upon being told that dinner was finished, we always threw ourselves into a pathetic, mourning stance pleading, 'Is that all Mum? We're starving.'

While Nana lay down to recover from 15 minutes of Joseph forgetting his lines, Mary in a paroxysm of holiness, a shepherd farting and screaming with laughter, and the baby Jesus getting out of his crib and crawling off the set, we threw ourselves into setting the table for Christmas dinner.

Mum to me: 'Get the white tablecloth, please. The lacy one.'

Me to sister: 'Get the white tablecloth. The lacy one.'

Sister to Mum: 'What white tablecloth? Why do I have to get it?'

Mum to sister: 'Do what your sister asks.'

Me to sister: Sneer.

My mother began cooking the Christmas chicken three hours before the event, which was only correct in 1959. In those days chicken was an expensive treat, and you went to the chicken farm to pick the bird out. Everything was free range. These were the days before there were psychotic battery creatures that committed suicide and suffered from chronic depression. That went for the chickens too. Nobody got depressed in 1959 – they just went on a retreat to the Carmelite nuns and everything was all right again for six months.

'Dad, why does the chook have its head on still?'

'It's a cry for help.'

'Dear!'

'Sorry.'

As much as I loved the drama of performing in and directing my own plays, I loved the drama of food even more. It had to take a long time to prepare and cook otherwise I didn't enjoy it as much. My mother, though not a good cook in the technical sense of the word, did rise to the occasion in the romantic sense, doing all the traditional things at the appropriate times. The ham was cooked on the day and served hot, the chicken was roasted to within an inch of itself, the vegetables were carcinogenic time bombs and the onion sauce was nice and gloopy. The plum pudding was homemade, hung for weeks, then steamed in muslin for hours and served stuffed with sixpences and threepences. Dad threw brandy all over the mysterious dark mound and lit it with a match so that Mum could find her way to the table as electric light hadn't been invented then it seemed. Nana would arrive at the groaning board fully recovered from the play and smiling.

'Nana! Nana! Are you all right now?' We would crowd around, stroking her.

'Yes darlings, and thank you for the wonderful play.'

Although I didn't know it, I think the future chef and entertainer was born in those deeply magical moments.

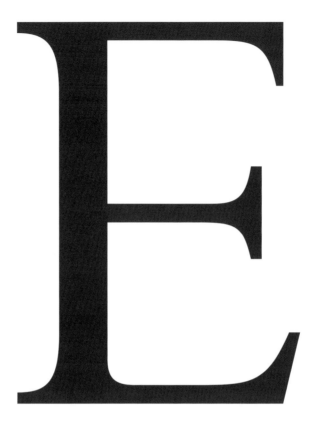

EASTHERBROOK FARM

Any New Zealander born in the first half of this century would recall eating rabbit regularly. In the hands of a good cook it was delicious but, like bread and dripping, it was often seen as food for the poor. By the 1950s, in the name of progress, any vestiges of pre-war depression food was sloughed off. But the bunnies kept breeding as bunnies do, so to control the population, rabbit diseases were deliberately introduced. This was very successful, but it naturally made people terrified of eating bunnies. Even now when most rabbits are farmed and even wild ones don't have disease anymore, people can't get over feeling edgy about it.

The farmed rabbit produced by Ray and Glenda Easther of Eastherbrook Farm in Pukekohe, Auckland, is succulent and mild tasting, and I don't understand why we don't eat more rabbit in New Zealand. Wild rabbit is very good too – it has more texture and flavour.

Most of Glenda's rabbits have names and, like most animal farmers, she is quite straightforward when talking about their sex lives. Even though rabbits are known to be rampant reproducers, the bucks are quite sensitive and can be put off their stroke by the more aggressive does. Life is tough at the farm, and if the buck doesn't come up with the action, he gets the chop. Does are chosen for breeding by their size, milking ability and the number of offspring they produce.

Eastherbrook Farm distributes all over New Zealand, and you can buy from them direct. They grow rabbits and ducks, and supply all sorts of exotic animal meat like wild venison, hare, goat and pork, as well as pigeon, buffalo, kangaroo and veal. Eastherbrook Farm is the only outfit I know that

Moroccan pigeon pies (b'stillas)

This pie is often made with chicken. Although a savoury dish, it is very sweet in Morocco. I have cut out the sugar, but if you prefer, you can add 1/2 cup of sugar to the ground almonds. The b'stillas are served as starters, and Moroccans eat them with their fingers. You can find spring-roll pastry in the frozen section of the supermarket. It is the closest thing to Moroccan warka pastry. Recently we have been able to buy real warka at the Epicurean Workshop in Auckland.

for the pies:

3 PIGEONS OR 1 SMALL CHICKEN WEIGHING 1–1.5KG

1 MEDIUM ONION, FINELY CHOPPED

4 CLOVES GARLIC, FINELY CHOPPED

2 PINCHES SAFFRON, SOAKED IN BOILING WATER FOR 30 MINUTES

1/4 TEASPOON TURMERIC

1 TEASPOON GROUND GINGER

2 CINNAMON STICKS

1/2 TEASPOON GROUND CUMIN

1/2 TEASPOON SALT

1 TEASPOON FRESHLY GROUND BLACK PEPPER

1 CUP WATER

1 TABLESPOON OLIVE OIL

140G (3/4 CUP) WHOLE BLANCHED ALMONDS

1/2 CUP SUGAR (OPTIONAL)

1/4 CUP LEMON JUICE

6 EGGS, BEATEN

1/4 CUP CHOPPED FRESH CORIANDER

1/4 CUP CHOPPED FRESH PARSLEY

1 PACKET SPRING-ROLL PASTRY CONTAINING 20 LEAVES EACH MEASURING 20 X 20CM

EXTRA VIRGIN OLIVE OIL FOR BRUSHING OR SPRAYING PASTRY

for the garnish:

ICING SUGAR

GROUND CINNAMON

1. Quarter the chicken or leave the pigeons whole. Place in a saucepan with the onion, garlic, spices, salt, pepper and water. Bring to the boil, cover and simmer for 1 hour.

2. Heat a little oil in a pan and brown the almonds lightly. When cool, grind to a powder in the food processor. (You can add sugar now if you wish.)

3. Remove the poultry and cinnamon sticks from the cooking liquid, and put aside to cool, then reduce the sauce to half by boiling. Lower the heat, add the lemon juice and the beaten eggs and stir until just scrambled. Add the coriander and parsley and allow to cool.

4. Pull all the flesh off the poultry bones and shred coarsely. (Up to this stage, the b'stilla can be prepared in advance.)

5. Preheat the oven to 180°C. On the work surface, lay out 10 pastry sheets and have the other 10 ready. Brush or spray each sheet with olive oil. Divide the poultry into 10 portions and place in a mound in the centre of each pastry sheet. Spoon the egg mixture on top, and on top of that sprinkle 2 teaspoons of ground almonds on each one.

6. Fold the overlapping pastry sheet around the filling to form a round pie. Turn over so the folds are on the bottom and repeat with another sheet, spraying it with oil.

7. Place the b'stillas on an oiled baking sheet, brush with more olive oil and fan bake for 20 minutes until golden.

8. To serve, dust the b'stillas with icing sugar and make criss-cross lines of ground cinnamon over the top.

makes 10 small b'stillas

Rabbit in mustard sauce

1 PLUMP RABBIT
4 TABLESPOONS DIJON MUSTARD
SEA SALT AND FRESHLY GROUND
BLACK PEPPER
100G BACON IN ONE PIECE
1 CUP DRY WHITE WINE
1 CUP CREAM

1. Have the butcher section the rabbit. Preheat the oven to 180°C. Place the pieces in a roasting pan and spread the mustard all over both sides. Sprinkle with salt and pepper.

2. Cut the bacon into 'lardons' or matchsticks and throw over the rabbit. Pour the wine over and bake for 1 hour, basting occasionally.

3. Remove the rabbit pieces and keep warm. On top of the stove heat the sauce, scraping the bottom of the pan. Add the cream and more mustard if you love it as much as I do.

4. Place the rabbit on a serving platter, pour over the sauce and serve with fresh pasta.

serves 4—6

occasionally supplies pigeon. I make Moroccan pies (b'stillas) with pigeon, rather than chicken, when I can get it. The difference is remarkable – much more intense and pleasantly gamey, and absolutely beautiful with the lemon, egg and sugar of the b'stillas.

EELS There was time in New Zealand when you couldn't walk out into certain lakes without standing on eels. All eels processed in New Zealand are wild. The ones at Aquahaven on Lake Ellesmere near Christchurch, once gathered, swim in tanks of pure, cool water from 40-metre deep artesian wells fed by the melting snow of the Southern Alps. Eels go through several dramatic body changes before they settle on their adult shape. Upon hatching, the eel is long and skinny around an egg sac. It then passes through a larval stage where it is flounder-shaped and the size of a leaf, progressing on to become a transparent glass-like eel and ending up a coloured elver. Interestingly, eels head out to sea to breed, sometimes travelling huge distances. On winter nights, all over New Zealand, when everyone else is drinking G&Ts by the fire, the mysterious eels slither out of fresh-water rivers, lakes and swamps and move unseen over farmland, making for the open sea. They rest under cover during the day and continue slithering again once night falls.

Farmed eels are killed by tumbling them in salt inside closed containers, which supposedly knocks them out quickly and also takes the slime off them. New Zealand eels are relatively low in fat and have quite tough skins. They are divine cooked fresh and also smoked. The Japanese, who consider eel to be stamina-giving, an effective way of avoiding heat exhaustion (don't ask me how) and – surprise, surprise – an aphrodisiac, have a delicious way of grilling them called *kabayaki*. To make *kabayaki*, first fatten your eel, kill it, then split it down the back. Next you skewer it and steam it. The bones are removed and boiled to make stock, to which is added soy sauce, mirin and sake then boiled down to make a treacle-like marinade. The eel is dipped into this mixture and grilled.

Smoking eel is a real labour of love. First you brine the prepared eel, rub a bit of salt in, then smoke in manuka and kanuka wood for about nine hours. The absolute secret lies in managing and controlling the heat. A good smoked eel should be moist, oily and sweetly smoky-tasting, not tough and strong-tasting. Matt Paku suggests brushing the smoked eel with honey, then grilling it skin-side up so it bubbles and blisters. It's also good simply sprinkled with pepper and lemon juice and eaten on a slice of crunchy baguette. Maori have always caught and eaten eel both smoked, dried and fresh, but other New Zealanders seem to prefer it already done and packaged so it doesn't look too much like a snake.

Some good eel smokers are Paku & Sons in Masterton, BV in Stratford, Taranaki, and New Zealand Eel Processing Co. in Te Kauwhata, Waikato.

EGGS Thank goodness we're allowed to eat eggs again. The eggpire strikes back and the dark days of egg-white omelettes are over except for those who truly do not enjoy eating or who are American. Eggs are a great source of protein, amino acids, vitamins and minerals and are eaten by over

E

75 per cent of New Zealanders. They are good for both the heart and the soul, and they taste absolutely delicious, especially if they are free range.

My favourite egg man is the inimitable and witty Ian Thomas of The Other Side Free Range Chook Park in Hastings. On his website Ian says:

'To the true free-range egg-lover the question is not just why the chicken crossed the road but also where? And what happened to her when she reached The Other Side? Once you've visited The Other Side, you'll know. The identity of that original pioneering road-crossing chicken may have been lost in the mists of time – but we can show you the fun-filled and fulfilled lives of her descendants. That's right … come on over to The Other Side and you can cross The Road yourself – retracing those famous chook tracks that started the legend. This is truly Hen Heaven – Pullet Paradise – the Garden of Eggden. This is the place where the Flock of the Free-Range gather in harmony to scratch, flap, sunbathe, dustbathe and strut their feathery stuff. When you reach The Other Side Free-Range Chook Park you and your family will find yourselves on the other side of so many things – that daily grind, that busy schedule, that unwanted stress, that school holiday boredom … maybe you have a few "henecdotes" of your own you'd like to share.'

Ian not only sells good eggs but encourages visits to his farm. It is one of life's pleasures to visit his stall at the Hawke's Bay farmers' market. His latest venture is 'Crappé', a 100 per cent pure compost based on poultry manure. He says it is a premium product – carefully blended crap, green material and hay, seasoned and aged for two years.

ELDER-FLOWER CORDIAL

Elder flowers grow on large trees all over New Zealand but they have a relatively short summer season.

The cordial gushes with warm evenings in the garden and a world bereft of worries. The citric acid makes it last longer but isn't essential. The lacy flowers of the elder tree are also divine cooked in fritters.

My sister Keriann makes really good elder-flower cordial every summer. The recipe produces a cordial to which you add water or, even better, sparkling water to drink. It keeps in the fridge for a couple of weeks, freezes well and is a lovely flavouring for panna cotta, apple pie and ice-cream.

Keriann Lancaster, Havelock North

Elder-flower cordial

25 ELDER-FLOWER HEADS
3 ORANGES
3 LEMONS
60G CITRIC OR TARTARIC ACID
1.5KG SUGAR
2.5 LITRES BOILING WATER

1. Wash and slice the oranges and lemons, and place in a large container with the other ingredients.

2. Pour over 2½ litres of boiling water and leave to soak for 1 or 2 days, stirring occasionally.

3. Strain through muslin and pour into sterilised bottles.

makes 2 1/2 litres

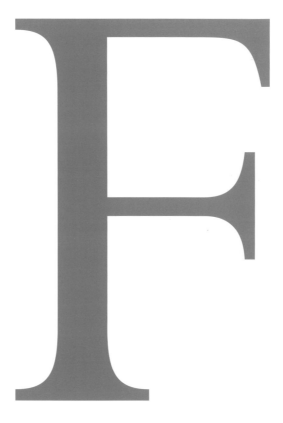

FAT Fat gives flavour and texture to food – it makes it taste and feel good in the mouth. How does it do this? It acts as a transporter for flavour-carrying molecules in food and slows down absorption by the taste-buds. You can taste this process if you eat a mouthful of marbled steak slowly – the longer you let it linger on the palate and tongue, the better it tastes and the more pleasure you have. In fact to take it a step further, fat is so important to meat that if you cut the fat off and eat completely lean meat from different animals it all starts to taste the same. It's the fat that tastes different in every meat. Beef, for example, should have some fat in it as it keeps the meat moist during cooking. Fat on an animal shows it is healthy and it is necessary for proper hanging. We are now pathologically terrified of fat. But it is not the obvious fat we should fear; it is the hidden fat in fast and processed food we should shun.

Everyone bangs on about how bad fat is for you but no one has looked into the effect of eating artificially (biochemically) altered lean meat. If the worst comes to the worst, cook your meat with fat on it, which is when it needs it, then cut it off just before you eat it . . . if you must.

We like a little fat on our ham, we like butter on our ciabatta and we love deep-fried fish and chips. This was never a problem until we stopped walking everywhere and someone invented computers. Now we're getting fatter and fatter because we have started to substitute our healthy New Zealand meat and three veg and our sporting lifestyle with American-style fast food and sitting or standing in front of labour-saving devices. This will not only shorten our lives but will make what life we have left in us not worth living because it will affect our mental and physical health. The slimmest people in the world are Lithuanians because they don't have many junk-food outlets and are too poor even to buy snacks. The poor things have to survive on dill, berries, potatoes and vodka.

I'm very interested in the migratory habits of fat cells. How is it that fat cells ingested in the form of delicious lamb chops, oil-drenched mozzarella and coconut-marinated raw fish find their unerring way to certain parts of the body? Why doesn't adipose tissue ever form on your breasts or hips where you really need it? Why do we end up looking like tellytubbies instead of Sophia Loren?

FARMERS' MARKETS

A farmers' market is like the kitchen of a French restaurant – unique in its capacity to provide succour to the intellectually and gastronomically curious. In my restaurant in Paris, friends and customers wandered in at moments of greatest fermentation to engage in conversations ranging from discussing Nietzsche to finding out the ingredients of a sauce. This is just what it's like at a farmers' market. Over and over again people told me what they like most about farmers' markets in New Zealand is the exchange, the gossip, the bonding. The buyers say, 'We love being able to talk to the person behind the product; they tell us if the fruit has been sprayed, which field it was picked from, what the deer had for breakfast, and how long to cook things for.' The sellers say, 'We really value people's comments because we never get to meet the buyer normally and it provides us with a social life.'

New Zealand farmers' markets are slightly less rigid than their English and American counterparts. The Islington market in London is very staunch; they won't even let a coffee stall in. The wonderful American markets will only accept produce from within a certain radius. The French *marchés agricoles* are yet another story. Growers sell out of the backs of trucks, gypsies sell baskets, and one guy can be just standing there selling his three precious truffles.

New Zealand markets each have their own flavour and emphasis, and are strictly seasonal and strictly owner-operated. The person who grows the asparagus is the person behind the trestle; the eggs belong to the chook that belongs to the farmer you are in congress with, thus cutting out the middle man and keeping prices down. The simple fact is everyone likes farmers' markets – farmers, consumers, environmental groups and even the local councils, because they revitalise small towns. Of course farmers' markets are very old, but they had died out, only to be reinvented in the last 25 years. In Britain there are over 120, and the government plans to have 900 in the near future. In America there are more than 2500 and the turnover is $US1 billion. I predict that they are here to stay. In the near future I want to see organic-hog roasting, calypso bands, night markets and lots more cheese, and I've got my flax bag all ready.

MATAKANA FARMERS' MARKET
'You're now on Matakana time' says the sign on the side of the road as you bear down from the south, leaving behind the cares of Auckland. A lot of folk who used to live in Auckland now live in Matakana. When Aucklanders say they want to get away from it all and lead the quiet country life, they don't really mean it. What they mean is, we want to retain the good stuff like flat whites, imaginative food and smooth pinot noir but chuck the noise, dirt and overcrowding. Here's where Matakana has hit the nail on the head, literally. They took some wood and nails and built an authentic farmers' market in a square, each stall beautifully designed and honed by Joe Polaischer, famous in the area for his and wife Trish's biodynamic, permaculture home and farm. The Matakana market is a small market with a large central stall, a place for sitting and gossiping and a stand for the band. The coffee is serious, it is a plastic

bag-free zone and the eggs are still warm from the hay. Set up by Christine and Richard Didsbury, the market is really charming and useful.

Kal Lovell makes very good fruit cheese – my favourites are guava and damson. There's Namida wasabi. You can find gourmet spuds like Cliff's Kidneys, funny-looking yellow tomatoes, and Salumeria grilling their delicious fennel and pork sausages right in front of you. You can buy a rooster, fresh horseradish, Omaha blueberries, all sorts of breads, Pacific oysters and pick-and-eat-immediately peaches. The market also has special Saturdays with themes – for example, Middle Eastern, with belly dancing, lamb on the spit, Turkish pide bread and exotic music.

The whole thing is run by Sally Meiklejohn and Dorothy Anderson, and these gals have big plans for the future. They are forming a federation of farmers' markets and turning the whole of Matakana into a Slow Town (for more information on this see Slow Food, page 194). Matakana market is open every Saturday morning until lunchtime.

VILLAGE GROWERS' MARKET IN HAVELOCK NORTH

Having visited farmers' markets all over the world, it came to pass that I found myself in the welcoming arms of Black Barn vineyard owners Andy Coltart and Kim Thorp on a sunny slope of the Te Mata hills. The Village Growers' Market, in this vineyard, is the magic circle, the protective womb of goodness and harmony into which you may enter tired and irritable and surely exit docile and joyful. It's a unique market in that it is small, round, closed in by hessian curtains and open to the blue sky. The sense of security and wellbeing is enhanced by a tree growing at each of the 21 stalls, trees planted years ago for that express purpose. In the middle is a circle of seats and a bit of shade where one can sip Hawthorne coffee or slurp up a feijoa Rush Monroe ice-cream, all the while gossiping, showing-and-telling or even courting. Surrounding the market are the Black Barn vineyards, in turn girdled by artichoke plants.

You can buy bread from Harold's Bakery and happily, as fate would have it, Black Barn wines have the stall next door selling the two things made to go with good bread – wine and extra virgin olive oil from the Village Press. Some of the fresh produce sold is organic – shining purple aubergines for ridiculously low prices, corn picked that dawn so fresh the sugar hasn't yet converted to starch, sweet, crisp Orin apples that taste like a spring morning, and the first of the figs, the sight of which immediately makes you dream of

OUTDOOR TOMATOS
$1.99
kilo

PURITY FOODS CO
PHONE 262 7712

roast duck. Back for another flat white … running out of cash … no problem … whiz over to the Black Barn stall where they have EFTPOS. On to St Andrews Limes, Prime Cuts with their lamb, salami and deli products, Casa Lavender for a spot of body cream, fabulous Hohepa cheese, and Terraza Saffron for you-know-what grown down the road – not forgetting the Squirrel's Pantry for delicious preserves. And they tell you all about it. It's all very poetic; growers and punters all around the magic circle are head to head in smiling conversation, snapping information out of each other.

The Growers' Market insists on high-quality Hawke's Bay produce only and on desperately good presentation. Aside from that, Andy and Kim are not the kind of guys who like rules. They modestly say the reason the market looks so good and has such a chic reputation is more to do with the clients and stall-holders than them. Okay, so the punters turn up in their Mercs and Range Rovers wearing boat shoes and their collars turned up, but these people are serious shoppers – they have extensive wine-and-food knowledge, plan their weekend meals around what they find at the market and wipe it out by 11 a.m.

The market operates on Saturday mornings in the summer.

FARMERS' MARKET IN HASTINGS

The Farmers' Market at the Hastings showgrounds is another very good market and is not completely stuck on the idea of food only; they would like to allow room for other farm produce like sawdust, and logs for the fire. There's the clever couple who fry their handmade beef sausages right in front of you to drive you nuts. The bespectacled and endlessly enthusiastic Clive Potter has spread his Epicurean supplies over two stall spaces, where the tables are groaning with organic celery root, chard with its gorgeous red stalks, huge fennel bulbs, Urenika and Agria potatoes, cavolo nero (black cabbage), tomatillos and generous bunches of fresh herbs. Wonderful Rangiuru cheeses are there, along with the avocado stalls, and gelato and hand-reared beef and lamb products. The market operates on Sunday mornings all year, rain or shine.

OTHER FARMERS' MARKETS ARE:
- Whangarei Growers' Market on Saturday mornings
- Kerikeri Farmers' Market on Sunday mornings
- Marlborough Farmers' Market on Sunday mornings from November to April at A&P Park, Blenheim
- Otago Farmers' Market in Dunedin on Saturday mornings

WWW.FOODLOVERS.CO.NZ

Check this out for a clever idea: www.foodlovers.co.nz has launched an online farmers' market where small producers can showcase their wares nationwide without leaving home. Many New Zealand producers enjoy having a direct relationship with the customer, so rather than have product lists with order forms, they personally respond to e-mails advising customers of their product availability. The foodlovers website receives around 1000 visitors per day. Now in its sixth year, it won for Helen Jackson the electronic media award at the New Zealand Guild of Food Writers Culinary Quill Awards in 2003. Visit the site at: www.foodlovers.co.nz/market.

THE AVONDALE MARKET IN AUCKLAND

The Avondale Market is held on Sunday mornings at the Avondale racecourse and is a riot of colour, noise, smells and exotica. Once you have ploughed your way through hula dolls, Polynesian doughnuts, velvet paintings, cheap blankets, girls' frilly frocks and Thai takeaways you reach the promised land of fresh Asian food. The market opens at 6 a.m. – by 8 a.m. it is pumping and by 10 a.m. it is the equivalent of downtown Calcutta. Everything is cheap and everything is desperately fresh – desperately fresh. The eggs are still warm from the chook's bottom and the herbs still have earth on them. The Indian stalls provide okra, snake beans, cow peas, little white eggplants, bitter melon, fresh brilliant orange turmeric and my favourite – curry leaves. The Asian stalls, usually run by Cambodians, Chinese and Vietnamese, are bursting with all sizes of bok choy, mustard greens, chrysanthemum leaves, daikon radish, vines and tendrils of various vegetables, lime leaves, coriander, Thai basil, banana flowers and Vietnamese mint.

Everyone is friendly and helpful about how to use the ingredients and if you're lucky you might well bump into our very own Asian-food expert, Jenny Yee. She'll be the one sniffing everything and seemingly on first-name basis with the entire market.

Before you leave the market you mustn't forget to buy some warm pork buns from the bun shop up on the hill.

LA CIGALE MARKET IN PARNELL, AUCKLAND

This is a very cute and surprisingly good French-style market in the car-park of La Cigale shop, held on Saturday mornings, which specialises in everything French from antiques to clothes to kitchen supplies. The first thing that hits you as you round the corner is the outrageous smell of a huge, golden paella cooking in a giant pan. The chalk sign says 'Ready at 10 a.m.' – extremely cruel if you have turned up early to get the best vegetables. However, Jason the vegetable man who comes down from Whangarei is likely to be running late and still trying to get all his produce out of the van half-way through the morning, so you may as well relax and make a morning of it. Jason has good mustardy rocket, fresh herbs, unglamorous but meaty acid-free tomatoes, baby pears, pink garlic, spuds, leeks and if you're lucky, courgette flowers. Fionna Hill is there with her beautiful flowers, there's the cake ladies, the honey man, the Rakaia salmon man who comes up once a month from the South Island, the sausage man, people selling olive oil and wine, and chickens turning on a spit with the fat dripping seductively on to the potatoes roasting below.

La Cigale also imports beautifully ripe French cheeses like Coeur du Barry goat's cheese, Fourme d'Ambert blue, Brie de Meaux and Cantal. This is a very hard stall to get away from and it is right next to the wine stall. And of course they have what every market needs – a good café on site where you can sit down with your friends and gush over your buys. I particularly like the food in this café because they do small manageable things like ribbon sandwiches – finely sliced club sarnies – excellent fare for a person who has just read *French Women Don't Get Fat* and is trying to assimilate the message of less is more.

There are other regular markets in Otara, Kaitaia, Thames, Gisborne, Palmerston North, Nelson, Christchurch, Westport and Otago.

FEIJOAS
This is another iconic New Zealand fruit, grown from Northland to Blenheim and usually on the market from March to June. The feijoa has a very distinctive, aromatic flavour with tropical overtones that include pineapple and guava, and a wonderfully creamy texture. In California it is called pineapple guava. The feijoa was collected in southern Brazil by a German explorer Freidrich Sellow in 1815 and introduced to Europe by French botanist and horticulturist Dr Edouard André in 1890. It was named after the Brazilian botanist, Joam da Silva Feijo.

Feijoas were introduced into New Zealand in the 1920s and have a very restricted gene pool – they are all basically cultivars of one variety, cultivated by the DSIR. New Zealand's ideal climate produced large fruit, and few pests enabled feijoas to be grown organically (chemical sprays therefore are not applied to New Zealand fruit, making New Zealand feijoas some of the most natural fruit available). They seem easy to grow in everyone's backyards, and late summer in New Zealand is defined by all the plastic bags of green feijoas friends leave on your doorstep.

Feijoas dry and freeze really well and a lot of them end up in Dick Hubbard's cereals or in ice-cream. Strangely enough they are also good with pork. They are ready to eat when slightly soft and when the jellied sections in the centre of the fruit are clear. This may happen on the tree or within two to five days of natural fruit drop. The fruit is unripe when the jellied sections are white, and is past its best when they are browning. Unpleasant flavours develop when browning occurs and the fruit should be discarded. Handle feijoas very gently, as you would ripe peaches.

FISH SHOPS
New Zealand has led the world in careful and sustainable management of fish harvesting through the quota-management system. Its exclusive economic fishing zone covers 1.2 million square nautical miles, 15 times the land area. There ain't much we don't know about catching fish, but strangely we don't eat enough of it. We only eat about 25g a week and should be eating 100–400g a week, or a fish meal twice a week. The shops listed here are doing what they can to remedy that.

SEAMART IN AUCKLAND
This is a very good fish shop which sells fresh fish straight from the boat to the public. They were also the first people to set up a takeaway sushi bar. You can buy the fish filleted or whole to be scaled, cleaned and filleted before your very eyes – snapper, terakihi, eels, crayfish, whitebait, blue cod, marinated raw fish, smoked fish, crabs and mussels. There is also a great deli department with a stand-alone Sabato section.

AUCKLAND FISH MARKET
A newcomer, this market is lots of fun and even has a fish auction. One morning I arose from my downy sheets to attend the auction at 5.30 a.m. I was met by lots of shell-shocked-looking buyers heading straight for the espresso machine. It's all very staunch and not a job for wimps; there were lots of jokes about my clothes and lots of serious

Stephanie Dean, Mt Eden Fish Shop, Auckland

eyeballing of the crates of fish fresh in from the night's fishing. In the viewing room there were huge, ugly, big-mouthed, pop-eyed hapuka; firm, yellow-fin tuna from the islands; the much cheaper albacore tuna; ruby fish; hoki; grey mullet – both fresh-water and sea-water varieties – and squid. When you've done your eyeballing you move into the electronic auction room. This is what's called a Dutch auction, which is silent and goes backwards. Instead of starting low and selling to the highest bidder, they start high and drop until there is a bid. Buyers bid on the electronic keypad in front of them.

There are several fish companies under their roof, a café, a sit-down sushi bar, a fish-and-chip shop, a deli, a grocery and a cooking school. You can get prawns, crayfish, octopus, paua, frozen fish, live fish, oysters, salmon – you name it.

MT EDEN VILLAGE FISH SHOP

Stephanie and Mario Dean are a handsome couple who make the best fish and chips in Auckland. Their chips are straight cut and large, the beer batter is light, and everything is cooked in cottonseed oil. Every night the oil is filtered and the fryers are drained, scrubbed and cleaned. One of their secrets is to drain the fried food properly then wrap it carefully in two sheets of white newsprint and two sheets of newspaper. They don't waste time reading the newspaper while they're wrapping either because Stephanie and Mario believe in giving their customers the best – fresh fish, warm and not soggy. Mario rises at 5 a.m. every day to buy the fish. They also sell fabulous quality, wet fish and have a smoker out the back. They don't over-smoke the fish, so it is always tender and succulent.

WELLINGTON TRAWLING COMPANY

Tony Basile also cooks his fish and chips in cottonseed oil like the Mt Eden Fish Shop does because, even though it's more expensive, it leaves a very fresh taste in the mouth, as though it is homemade. Tony is of Italian heritage and a real, traditional fishmonger, selling wet fish of every imaginable description, as well as running a big exporting business out back.

PACIFIC CATCH

Pacific Catch has an outlet in Wellington at Moore Wilson Fresh, Lambton Quay, and a truck at Paekakariki. Their seafood is always fresh and they have a great website explaining how to buy fish, look after it and cook it. They have a huge selection of fish, depending on the season, like groper, blue cod, eels, flounder, swordfish, skate and orange roughy. The shellfish ranges from clams, paua, pipi and queen scallops to octopus, paddle crabs and kina. They provide seafood salads, frozen meals, takeaway meals and fish filleted to order, and the sellers are very friendly and helpful.

You can find a range of simple, contemporary recipes designed for maximum natural flavour on their website: www.pacificcatch.co.nz.

OTHER GOOD FISH SHOPS:
- City Seafood Market in Christchurch
- Fresh Freddy's Fish Supply in Dunedin
- King's Fish Market in Invercargill

FOODIES

Foodies are a ghastly brand of creature usually found pontificating in restaurants – disciplined, driven, gastronomically chauvinistic and utterly thrilled with themselves. Foodies always drink designer water, know that you don't butter bread because the French don't, are not put off by bad decor because it's the food that counts, encourage their dreadful children to drink baby-cinos and eat *foie gras*, and insist on tasting everyone else's dish, cooly marginalising anybody who wishes to quietly eat their own meal. In the foodie world there are characters we all know – the serious thrill-seekers, the thin hypocrites, the aesthetic gourmands, the happy fatties and the loveable analysers. Foodies are often exhibitionists who gorge on the public consumption of fashionable food at any price. It's about performance and letting the lower social and gastronomic orders know that reward comes in the form of original, flamboyant and costly food. Conspicuous culinary consumption is a clever and tasty form of social climbing. *Mais attention!* – rotting fruit, the extinction of rare foods and overabundance are the undeniable signs of decline.

Then there are the anti-foodies, who control the universe by controlling their food. They go to a haute cuisine restaurant and order a green salad with no dressing, thanks. They force the chef, who has spent his or her life inventing the dishes on the menu, to make something special for them, telling the diabetic lie. Why chefs put up with this is a mystery to me – I think the mortality rate in good restaurants is abnormally low. Interestingly, foodies and anti-foodies share one trait – neither of them smoke.

FOOLISHNESS

Not a lot of New Zealanders like making a fool of themselves. We have an earnestness that is rewarded in our literature but means we can't do comedy terribly well. The best entertainment we achieve is accidental, as is the case with that derived from scoundrel politicians, phone calls between competing comedians that are so expletive-ridden you have to play spot the noun, and wine- and food-makers so thrilled with themselves you want to say, 'it's only food, love,' and watch them come out in boils. I blame our lack of humour on the puritanical dour Scots – Presbyterians couldn't laugh if their bowels depended on it. We should have had more Irish immigration; at least Catholics drink and have sex, which leads to dancing and singing, and the next thing you know you're making a fool of yourself. Hence the intonement: 'Beware of strong women – they'll eat you alive before you even notice your tie is missing.'

April Fools' Day is an occasion to indulge in a formal kind of trick humour New Zealanders adore – not only because it's clever, but because huge numbers of people are inconvenienced, which makes us scream until we fall over. It is normally committed by people who have not fully recovered from boarding school. The tradition may have originated in an ancient Roman festival, the Feast of Fools, during which they made fools of their arch enemies the Druids. Or the tradition may have started in 1582 when the reformed Gregorian calendar was adopted in Roman Catholic Europe. April was the first full month to be affected by the ten-day change and April the first came a week and a half early, fooling anybody who was behind the times. Or the tradition may have been brought back to England from colonial India, where the maharajas loved playing elaborate stunts on one another on the April 1st.

Only recently a radio station announced on April Fools' Day a government initiative where the next two Thursdays would be cancelled, because we had changed the clocks so many times, what with wars and daylight savings, and so on. Many employers called in to enquire if they had to pay their employees for the lost Thursdays. But the most famous April Fools' story of all was the spaghetti harvest. A well-respected reporter did a piece on the spaghetti harvest, showing trees dripping with strips of white pasta, and talking in hushed tones of vast, secret spaghetti plantations. Happy peasants were shown dragging baskets of flaccid spaghetti into the sun to dry. Many people called in to ask how to get hold of the spaghetti trees for their own back gardens.

GAME

PREMIUM GAME IN BLENHEIM

Without doubt the best-flavoured game meat is from wild animals. Wild-game meats tend to be darker in colour than farmed meats and the animals are not drenched or sprayed, making it a truly natural product free from residual chemicals. Allan Spencer is a wild and woolly kind of guy, and what he doesn't know about a wild black pig ain't worth knowing. About seven years ago he and three hunting buddies started a processing business specialising in wild meat, fresh from the field. It was supposed to be a business hobby, but a few bankruptcy scares later it's a thriving, award-winning business, growing by 50 per cent last year. Allan says, 'We used to get calls from restaurants asking for

game but we were not legally allowed to do that, so we built a proper factory and got a licence. Obtaining a MAF licence was incredibly expensive, and then we had to find the market to make it all worthwhile. Now we can't get enough rabbit, wild venison and wild pork.'

The clear, clean atmosphere of New Zealand's high country is the source of the fine game meats supplied by Premium Game. Allan and his partners hunt on the ground and in helicopters, and also contract about 30 registered hunters to hunt rabbit, hare, wallaby, thar (Himalayan mountain goat), wild goat, wild pig and venison. On an average week they process as many as 20 to 30 deer, 200 rabbits, 100 hares, 20 goats and 20 pigs. Thar and wallaby are usually hunted to order. The company has two master butchers and a customer base that spans almost every restaurant in Blenheim and up to 30 local wineries. They also supply fine restaurants all over New Zealand and some supermarkets.

Not only are MAF inspections expensive, they are tough. Every time a hunter comes in they have to fill in a form to show the area they were hunting in, what time each animal was killed and what time they arrived at the factory. They also have to fill in a landowners' declaration form to ensure no poison was laid there. And that's just the field work – at the factory the carcasses are checked minutely for damage, TB and any other diseases. The meat is processed, aged and vacuum-packed into dozens of cuts, ready to cook. They make their own bacon, sausages, ham and salami, and now sell a range of Maori herbs to go with the meat. Their website is: www.game-meats.co.nz.

GARLIC

Garlic not only tastes good but is also desperately good for you – there is no such thing as eating too much, as it is sacred, medicinal, erotic and restorative. Garlic grows very well in Marlborough – it loves the cold winters and hot, dry summers. It's planted in midwinter, the planting sometimes going on all night, and harvested in midsummer. Like olives, garlic has been around for a long time, dating back to 2000 BC. They say that slaves working on the great pyramids downed tools when their garlic supply was stopped. They believed it gave them strength and protected them from illness. I find that my slaves won't do a thing without it. Its medicinal properties are well known – it lowers cholesterol, prevents bowel cancer, is an antibiotic, thins the blood, cures colds and sore throats, and gets rid of anybody standing within a mile of you. The pungent odour of garlic is detectable on the skin up to 72 hours after ingestion, but if you suck on a lemon or eat parsley, it helps get rid of the smell. Horace was of the opinion that one garlic kiss would drive a lover to retreat to the far side of the bed. My opinion is give the lover some garlic and he'll come right back again. Roasting is a good way to cook it, as it loses its tang and becomes sweet and mellow.

Printanor is the most commonly grown variety of garlic in New Zealand. Sporting ten cloves to the head – it is firm and has white skin. It is particularly juicy, has a fresh, tangy taste and is available all year round. New Zealand garlic never gets that dried-out look because it is not cool-stored – we grow it from January to November. You can tell if it is New Zealand garlic and not a beastly import from China by checking the roots and looking for labels. Our garlic has its roots trimmed one at a time and is never labelled, because it sheds its skin if labels are stuck to it. When you get your garlic home, keep it in a cool, dark, dry place just as you would potatoes, and only break off the clove you are going to use immediately. Leave the rest intact to prevent drying out. We also grow what's called elephant garlic in New Zealand, which is five times bigger than regular garlic and less pungent but sweeter. It's also more fragile and bruises easily, but you can eat lots of it because of its milder flavour. Lately various people have been producing smoked garlic with quite a delicious result. You use it the same way as fresh garlic – it is not a cooked product. One of the smokers is The Original Smoke and Spice Co. and their website is: www.smokeandspice.co.nz.

Roasted garlic & fresh goat's cheese on toast

3 HEADS GARLIC
EXTRA VIRGIN OLIVE OIL
FRESH THYME
SEA SALT AND FRESHLY
GROUND BLACK PEPPER
100G FRESH GOAT'S CHEESE
1 BAGUETTE, SLICED
CUMIN SEEDS

1. Preheat the oven to 180°C. Trim the top quarter off the whole garlic heads to expose the cloves. Blanch in boiling water for 10 minutes. Drain well. Discard any loose skin and puncture the sides and top with a fork.

2. Place in a ceramic dish and drizzle generously with oil, then sprinkle with thyme, salt and pepper.

3. Roast until the cloves start popping out of the skins (about 40 minutes).

4. To serve, toast the baguette slices, spread with goat's cheese then top with some soft cloves of garlic and sprinkle with cumin seeds.

serves 6

HANDS

There is only one essential tool you need in a kitchen and that is your hands. A cook is a handcrafts person, like a potter or a painter. The tools of cooking have not really advanced since the invention of the fork. Cooking implements help, but they can't make you a good cook. Hands are dextrous, don't change temperature, are sensitive and are nice to lick things from. I have the hands of one who has cooked for a living – lined, tough and scarred. Just as you should never trust a thin chef, you should never trust one with smooth hands. How could you have smooth hands if you have chopped, burned, stained and drenched them all your life? The French say you end up with the face you deserve. Chefs' kitchen years are written on their hands. How many crabs, crayfish, oysters and mussels have I stabbed myself with? I still have the scar where I severed tendons in my forefinger while attacking a roast. Cooks can't grow their nails and wear polish. Is it any wonder we are cranky, unstable and nonconformist? If you nevertheless feel you could do with some flash kitchenware, besides your hands, refer to the entries on cookware, see page 63.

HEROES

KAY BAXTER

Kay Baxter is a one-woman cultural icon and is probably the food person I most admire in New Zealand. She runs Koanga Gardens in Maungaturoto, just before the Brynderwyn Hills. Koanga Gardens is a charitable trust which has been growing and collecting old fruit trees, vegetables and flowers and their seeds for 20 years. As she has come to know the seeds, Kay has become aware of their importance and value in our lives and our future. They are the strongest seeds we have with the widest genetic diversity and have been developed over thousands of years to sustain and support human life. Since 1920 we have irretrievably lost a staggering 90 per cent of our vegetable seeds, 85 per cent of our fruit varieties, and flowers are following close behind. We are living today in an era of unprecedented extinction – 20,000 species a year are being lost and this is now threatening the balance of evolution itself. From a biological point of view, genes are the thread linking our tenuous lineage between past and future, but this thread is quickly disintegrating.

Kay maintains a collection of New Zealand heirloom plants, along with records of their history and culture, to ensure their survival and availability for future generations as a resource for cultivation and genetic diversity. She is at pains to promote the collection as a taonga (treasure) and establish and maintain an educational resource and research centre where people can learn to garden with heirloom plants. Koanga Gardens has approximately 500 accessions in their collection, around 200 of them New Zealand heirlooms.

Maintaining heirloom vegetables is not about nostalgia. We are now living in a monoculture environment. The problem is that over the years we have bred our vegetables to look good, grow efficiently and be disease-resistant but this could lead to disaster. It was monocultural thinking that caused the potato famine in Ireland. The problem with the clone potato breeds of the 1840s was that they were all too closely related; they carried the same genetic strengths but also the same genetic weaknesses. When the Irish crop got the blight it was wiped out quickly because of its weak genetic base, and millions of people died as a result. Kay grows heirlooms as a hedge against massive crop failures in the future.

However, for home growers, heirloom veggies and fruit are mostly about taste. We all remember the incredible taste of the spuds our fathers grew in the backyard and long for that nutty sweetness in our adulthood. Returning to old varieties almost always means a return to better taste and nutrition. When you taste Kay's wiggly Dalmatian beans, her pre-European kumara, her Bohemian sugar peas and her knobbly Maori potatoes, you are in heaven.

Her website is: www.koanga.org.nz.

DICK HUBBARD OF HUBBARD FOODS

'Good morning, Peta,' beamed a man with a big nose, big ears and big smile, 'would you like to join me?' Cereal king Dick Hubbard rose from a container of cereal, covered in cornflakes and wearing a snorkel and goggles. He roared with laughter as his staff looked on indulgently. They're used to this stuff in the factory. Dick wanted to prove to me that he examined all his product with a fine-tooth comb to ensure it was perfect before you and I put his fabulous Berry Berry Nice muesli in our mouths.

Dick Hubbard is a man with lots of brains and a huge heart. Once in a very blue moon the universe provides us with an altruist businessperson along the lines of Anita Roddick of the Body Shop. Dick was brought up on a dairy farm in Komata just out of Paeroa and has been in the food industry all his life. He's very down-to-earth, and proud of it, his personal values of honesty and integrity filtering on down into his business practice. Like many successful people, Dick was let down early in his career by a broken promise – in the 1960s the dairy company agreed to give him a dairy-technology cadetship at Massey University which they later reneged on, citing bad marks. Enraged, he set out to prove them wrong, worked hard, financed himself and surpassed the cadets. Deliciously, he was offered a job lecturing at Massey and also a job as project manager for a tropical fruit-processing factory in Niue, which was a New Zealand/United Nations combined project. He chose the latter and this set him on the road to commercial ventures with social objectives.

Several high-powered jobs later and at the age of 40 Dick had a catharsis regarding his contribution to life. He wondered what he would have on his tombstone – would it maybe be, 'Here lies a man who made a wealthy man wealthier'? He decided to start up his own business with a social responsibility. In 1988 he and a financial partner set up Winner Foods, which in 1990 became Hubbard Foods under his sole ownership. His brilliance was in taking a common foodstuff – breakfast cereal – and revolutionising it. In a grotty factory in Onehunga with five staff and doing the accounts at home at night, he took on Sanitarium and Kellogg's. He created a Foodtown muesli that was so good it soon took over the market leader. The first cereal Dick launched under his own name was called Fruitful Breakfast – a muesli full of fruit and the now famous yoghurt-coated raisins. It is now New Zealand's number-one muesli and the sixth most popular cereal in New Zealand. His cereals have crazy names like Café au Lait – coffee-flavoured wheat flakes mixed with yoghurt-coated cornflakes; Bugs 'n' Mud – cocoa-coated rice pops with rice 'bugs' that sport natural orange stripes on their backs; 'Thank Goodness' – a wheat-and gluten-free mix of rice pops, fruit, sunflower seeds, linseed and almond flakes. His 'Light and Right' brand won the National Heart Foundation's Nutrition Award in 2004.

Hubbards have 180 staff, an annual turnover of $35 million, and the Hubbard brand represents a third of New Zealand breakfast-cereal sales. Dick is widely respected as a role model among business leaders for his work as chairman of Business Grow and board member of Business in the Community, an organisation that assists small businesses. He is involved in all sorts of other organisations that revolve around the concept of corporate social responsibility, fund-raising with World Vision, Outward Bound, school camps and book programmes. It is his philosophy to treat every staff member with dignity. There is no corporate carpark at the factory at Mangere – it is first come, first served – and everyone is on a first-name basis. And they source all their ingredients from New Zealand where possible.

The in-house newsletters are full of naff sayings like, 'a backbone is a stronger bone than a wishbone' and 'a diamond is really just a small and insignificant piece of coal that has adapted brilliantly to extreme pressure'. He famously took his staff on holiday to Samoa to celebrate ten years of operations. It was all over the news, with Dick resplendent in lava-lava and flowers in his hair – he was ecstatic. Sadly his staff thanked him by then protesting their contracts, so he gave them a wage increase.

Dick Hubbard has now done the obvious next thing in his wonderful career – he has become Mayor of Auckland. He had my vote with bells on.

PADMA AND SWAMY AKUTHOTA OF SATYA SOUTH INDIAN CAFÉ

I met these stirling people when Taste New Zealand filmed the chef/owner Padma Akuthota and her husband Swamy Akuthota making various unleavened Indian breads. After that they got lots of positive press, moved to bigger premises and have opened another little restaurant. I eat at these restaurants often with my gastronomic colleagues and friends. We are all in agreement that Padma's food is the best we have eaten outside India. There are over 200 Northern Indian restaurants in New Zealand but few Southern Indian ones, and the cuisine is quite distinctive. Padma is a brilliant cook producing rich, complex and profoundly flavoured dishes from her homeland. She is the best dhosa maker in Auckland, with Indian chefs coming from all over the country to eat hers. Her food is not only

made with love and care as if she were cooking for her family, but is always visually beautiful and harmonious. Swamy serves the food with politeness and charm and loves getting into complex conversations regarding the origins of the dishes. Satya Café makes a unique contribution to the rich gastronomic cultural mix we have in Auckland.

ROSS MCCALLUM

When I think of Ross I think of Kapiti and of mouth-watering Kikorangi Blue, surely New Zealand's most-loved and most-consumed blue cheese. It has a rich golden curd and creamy spoonable texture marbled with a dense blue veining. Mildly pungent, its flavour develops as it ages to create a smoother, more delectable taste. For years, when we only ate Cheddar, we also loved imported blue-vein cheese. And it was strong – much more pungent than Kikorangi. But now we're much flasher and more sophisticated, and we lap up the creaminess of this milder cheese.

It is hard to imagine there is a household in New Zealand whose cheese-eating habits haven't been touched by Ross's vision and entrepreneurship. In his quiet unassuming way,

Padma and Swamy Akuthota ,Satya South Indian Café, Auckland

Ross has been one of the important food heroes in New Zealand. In 1984 he and his wife Glenyss and another couple opened the doors of Kapiti Cheese at the Lindale Tourist Centre, north of Wellington, making Edam, Gouda and Cheddar. They went on to make many other cheeses – including feta, camembert, brick and Parmesan. By the time Ross sold the company last year to United Milk they were making an unbelievable 51 products. Kapiti Cheese now has a turnover of nearly $19 million and is probably the most awarded brand in the New Zealand food industry. It also has a high international profile, partly due to the appearance of its products on the menus of at least 50 different airlines.

Some of the more outstanding cheeses are whisky Cheddar; Kohu, a goat's milk Gouda; mascarpone, an Italian-style cream cheese; *fromage blanc* and Aorangi, a double-cream brie. My favourite is Mt Hector – a little goat's cheese in the shape of a truncated pyramid, meant to resemble the tabletop mountain overlooking Kapiti Island. It is a seasonal summer cheese and the milk comes from one farm in Takapau, Hawke's Bay, where the farmer has two breeds of traditional Swiss milking goats. It is designed to have a high acidic body and high moisture content, ensuring that when ripe it will run. When perfectly ripe it is heavenly – soft and chalky. Kapiti is also famous for its 50 flavours of super-sensational ice-creams, its crème anglaise (custard) and its sorbets.

Ross is a tall, loping gentle giant who laughs easily and works hard. He is a member of Slow Food and has applied Slow Food ideas to many parts of his business. The big, new cheese factory in Paraparaumu, which enabled him to quadruple production, remained true to its artisanal roots. All the cheese is still made in open vats, but there are now six instead of one, and techniques have become more streamlined. Mechanical rather than human arms now draw the knives through the curd. Rather than laboriously transferring the curd into the hoops with buckets, Ross decided to let gravity do the work. Positioned on a mezzanine floor, each vat is built so it can be tilted and drained, with the curds flowing down a chute into waiting hoops on the floor below. All cheese is matured on site before being sold. The zesty Riverdale Cheddar, for example, is matured for three to four years before it is put on the market.

So Ross took the money and ran. But did he and Glenyss lie around and smell the roses? Why, no! Ross now has a flash new business card that says 'Gourmet Guru' and has set up a business mentoring food companies. I wouldn't mind having him on my books.

ANDY COLTART AND KIM THORP OF BLACK BARN VINEYARDS

These two fine gentlemen run the most glamorous food and wine-related mini-empire in New Zealand, and they always look like they're having the greatest time, and anyone could do it, and 'Have you tasted our reserve merlot yet, darling?' They are unremittingly gracious, generous and unpretentious and have many arrows to their bow. Their operation is called Black Barn Vineyards and under that brand comes the vineyard, the retreats and accommodation, the functions, the bistro, the amphitheatre, the growers' market and the art gallery. Hawke's Bay is a very switched-on gastronomic heartland and it has succeeded in creating a real HB brand. (See Tourism, page 204 for information on the input of Graeme Avery at Sileni Estate vineyard, and page 203 for information on the Hawke's Bay Wine Country.)

The vineyards are on the warm north-facing slopes of the Te Mata hills just outside Havelock North. The production is small and premium, with a total planted area of just 20 acres. The vineyards are divided into no less than 28 tiny sub-blocks, which are all monitored and harvested separately. All the grapes are estate-grown and selectively hand-picked to ensure optimum ripeness and fruit quality.

They offer five unique properties for nightly rental, fully self-contained and exclusively yours for the duration of your stay. Each is selected for its prime location, unique character and original style. They are all luxuriously appointed to reflect their individual character and contain the very best in furnishings, bedding, fabrics, kitchenware and amenities. From an eight-bedroom luxury retreat to a two-bedroom turn-of-the-century cottage in the heart of the vineyard, these properties are recognised as among the best available in New Zealand. They do not wholesale or advertise their properties; all bookings are made directly with the winery. Therefore you will not find them in travel shops or discount brochures, and 80 per cent of their guests are either repeat visitors or personal recommendations through word of mouth. They are happy to organise anything you require to make your stay more enjoyable. From food shopping to a personal assistant, to fly fishing, to guided walks, to fully prepared meals, they can book it for you in advance if you wish. They do not add any surcharges or mark-ups for these services, so they can provide you with the one they believe is the best for the job.

The bistro is only open for lunches, so they can use this space for evening functions as required. It can seat up to 100 people and double doors open out on to a beautifully

H

BLACK BARN
VINEYARDS

WINE SALES
SEVEN DAYS

lit sunken courtyard covered by a canopy of grape vines. The restaurant and courtyard are in the heart of the vineyard and look right out across the vines to take in all of Hawke's Bay. This space can be used for small gatherings, musical evenings, private dinners and weddings.

The amphitheatre has been described by internationally recognised singers and musicians as probably the best outdoor venue in the country. Renowned for its acoustics and atmosphere, it is a truly memorable location. Rather than simply being an uncomfortable slope on a hill, the amphitheatre was carved out of the hillside and purpose-built from scratch. Large, flat, grassed terraces mean concert-goers sit in comfort with close uninterrupted views of the stage and the whole of Hawke's Bay as a backdrop. Every terrace is fairy-lit for concerts and the entire amphitheatre is surrounded by a circle of 50-year-old muscatel grapes – approximately three big events are held there each year. Many of these concerts are accompanied by private dinners before the main event. The website is: www.blackbarn.com.

ALISON HOLST

Wellington's Alison Holst is living proof that a Bachelor of Home Science can go a long way. This well-bred, high-achieving girl from Dunedin has become the gracious, charming mother of everyday New Zealand food. There are several pretenders to the throne, but none have hit the mark and are as trusted and loved as Alison. Before I met her, I couldn't imagine what I could possibly have in common with a woman who was everything I was not – a home-maker, a muffin-maker, and a writer of over 75 cookbooks with names like *Alison Holst's Best Mince Recipes* and *Baby Food and Beyond*. My life was so different from hers – she wouldn't think I was up to much. I am here to tell you that Alison has another side only her friends know about – she's funny, intelligent, well-travelled and makes everyone who comes into her orbit feel as if she was just waiting for them to come into her life. The first time I met her was when we were both judging the cheese awards in Auckland, and I was struck by her diligence and agonising detail over the cheeses. She went back and back, tasting, asking questions and advice from expert Juliet Harbutt, making sure she had made the right decisions. She was the judge of the supreme award-winner and it nearly threw her into a state of catharsis, so concerned was she about the impossibility of choosing a best-of-all-cheese from categories which bore no relationship to each other. I agreed with her concern but was not prepared to lose weight over it. I admired her unreservedly from that moment on.

Alison has made television cooking shows, sold over three- million copies of her cookbooks, and is a journalist, broadcastor, cooking teacher and businesswoman. She received a Queen's Service Medal in 1983 for services to the community, was made a CBE for Services to Home Science in 1987, and in 1997 was given an honorary Doctor of Science degree from the University of Otago. Her focus has always been to encourage home cooks to produce interesting, tasty, varied, nutritious meals that don't take too long or cost too much to prepare. 'When you cook at home you know what you are putting into your mouth,' she says. She is concerned that people have forgotten how to plant a garden, cook meals from scratch, make and repair clothes, fix houses and make their own entertainment. Alison loves, respects and is proud of her family and considers family life to be much more important than professional success.

She now writes books with her son Simon Holst and loves fishing, long-distance gossiping and gourmandising with her marvellous, equally tall and impressive sister Clare Fergusson. Clare is a fabulous cook, recipe writer, broadcaster and food stylist based in London and is the queen of big hair, the big laugh and joie de vivre. The other equally tall and impressive sister is Patricia Payne, a mezzo-soprano of no small talent. When these three get together, lock up the boring people because they couldn't cope. They laugh until they cry, and they sing, cook and tell stories until the cows come home. And Alison is all ours – all you have to do is tap in: www.holst.co.nz and she is smiling out at you.

GRAHAM HARRIS

There he was, up on the stage at the International Slow Food Awards in Bologna, patiently explaining to the large audience that he had been short-listed for his work on Maori potatoes, not kumara. Unfortunately most people, including the enthusiastic television personality who was MC-ing the award ceremony, don't know the difference. But Graham Harris does, because he's been working with Maori potatoes for most of his professional life. And if any man in New Zealand knows the difference between a potato and a kumara, it's Harris.

While researching Maori potatoes, I fell into the intellectual hands of this senior lecturer at the Natural Resources Centre of the Open Polytechnic in Wellington. Harris not only grows and eats 16 varieties of these strange-looking, heavenly tasting, tuberous root vegetables but is also writing a thesis on the history of Maori potato cultivation for a Master of Philosophy degree in ethnobotany. Harris is particularly interested in the connection between the Maori spiritual attachment to land and their growing of crops, employment, nutrition, gift giving and the transfer of knowledge between the generations.

At the time I discovered Harris, I was asked to be one of 400 international judges for the Slow Food Awards in Italy and was casting around for a suitable candidate to submit. Slow Food wished to reward, acknowledge and help any person or group who fitted into the criteria of their anti-fast-food, pro-conservation of the food culture of the past for the future agenda. In other words they were looking for people who really make a difference, not just with their food job but also for its social, historical and practical effect. Graeme Harris, quietly and without flamboyance, is one of New Zealand's largely unsung heroes – a true guardian of these neglected treasures. Only ten years ago most people knew nothing about the delicious Maori potato, except, of course, those Maori who had always grown it in their gardens. In a world degraded by fast life, fast food and disappearing agricultural traditions, a good spud, simply steamed, is like edible gold.

Purple urenika (peruperu) are small and have a fine, dark blue flesh with white flecks. When cooked they become very floury; but they hold their shape, so can be used in salads as well as mashed with lots of extra virgin olive oil and milk. It is a particularly bizarre experience to eat purple food because blue is associated with poison. You don't expect it to taste like a potato, but it tastes like the spuds you think you remember from your childhood – sweet and nutty. Yellow kowiniwini look like warts, taste like hazelnuts and are very waxy. Karupararera have chocolate-brown skin and yellow eyes. Once tasted, they are never forgotten, and the reason that they taste so good is because they have never been commercially cultivated or modified in any way. The sensual, flavourful appeal of the Maori potato fits in perfectly with Slow Food's 'defence of quiet material pleasure and slow, long-lasting enjoyment'.

According to Harris's tireless research, these superior-tasting and disease-resistant potatoes probably came to New Zealand with the first European ships, but many Maori believe their ancestors had been cultivating potatoes along with kumara as long as a thousand years ago. The interesting thing is that centuries ago all potatoes were small, rather ugly and sometimes taking a very long time to cook. Maori stored their potatoes in pits in the ground. Layers of ponga fronds were placed among the potatoes, the spores from the ferns keeping pests and disease away. Imagine how fabulous they must have tasted, coming up from the hangi pits?

And that's why Slow Food sat down at the groaning board, had a good look at their 400 entries and voted Graham Harris on to its top 13 influential food people in the world.

Jane Hunter, Hunter's Wines, Marlborough

JANE HUNTER OF HUNTER'S WINES IN MARLBOROUGH

Jane has been owner, viticulturist and managing director of this well-known New Zealand wine company since 1987. She is an extraordinary woman in her quiet, undramatic way. Jane had no intention of becoming the public face of Hunters; it was her extrovert husband Ernie who was supposed to do all that. He died suddenly and tragically, and Jane was faced with running the vineyard all on her own. Other members of her family assist her and no matter what happens, Jane is always calm but feisty if needed, looking you straight on with her stunning green eyes.

The 1991 Hunter's Sauvignon Blanc won gold at the Air New Zealand Wine Awards just ten days after being bottled. In 1992 Hunter's won the Marquis de Goulaine trophy for the World's best sauvignon blanc. Jane's commitment to the industry has been instrumental in placing the Marlborough region firmly on the map – a fact that was recognised in 1993 when she was awarded an OBE for her services to the wine industry. Jane has won national acclaim and was presented with an Honorary Doctorate in Science from Massey University in 1997. She and faithful shadow Paddy, a ten-year-old British Clumber spaniel, work daily at the

winery together and enjoy long walks through the vines, all the time keeping an eye on the vineyard's development. Hunter's and Marlborough are, of course, most famous for sauvignon blanc, the flinty wine we export the most. Jane also keeps winning awards for her riesling and chardonnay, makes beautiful, sparkling pinot noir and even a rosé for those long, hot summer months of barbecues and grilled snapper. Her property is absolutely delightful, with gardens, artists' residences, a gallery and a restaurant. In November Hunter's sponsors the top garden festival in New Zealand, where green-fingered individuals gird their loins and travel from all over to spy on other people's gorgeous gardens.

In 2004 Jane won the inaugural international Women in Wine Award, designed to recognise a woman who has made an exceptional contribution to one or more of the year's award-winning wines or wineries. The international judges made the following remarks: 'Jane Hunter OBE has spent 20 years at the forefront of the New Zealand Wine industry where she has not only built her own Hunter's Wines into a successful company, but also worked tirelessly to promote the profile and reputation of the Marlborough region. She has shown total commitment to the New Zealand cause over a long career and enjoys enormous respect from her peers both at home and internationally. Jane's example is an inspiration to women working in any area of wine. Her experience covers everything from viticulture, through company management to international trade and liaison with governmental agencies. What a lot of different skills that all requires, and with what dexterity has Jane mastered all the challenges she has faced! This is a woman who has shown long-term commitment to the industry, tireless support for her fellow pioneers and a clear focus on the challenges ahead. Moreover, she has achieved success while maintaining a very female attitude, a level head in crisis and an understanding of the true worth of friends. She is an inspiration to us all.'

The Hunter's website is: www.hunters.co.nz

MOHAMED ABBARI OF SIMO'S MOROCCAN RESTAURANT

When I launched my book on Morocco, *Sirocco*, a Moroccan chef in Christchurch I had become friendly with called me up and said, 'I'm doing the food at your launch.' So he prepared all these fabulous titbits in his Christchurch kitchen, then flew himself and his boxes of food up to Auckland, stunned everyone with his perfumed jewels of deliciousness and went home again the next day. This is

entirely typical of generous Moroccans and especially of Simo. We need more Simos in New Zealand – a lot more. Mohamed Abbari (Simo) who was classically French trained in Rabat, has done much for New Zealand cooking and now is thrilling us with his native cuisine in his multi-award-winning restaurant Simo's in Christchurch.

His New Zealand wife, Julie, has taken on the graciousness, warmth and hospitality of the Moroccans, and is the most gentle, loving hostess you could meet. Their kids are fantastic and even her parents help out with the business. Everyone believes in Simo. At the stylish, traditionally decorated restaurant they spray you with rose water, ply you with mint tea and finish you off with date and pistachio baklava. I ask you! He is one of the few chefs that does not believe in fusion cuisine, insisting that a country's cuisine should remain pure and not muddled with ingredients and techniques from other cultures. Moroccan recipes are centuries old and, apart from modern presentation, Simo doesn't really mess around with them much. His *briouats* are light, his *harira* soup is just like at the *souk* (market) in Marrakech, his preserved lemon, chicken and olive tagine is thick and complex just like the first one I ever ate in Casablanca, and the *b'stilla* is flat, eggy and lemony, as it should be.

Simo not only wants you to come and eat his Moroccan food, he wants you to use the flavours at home. To this end he teaches cooking classes, and has a range of spices and condiments in the most stunning burnt orange and midnight blue packets. Because he hasn't enough to do with the restaurant, his products and his family, he has started up another business called MoJo with partner Jonny Schwass. MoJo bridges the gap between supplier and restaurant, offering menu design, product development and cost analysis. The main focus of the business is supplying commercial kitchens with prepared, portioned and cost-controlled product. He has also just started importing argan oil, made from the berries of the argan tree, *Argania spinosa*, which are left to dry, then cracked open to release their seeds, and about which I wrote in *Sirocco*. In Morocco it is mostly women who produce this honey/amber-coloured oil by a hand-grinding process, and it is principally used to make the delicious spread, *amlou*, but also as a cosmetic and for cooking. Argan oil has a nutty, sharp flavour and can be rubbed into couscous, plopped into tagines, with fish, in salads or dribbled on to bread.

Simo is a member of Slow Food and is a walking example of what that means – passion, taking your time over a meal, using only fresh, top-quality primary produce and preserving cultural identity. He hates fast food and sees it as the destruction of pleasure, of the importance of dining together and of taste itself. He doesn't understand why you would choose to eat alone and in a rush. Simo loves New Zealand and sees his food businesses as a way to give something back to his adopted country.

HONEY

Honey is an elixir of sex. Flowers use bees in their surreptitious sex dance. They can't get together and hold hands themselves and sometimes the wind doesn't prove a very good carrier of pollen, so bees do the job. Flowers produce nectar to attract the bees, which when they dive into the flower to suck up the sugar get pollen stuck on their hairy bodies and transfer it to the next flower, thus fertilising it to reproduce. The reason flowers are colourful and beautiful in shape and form is not for your dining-room table, but to attract the bees. Just as a woman will wear a pretty dress and lipstick to attract the male, flowers do the same thing. Conversely, bees need nectar to feed, provide fuel for flying and to preserve the hive. No matter how hard the flower makes it for the bee to get at the nectar sac, the bee can always get in because of her jointed body which will bend easily. Honey is a wild food, and you have to respect the bees' nature or they will attack you, even to their detriment – when a bee stings to get rid of intruders, it dies. We need bees, for without them the earth couldn't regenerate her trees, grasses, flowers and plants.

BEESONLINE

BeesOnline is the best honey shop in the country and Maureen Maxwell is one switched-on operator – always professional, always smiling, even when she's in the thick of it. And she's utterly committed to the production of good honey, organic and GE-free if possible. To intensify the natural flavour, the honey is minimally filtered and not heat-treated. Maureen seems to be in love with honey. The taste of fresh honey dripping off the wax changed her life, and she is inspired by the complex lifestyle of bees. She can look quickly at a display hive, the embodiment of pure energy, and tell you exactly what sort of bee each one is and their job. 'See, that one's cleaning, that one's taking bodies out, that one's doing the waggle dance to signal where the food source is outside the hive, and that big one with the red dot on her back is the queen.'

Speaking of waggling, bees can unbelievably 'remember' that a certain flower produces good nectar and pollen for 12 days. Even if they're only hanging out in the hive, bees are always fanning to keep it cool. Maureen's honey centre covers everything from petal to palate. She describes her single-flora honeys like wine and makes you fall for the slightly salty, snow white, delicate flavour of the honey from the flame-flowered pohutukawa tree. Depending on the month, she will also have manuka, rewa rewa, clover and bush honey.

I've always wanted to know how you can control which flowers the bees will go to in order to obtain your single-flower honey. Well, the bees will work with whatever flowers are closest to them, so when Maureen wants a tawiri honey she moves the hives to the where they are growing. Different flowers and trees produce the precious nectar at different times of the day and month, and obviously only in the summertime. As Hattie Ellis says in her wonderful book about the mysterious history of bees, *Sweetness and Light*, honey is 'a sweet, fragrant river from a million tributaries, carried across the air and flowing gold into the pot through the transforming power of the bee'.

Maureen has made her large, modern honey centre in Waimauku, Auckland, a 'must-experience' destination. Visitors can observe the working factory, watch the bees making honey in a glass chamber and two-storeyed bee theatre, taste anything they want for free, buy anything they want for money, including honey-related products like honeygar, honey syrup with vanilla and citrus added, honey mustard, bee pollen (which she has got me taking), honey-roasted nuts, beauty products and her recipe book. Best of all, you can enjoy a good nosh in her award-winning café, which serves hearty helpings of fresh, tasty food and a good selection of New Zealand wine. The place is packed every day and the view is of calm countryside, native gardens and sculptures.

BeesOnline is a completely sustainable, self-sufficient site – there is a spring and they harvest and recycle their own water. The roof of the honey centre is covered in grass for its insulation properties, the land is landscaped with natives and local artwork, and the cows produce organic milk from grass that has been pollinated by their bees. There are redeveloped wetlands in front of the building, so it's more eco-friendly for the fauna, not to mention the ducks which wander in periodically for a treat. Maureen believes New Zealand honey is the best in the world and the demand for our GE-free and natural products is about to go through the roof.

My favourite of her honeys at the moment is her rose-infused one which has a limited release each year timed for Mother's Day – it's just too divine drizzled over fresh croissants and in North African-inspired recipes.

H

Rose honey & honeygar chicken with couscous

4 TABLESPOONS ROSE HONEY
4 TABLESPOONS HONEYGAR
2 TABLESPOONS WATER
1 TEASPOON GERANIUM WATER
½ TEASPOON CARDAMOM SEEDS
½ TEASPOON CRUSHED PEPPERCORNS
1 BAY LEAF
6 SINGLE ORGANIC CHICKEN BREASTS
OLIVE OIL FOR FRYING
1 TEASPOON SESAME SEEDS FOR DECORATION

1. In an ovenproof dish, warm together the honey, honeygar and water, then add the geranium water, cardamom, peppercorns and bay leaf. Allow to cool.

2. Marinate the chicken breasts in this for 30 minutes. Preheat the oven to 180°C.

3. Remove the chicken from the marinade and place the dish with marinade in the oven to warm up. Pat the chicken dry and quickly fry or grill on a high heat to brown both sides.

4. Place the chicken back in the marinade and cook, covered, in the oven for 10 minutes. Remove and allow to rest in its juices for 10 minutes.

5. Slice chicken thickly on the cross, pour juices over and sprinkle with sesame seeds. Serve with couscous.

Couscous

300G INSTANT COUSCOUS
HALF OF A PRESERVED LIME AND
1 TABLESPOON OF THE JUICE
FRESHLY GROUND BLACK PEPPER
2 TABLESPOONS EXTRA VIRGIN OLIVE OIL
60G RAISINS
1 TABLESPOON GERANIUM WATER
60G WALNUTS
60G BLANCHED ALMONDS
½ TEASPOON CINNAMON
½ CUP CHOPPED FRESH MINT

1. Place the couscous in a large bowl. Add the preserved lime juice, pepper and oil and rub them in with your hands. Pour over enough boiling water to just cover the couscous and set aside to 'swell'.

2. Soak the raisins in the geranium water for 30 minutes.

3. Chop walnuts and almonds coarsely.

4. Discard preserved lime flesh and thinly slice the skin.

5. Fluff up couscous with a large fork and toss in the raisins and geranium water, nuts, preserved lime, cinnamon and mint.

6. To serve, pile the couscous in a pointed hill on a serving dish. Couscous is best served warm or at room temperature – nothing is worse than fridge-cold couscous.

serves 6

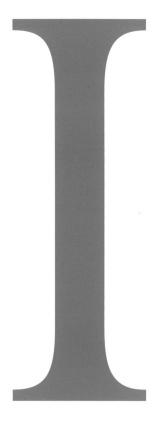

ICE-CREAM

New Zealanders are the second-highest per capita consumers of ice-cream in the world. This is not only testament to the quality of ice-cream produced here over many years, but evidence of extremely good taste on the part of New Zealanders – we love our dairy products and know our ice-cream. As a result, the ice-cream market is historically very innovative and extremely competitive for its size. New Zealand seems to be most famous for its hokey-pokey ice-cream, which as teenagers we called hope-he-pokes-me, then collapsed with the hilarity of it all. Almost universally, the top three ice-cream flavours around the world are vanilla, chocolate and strawberry. But not in New Zealand – here hokey-pokey, which is like brittle golden syrup or toffee through the ice-cream, comes second after vanilla. When hokey-pokey ice-cream melts in the summer sun it becomes memorable, gooey, New Zealand gold. When it comes to hokey-pokey we won't be trifled with, if you'll pardon the pun. If the ice-cream-makers don't get the blend just right the complaints start flowing. Some people love it melty and gooey but others like it crunchy – if you err too much on the soft side, all the crunchy people complain, and if you err too much the other side, the soft people complain. When I was a child you could buy chewy, slightly over-caramelised tasting hokey-pokey bars from the dairy.

KAPITI ICE-CREAM

The secret of Kapiti Ice-cream is simply that they make it properly with egg yolks, milk and cream. If you want to know why some ice-cream tastes better than others, it's because of the fat content. This ice-cream is real ice-cream and has a heavy, dense, creamy texture that is the result of

Hokey-pokey ice-cream

to make the ice-cream:

1 ¹/₂ CUPS MILK OR CREAM

4 EGG YOLKS

100G SUGAR

1. Bring the milk or cream to the boil.

2. While this is happening, beat the egg yolks and sugar together until they become thick and creamy (about 5 minutes).

3. Pour the boiling milk into the egg-yolk mixture, stirring with a wooden spoon. Pour this mixture back into the saucepan, stirring gently and continuously over a low heat. You will see and feel the custard slowly thickening until it easily coats the back of the wooden spoon.

4. Remove custard from the heat immediately and pour through a sieve into a clean bowl. Stir occasionally as it cools.

5. Whip in an ice-cream maker.

6. When you have made the hokey-pokey, break it up into little bits and stir it into the ice-cream, then freeze.

to make the hokey-pokey:

5 TABLESPOONS SUGAR

2 TABLESPOONS GOLDEN SYRUP

1 TEASPOON BAKING SODA

1. Grease a baking tray with butter.

2. Bring sugar and golden syrup to the boil, slowly stirring all the time. Boil for 6 minutes, stirring occasionally.

3. Remove from the heat and stir in the baking soda quickly, then immediately pour the frothing mixture into the greased tray. It will go hard almost at once.

serves 4—6

a low overrun – the term given to the increase in volume of finished ice-cream over the volume of the ingredients. Basically, this measures the amount of air whipped into the finished ice-cream. As ice-cream is usually sold by volume rather than weight, i.e. by the litre rather than by the kilo, cheaper ice-creams have high overruns. Kapiti Ice-cream uses a very low overrun, giving it its characteristic dense, real, 'homemade' texture. So, per scoop, there is more ice-cream in their ice-cream. Some of Kapati's flavours are fig and honey, gingernut made from actual Griffins Gingernuts, spicy apple crumble, feijoa, green apple, Maacha green tea, chai latte, and Tahitian lime.

FOUETTÉ ICE-CREAM

The ice-cream made by Di Sherratt really is homemade, but instead of using egg yolks she uses egg whites. This is a very common ice-cream style made all over Gisborne and Hawke's Bay. There is no churner involved and it all happens in the kitchen of a cottage next to her farmhouse in the back blocks of Tahunga, Gisborne. There is cream involved and sugar and whipping and folding, and more than that I am under pain of death or worse not to reveal. The result is a very light, unctuous mouth feel which carries inserted flavours really well. The day I visited her, Di made a lemon meringue ice-cream that tasted exactly like the aforementioned lemon meringue pie. She beat a lemon syrup into the mixture, then scrunched in cooked meringues at the last minute before freezing. Other flavours include lavender and honey, liquorice and prune, boysenberry and marshmallow, Celtic cream, marbled chocolate and coffee praline. She has just started making casatta cakes and drives an hour from her farm into Gisborne to deliver the goods herself, entrusting this journey to no one. There are no preservatives or additives in *fouetté* ice-cream and it's not churned but whipped (which is what the French term means) so has to be eaten reasonably fresh.

Di makes it to order and in summer, orders can run to 70 litres a week.

OTHER GOOD ICE-CREAM MAKERS ARE:
- Rush Munroe in Hawke's Bay
- The Gourmet Ice-cream Co. in Dunedin
- Deep South Ice-cream in Invercargill and Christchurch

INTIMACY, LOVE & FOOD

Food exists in an emotional context in which it can make us feel comfort, disgust, fear, happiness and sometimes even melancholy and pain. We clearly use it to influence other people's emotions, even the emotions of spirits, as when ancient cultures offer huge feasts or forbidden foods like human flesh to appease the gods. Sharing food with people is a way of sharing love, and you have only to read Laura Esquivel's *Like Water for Chocolate* to understand how your emotions can be conveyed in the food you cook. The boundaries between love and appetite are so diffuse that at times they evaporate completely. A cook transmits a very intense personal energy when he or she is cooking, and food has the ability to transport us back to our very essence. When one prepares food with energy and passion, those very qualities are transferred to those who eat the food.

Food and the smell of food invokes memories of people, places and emotions with almost the same intensity as music does. My paternal grandmother is linked forever with lavender-smelling pastilles. As I played serious card games with my grandfather, my grandmother would offer us some of her precious bonbons. When she found out they were going out of production, my grandfather bought up every last packet in Auckland for her. Her death left a huge void in my life that even now has not been filled. Just touching something that was hers makes me weep. By contrast, every time I smell onions cooking I laugh because it reminds me of a beau who used to fry them to trick me into thinking he was cooking a delicious meal, then heat up a frozen dinner in the microwave.

Herbs and spices are the heart of your kitchen, and the kitchen is the poetic centre of your home – these condiments sweeten your breath, improve sexual ardour, help you sleep, stimulate you and aid digestion. I will never forget the day an old Greek man put a bunch of wild oregano in my bag as I travelled around the islands. The bag smelt of that penetrating aroma for weeks, and it was the first time I had ever thought of herbs as anything other than something one eats. A bunch of fresh rosemary thrown in a hot bath is also a rather lovely experience. Of course herbs and spices were originally grown in monasteries and convents only for medicinal purposes. We have forgotten that knowledge today when we trip out into our gardens to pull a bay leaf off the tree; if we did that in medieval times we would have known that bay or laurel is a symbol of virility.

Could there be anything more intimate than someone picking up morsels of food with their fingers and placing them in your mouth? This is what mothers do with their children and it intimates trust, love and acceptance.

ITALIAN FOOD

MARIA PIA'S TRATTORIA

The best Italian restaurant in New Zealand is Maria Pia's Trattoria in Wellington. Her Puglia-inspired food is fresh, seasonal, down-to-earth and utterly delectable. She makes all her pasta with a rolling pin, not a machine, and she makes bread, cakes and sausages by hand every day. She wanders through the restaurant looking like the pretty, flour-covered Italian mamma she is, telling stories and dishing up 'twisted plaits' from a big bowl under her arm. She assures me that Italian women who make their own pasta have strong arms and beautiful breasts.

Pia's tomatoes are always perfect or she doesn't serve them. She brings in mozzarella fresh from Puglia herself. She makes unusual dishes like *cassoncei alla Bergamesea* (ravioli stuffed with meat, herbs, walnuts and raisins), braised goat, and steak fillet baked in tomatoes; and southern dishes like duck with aromatic couscous and vegetables, raw salmon marinated in lemon, orange and pomegranate seeds, linguini (always al dente at Pia's) with Queen scallops, pipi and mussels, and *tortellini in brodo*. Parmesan cheese comes in its wooden grater and you use as much as you like. Although Apulian cuisine is principally a poor cuisine, there is nothing scarce about the way Pia serves. All food decisions are made seasonally, and at the moment Pia is getting a grower to produce Italian vegetables from the seeds she brought back from her last trip to Puglia.

Pia's American husband, Richard, runs the joint, dishes out unusual Italian wines, is a fine musician and the convivium leader for Wellington Slow Food. As if this isn't enough, they

Antonio Cacace, La Bella Italia, Wellington

Maria Pia de Razza, Maria Pia's Trattoria, Wellington

have two beautiful daughters who wait tables on busy nights. The restaurant is exactly what you would expect a family joint to be – homely, unpretentious, covered in photos and always full of laughing, happy, well looked-after people. The sort of people who eat chez Pia are intelligent, cultured and arty – diplomats, musicians and homesick young Italians, who usually turn up at midnight after closing time when Pia whips up some fresh pasta dish to feed them. It's definitely not a place for flash-Harry yuppies. Don't even think about going there without reserving.

The latest on Pia and Richard is they are now importing Italian goods for sale to you and me, Pia has written a recipe book with family stories in it and she wants to set up an Italian cooking school for young people. You would almost want to move to Wellington just to be near these people. Every time I visit, Pia gives me something; one day it was a massage, another day some oil, another day some crystals. She knows what you need when you need it.

LA BELLA ITALIA
Happily there are lots of outlets in New Zealand to satisfy our craving for good Italian food. It is much easier to buy it than find it in a restaurant. Antonio Cacace is from Massa Lubrense in southern Italy. He came to New Zealand in 1991, and in 1996 opened his shop in Petone, selling the Italian produce he so missed from his homeland. When you walk into his warehouse it's pumping – lunch tables in three different areas, cookware, delicatessen, cheese, cookbooks, ingredients, wine, opera, noise, people, fun. You can buy Italian confectionery, mortadella, Parma ham, salamis, focaccia, sausages, pasta and sugo; and you also eat in the trattoria and they even arrange for catering to be done. You name it, Antonio does it. I found fennel liqueur there, which I didn't think I could get in New Zealand. Like all Italians he's very generous. On one occasion when I poked my nose in, he was still plying me with deliciousness as I was getting back in the car. He ran out with a serving of fish in a plastic container, the *plat du jour*, so I could taste it. This was after making me a huge buffalo mozzarella, ham and tomato sandwich. As I closed the car door he chucked in some Italian sweeties.

This is a wonderful place to visit and graze. I asked Antonio why there were so many tables for customers to eat at, and he told me that originally there were none, but he got so frustrated with always explaining to people how to eat and cook with his products that one day he said to a customer, 'Look, sit down here and I'll show you.' He

started with four tables and now he seats at least 50, teaches cooking classes and never stops being hospitable. You can eat Italian dishes like San Danielle prosciutto on melon; all sorts of cheeses; fresh tuna steaks drenched in oil, lemon juice, parsley, garlic and mint; and chocolate and almond cake, to name a few. If you feel you need a more authentic experience, you can fly to Italy and stay at his family's three-star hotel and restaurant called La Primavera in Massa Lubrense. It is situated between Capri and Ischia near Naples, and friends who have been there tell me it's wonderful and the food is very typical and good.

ITALIAN FOOD IN AUCKLAND
For Italian supplies in the Auckland area, try Sabato in Mt Eden (see Delicatessens, page 70) and the Italian Grocer in Ponsonby. If you are looking for a restaurant, Aqua Matta serves refined, high-quality food in an arty setting; Toto serves delicious, classy food in an operatic setting; and Delicious serves very good, fresh pasta in a casual, neighbourhood setting.

BRESAOLA
My friend Paolo Delmonte, who is the co-ordinator of the Slow Food Convivium in Auckland, has taken to making his own bresaola in desperation at not being able to get the real thing in New Zealand. Bresaola is a speciality of the Valtellina Valley in Lombardy. It is air-dried, salted beef fillet, a little sharper but more delicate and aromatic than prosciutto (dried pork) and one of the most elegant of all the dried meats. Paolo makes his by covering the beef fillet in salt, pepper and spices and leaving it for ten to 20 days. It is then hung in a naturally controlled drying room for a further 30 to 60 days depending on the size of the fillet. No chemicals, colorants or preservatives are used. This is a much slower method than commercially made bresaola, but the meat ends up more flavoursome. The first time I tasted Paolo's bresaola was in his home with his beautiful young daughters looking on. He slices it very thinly with a small domestic electric slicer, lays it out flat on a plate, drizzles it with extra virgin olive oil, adds a few drops of lemon, maybe some pepper and rains it with Parmesan. In Lombardy bresaola is sometimes wrapped around a filling of soft goat's cheese and then rolled up like cannelloni. Of course, now I'm addicted and have had to buy an electric slicer solely for my bresaola. Paolo sells to top restaurants, catering companies and deli shops. One can also buy it online at: www.aldente.co.nz/product.

JAM The best jam in New Zealand is made by Anathoth in Upper Moutere, Nelson. If you can pronounce it, you get a free jar. Just kidding. Anathoth jam is living proof that you can have an unpronounceable name, an unglamorous plastic pot and a humble background, but if your product is good, the people will come. Kaye and Owen Pope started selling Kaye's jam at the Nelson market and now their jams are in every supermarket in New Zealand. They make the jam in ten-pot batches, all cooking in a row while the cookers run up and down stirring them. The cooking method and simple recipes ensure you get the same old-fashioned taste of New Zealand that you remember from the very first time you tried a hot-buttered scone with freshly made jam. The most famous is the raspberry jam, absolutely bursting with fruit grown on the couple's own property. A close second is the three-berry jam made from strawberries, raspberries and blueberries. They also have a very charming website worth having a look at: www.anathoth.co.nz.

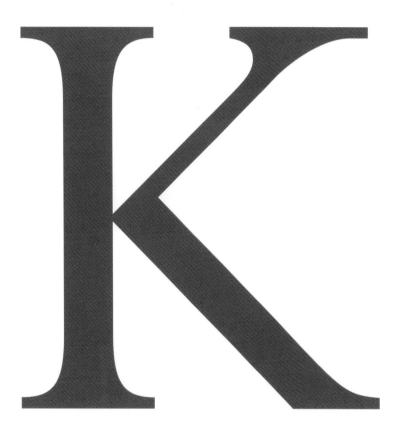

KAITAIA FIRE
This is New Zealand's answer to Tabasco Sauce. Kaitaia Fire Ltd was established in 1989 by Garry Sommerville on an organic two-hectare farm in New Zealand's winterless Far North. From those humble beginnings, they now export their sauce all around the world and produce a range of organic 'hot' products for the domestic market. The sauces have won many food awards in both New Zealand and the United States.

Scattered among the farmland is Northland's 'hot crop' and yes, this one is legal – chilli peppers, *Capsicum frutescens*, the main ingredient in the Kaitaia Fire organic hot sauce made at Lake Ohia and named after the local town. When the chillies are at the height of their maturity and the red colour is at its most intense, they are plucked off the knee-high bushes and brought in for sorting and washing. After being finely milled and mixed with organic sea salt, the chillies are sealed in barrels with air locks to undergo a quasi-fermentation process over the next few years. This process effectively removes all the sugars in the fruit and releases the volatile oils locked up in the peppers' cell walls. When the resulting mash has reached its optimum level of maturity, it is mixed to a secret recipe and bottled.

Garry says, 'People make all sorts of claims to justify their addiction to things hot and spicy. One thing is certain, however, a good healthy dose of chilli sauce heightens the awareness of any given moment by disrupting normal thought patterns and attention spans. Everyday cares and worries are forgotten as all the senses are focused on the site of application, and the body begins to release endorphins, the naturally produced painkillers. All of this and the potential to lift any culinary experience out of the mundane, and occasionally into the realms of the unforgettable. So do yourself a favour and live a little.'

Garry and his team love it up north, but they realise that not everyone has the good fortune to visit this subtropical paradise. They don't wish to let your bad luck impact negatively on your eating habits, so Kaitaia Fire is sold all over New Zealand and you can also buy it from their website at: www.kaitaiafire.com.

KINA
Kina, or sea-urchins, are a very scary seafood for just about everyone except Maori, who are glad no one else understands them. They wrench them off the rocks, break them open with a knife and slurp out the yellow-orange roe (the ovaries) before you can say 'What the ...!' Kina look like hedgehogs with spines sticking out in all directions. They are most creamy in the breeding season or when they are moulting. The best I ever ate was fetched for me by diver and adventure-tour guide Grant Davan at Herekino, Kaitaia (see Tourism, page 203). I had never liked kina before, finding it bitter and mineraly,

but the trick is to get it fresh and plump, straight from the sea. This stuff was utterly sweet, slightly briny and scallop-tasting. Like lobster and caviar, you can't eat too much kina, as it is very rich. There's no chewing involved – it melts in the mouth, leaving you longing for a glass of chardonnay and a roll in the hay – or if you're less ambitious, a slice of Vogel's bread thinly spread with wasabi butter.

Interestingly and inevitably, research is being done on kina aquaculture, because there is a gasping, appreciative market in Japan and we can't provide enough of the wild stuff, not enough of good quality, anyway. Kina grows all over New Zealand and is protected from over-fishing by our quota-management system. For you and me, the limit is 50 per person per day, which I think is a lot.

KIWIFRUIT
When I was a child this furry, brown fruit was called Chinese gooseberry. We never did anything flash with it – we just ate it either by pulling it open or slicing it in half and spooning the flesh out. It was also used in fruit salads and to decorate pavlova. It came here from China 100 years ago in the fingertips of a missionary, Miss Isabel Fraser, who had been visiting her sister in Yichang, China. She gave the seeds to a horticulturist and the rest is history. It is now one of the quintessential fruits of New Zealand along with passionfruit, feijoas, tamarillos and apples.

In 1959 Chinese gooseberries became kiwifruit for marketing reasons, establishing New Zealand as the world's principal supplier of kiwifruit. Te Puke is the place to be if you want to grow kiwifruit. The growers there produce 80 per cent of the national crop, exporting about $1 billion worth of fruit through Zespri International Ltd. In 1999 the government-owned company HortResearch developed a delicious yellow kiwifruit called Zespri Gold, which is really sweet and has been very successful. It's desperately good for you because it has ten times more vitamin C than a lemon, is high in antioxidants and fibre, and is full of potassium. Kiwifruit should be eaten fresh as it comes, as a juice or smoothie, and in a fruit salad.

KOURA
Koura are native New Zealand freshwater crayfish. They are a little hard to catch and meltingly delicious to eat with a wild, sweet flavour. Koura are hard to see because they are so well camouflaged – they are dark green and mottled like

the stones they live among on stream bottoms. Often their waving feelers and black beady eyes are all that can be seen, because they stay hidden during the day and move around mostly at night. Traditionally, only Maori have the right to harvest them from rivers, lakes and inland waterways, but if you have permission from the local iwi (tribe) you can catch them too. Of course if you want to breed them, you must also get permission from the Department of Conservation. Another reason they are hard to catch is because they perform a nifty reverse thrust when threatened, flicking the tail forward violently. Koura are environmentally important for our freshwater lakes. Because they are very slow-growing and many do not reach adulthood, there are never too many, so we must not over-fish them. They are a special treat to be enjoyed as such.

The first time I ate koura was with guide Emily Schuster, the famous and now deceased 'mother' of Rotorua. She steamed them in a flax basket in a thermal pool, where they went from green to dramatic dark orange. Then she showed me the correct way to eat them with your hands. First you say grace:

Manaakitia mai e te Ariki enei kai
Hei oranga mo o matou tinana
Whangaia o matou wairua
Ki te taro o te ora
Ko Ihu Karaiti hoki to matou Ariki
Amine

Bless for us this food, Lord
To sustain us in body and spirit
As does the bread of life
For Jesus Christ our Lord
Amen

'Get into it girl. Eat it like a Maori,' said Emily. 'Pull the back off, then using it as a pincer remove the yucky stuff from the abdomen. Suck out the contents of the head and body, then pull the tail out of its shell. Save the best bit for last.'

I think I ate it like a Maori; in any case my face was covered in sweet, melting koura bits.

SWEET KOURA ENTERPRISES IN ALEXANDRA

Francie and Peter Diver are pioneers in this industry, being New Zealand's first registered farmers of sweet koura. Peter came up with the idea and researched the resource consent, re-zoning of land and harvest permits. They do guided tours at their aqua-farm and Francie loves telling you about the koura's sex life. The females are very aggressive. They choose the strongest, biggest male, jump him, then dump him. The smaller, less interested males they force themselves upon. There is one huge male who hides in the dark as much as possible, but the girls inevitably find him, and sometimes Francie drags him out with as many as six females clinging to him!

Francie and Peter started farming them simply because they liked eating them. The business has grown hugely from its humble beginnings in the duck pond, and restaurants can't get enough of their koura. Demand exceeds supply by 20 times. Now they have 40 temperature-controlled ponds and water bores to ensure purity, but Francie still has to catch them. She used to do it with a net and waders. Sick of freezing to death in the ponds, she has invested in a pair

Lilian Gray of Lil's Kumara with her daughter, Tolaga Bay

of thermal gumboots and harvests them by attracting them into pots laced with bacon bait. If you want live koura for your very own dining table, they cost $60 a kilo plus courier to anywhere in New Zealand – just e-mail them at sweetkouraent@clear.net.nz.

KUMARA

The kumara is a sweet potato grown mainly in the north of the North Island. It was brought to New Zealand by Kupe from Hawaiki in about 1250. Maori legend has it that after the visit of Kupe, the Hawaiki priest Ruakapanga taught the cult of the kumara: the soil suitable for its cultivation, the lie of the land (whether it was lying to the sun or sheltered from the prevailing winds), the moisture content of the soil, soil temperature, the availability of moisture from the rains – all the conditions suitable to produce the sweet and delectable kumara. He sent out his scouts to check the best places to grow it in New Zealand and settled on the eastern parts of the North Island and Gisborne. When it was springtime, he sent his birds Harongarangi and Tuingarangihei with the kumara seeds to be planted in New Zealand.

The early variety was a bush with tubers much smaller than the kumara now grown. Further sweet-potato clones may have been introduced on voyages between the Polynesian homeland and New Zealand. In 1880 Colenso recorded 48 cultivars grown by Maori, with skin and flesh colours ranging from white through to red and dark purple, and with different root shapes. It seems probable the sweeter cultivar now used is the Rarotongan 'waina' introduced in 1850 by sailors from an American whaling ship. Kay Baxter at Koanga Gardens has nine varieties of pre-European kumara as well as gourds and kami kami. This vegetable was

K

stored in ground pits and covered with ponga fronds, grasses and rushes, where it was protected from rats and water.

Some of the best kumara grown in New Zealand is cultivated by a solo Ngati Porou mother with six kids in Tolaga Bay, Gisborne. Lillian Gray of Lil's Kumara is one of life's gems – big brown eyes, head-scarf tied like a pirate, work boots, tattoos and personality to knock your socks off. Lil is a woman who has seen hard times, and has given up the city life and moved with her kids back on to the family land and to her roots. She has got herself off the benefit and entirely supports her family with the kumara business, seeing herself as a role model for local Maori – you don't need to leave rural areas to make a living. She is one of 17 children. Her father grew kumara and she remembers giant feasts in her childhood with hangi in the back garden and people coming and going for days. Lil plants and harvests the traditional way, markets, distributes and accounts for her organic kumara herself with the help of her children and a few cuzzies. The sandy Gisborne soil produces thin-skinned kumara, making it edible without being peeled. The flesh is sweet and creamy and not at all stringy.

After picking the kumara, Lil stores them in boxes in a shed or in wardrobes to keep them cool. They last up to eight months wrapped in newspaper. She took me to her marae to show me the two birds Harongarangi and Tuingarangihei carved above the door to prove the story was true. Last year Graham Harris (of Maori-potato fame) took Lil to the Terre Madre Slow Food convention in Italy. Choice, thought Lil, I'll meet all sorts of cool people. I would love to have been there to see her charming the Italians with her stories and enthusiasm. Apparently she had to be stopped from lighting up a fag in the plane. Lil is always out in the garden fussing over her kumara and now only feeds her children healthy, organic food – junk is a thing of the past. She teaches her kids how to grow, cook and eat good food. A woman more filled with love, fun and integrity you would be hard-pressed to find.

My friend Raewyn wants to re-honour the kumara. She thinks they are completely undervalued and should have the same heady status as spuds. Her favourite way of doing them is baked in tinfoil in the oven for a long time until they are almost like cream. They are very versatile – you can boil them, roast them, fry them like chips, use them in desserts like sweet kumara pie and sweet kumara mousse with chocolate, and make kumara and chestnut soup and kumara ravioli. Here's a contemporary version of that Maori favourite, the 'boil-up'.

Boil-up

for the boil-up:
A BIG BUNCH OF PUHA OR WATERCRESS
2 LITRES VEAL OR CHICKEN STOCK
400G TRIMMED AND TIED PIECE OF PORK FILLET
8 SHALLOTS
8 SMALL GOLDEN KUMARA
2 CHICKEN BREASTS
4 COURGETTES CUT INTO 2CM PIECES
4 PUMPKIN DUMPLINGS MADE IN ADVANCE
(see recipe below)

1. Soak the puha in water and bash it a little to wring out the bitter white juices.
2. Bring the stock to a simmer and add the pork, shallots and kumara. Simmer for 15 minutes.
3. Add the chicken and simmer for another 5 minutes. Remove the pork and chicken to a plate.
4. Add the courgettes, puha and pre-made pumpkin dumplings. Place the plate of meat on top of the saucepan to keep warm and simmer stock for five minutes.
5. To serve, place a dumpling in the centre of a shallow soup bowl and arrange the vegetables around this. Slice the pork and chicken into four portions and place on top. Ladle lots of hot stock over everything. This would be good with Dijon mustard or onion jam on the side.

for the pumpkin dumplings:
2 CUPS COOKED PUMPKIN
SEA SALT AND FRESHLY GROUND BLACK PEPPER
4 EGG YOLKS
8 TABLESPOONS SIFTED FLOUR

1. Dry out the cooked pumpkin on a low heat, then mash finely. Season, then whip the egg yolks and flour into the mash.
2. Bring a pot of salted water to the simmer and using an ice-cream scoop or similar, shape four balls of the mixture and place in the simmering water. Poach for 5 minutes after they have floated to the surface. Drain and reserve until needed.

serves 4

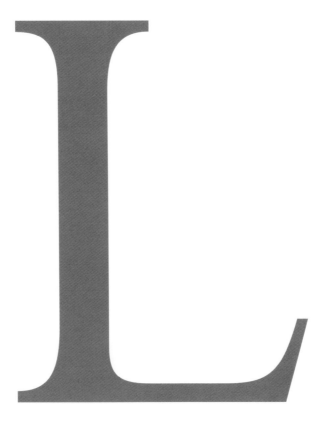

LAMB New Zealand is a country built on the sheep's back and there's not much about the raising of sheep that New Zealanders don't know. We have 45 million of them to be precise (and only four million humans). New Zealand has a temperate climate, ample rainfall in most areas and an abundance of land suitable for pastoral farming. Our sheep are raised on their natural diet of fresh pasture in wide-open spaces without the need to provide a grain diet with nutrient supplements. New Zealand farmers are extremely technically competent and know what is needed to consistently produce top-quality animals – the grass types, the farm-management techniques, the technology of genetics – and they use this knowledge to their best advantage.

There are no finer conditions in the world for raising sheep. New Zealand's farmers know this environment is special and precious and they make the most of nature's gift by applying sustainable agricultural practices. Such practices maintain and improve our natural resources of land, air and water. They involve the production of quality products without harming the environment or the community. These conditions enable New Zealand to be energy efficient. Extensive grassland systems for animal production favour sustainable agriculture because they are less wasteful of natural resources such as fossil fuels, which are used more widely in the production of grains and processed animal feeds. Grassland systems also convert solar energy to animal protein more efficiently than intensive systems. New Zealand sheep products are lean, nutrient-rich, and free of unwanted substances and harmful residues. We are also a world leader in farming without financial assistance from the government.

one hundred & twenty-three

The lamb we eat in New Zealand today is almost unrecognisable from the meat our grandparents and great-grandparents ate. They enjoyed strong-tasting hogget, mutton pies so laden with fat that it ran down their chins when they bit into them, and well-cooked roasts with acidic mint sauce and mutton broth. Now we faint at the sight of lamb fat and have the butcher cut off any that has not been bred out before we can be polluted by it. We eat sweet, mild-tasting, medium-rare racks of lamb, salads with barbecued lamb loin, and young legs of lamb with rosemary and anchovies sticking out of them. We order it 'pink in the middle, please'. I don't know one single person in New Zealand who has ever tasted mutton broth, although the excellent Cuisine Stocks make a delicious, fresh lamb stock.

Lamb is killed at around six months, hogget at one year plus and mutton at two years onwards. I miss terribly my mother's slow-roasted hogget and mutton roasts and slow-cooked Irish stews and don't understand why we have become a country of wussy eaters. Are we afraid of the real taste of a sheep? Hogget and mutton are as sweet and tender as lamb and not at all tough and smelly. Spring lamb, which has now become the norm, used to be a seasonal treat. Older lamb has to be hung for a few weeks, and therein lies the problem – producers can't be bothered. However, if one is a good detective, one can find hogget and mutton even in supermarkets. I predict that hogget will be the next big meat as chefs and cooks rediscover this lost flavour.

LEMONS

LAVENDER'S GREEN LEMON CORDIAL

Mary Biggs is a truly lovely, intelligent, witty woman who moved with her husband, Peter, and four kids from Wellington to the quiet life in Featherston in 1997. While Peter was in Wellington working, Mary looked around her 1886 rambling, colonial homestead with its 7.5 hecatres of trees and native bush and thought, mmm . . . what shall I do? The original plan was to grow organic lavender, but she started making lemon cordial to sell at school fairs and country markets. The rest is history. Her Lavender's Green Lemon Cordial is so good she now sells it all over New Zealand and in London in the distinctive cobalt blue bottles with the gorgeous yellow labels. She designed the labels herself in 20 minutes at the kitchen table using her children's

Stuffed Leg of Hogget

for the meat:

1 LEG OF HOGGET LAMB, TUNNEL-
BONED OUT, RETAINING THE SHANK
BONE — *ask the butcher to give
you the bones for the gravy*

1 TABLESPOON BUTTER

1 TABLESPOON OLIVE OIL

100G DICED BACON

1 MEDIUM ONION, DICED

100G DRIED APRICOTS, CHOPPED

100G HAZELNUTS, CHOPPED

1/4 TEASPOON FRESHLY GROUND
NUTMEG

3 TABLESPOONS CHOPPED
FRESH SAGE

3 TABLESPOONS CHOPPED FRESH
FLAT-LEAF PARSLEY

1 TABLESPOON LEMON RIND,
CHOPPED

1 CUP FRESH BREADCRUMBS

1 BEATEN EGG

OLIVE OIL

SEA SALT AND FRESHLY GROUND
BLACK PEPPER

for the gravy:

1 CHOPPED CARROT

1 CHOPPED SMALL ONION

1 CHOPPED STALK CELERY

1 BOUQUET GARNI

1 CUP DRY RED WINE

BONES CUT FROM THE LAMB

1/2 CUP WATER

1/2 CUP BEEF OR LAMB STOCK

1. Weigh the hogget to guage cooking time. Preheat the oven to 180°C.

2. Heat the butter and olive oil in a frying pan. Sauté the bacon and onion until golden.

3. Mix bacon and onion with all the other ingredients in a bowl.

4. Force the stuffing into the cavity of the meat and tie up with string. Rub oil all over and sprinkle with salt and pepper.

5. Place the gravy ingredients, except for the water and stock, in a roasting dish and put the stuffed hogget on top.

6. Roast in the oven for 40 minutes per 500g of meat.

7. Remove hogget from the oven, transfer to a platter and leave to rest for 10 minutes in a warm place.

8. Carve the hogget at the table and serve with the gravy.

1. To make the gravy, scrape up any crunchy bits sticking to the roasting tray.

2. Bring the gravy to the boil and add 1/2 cup of water and stock.

3. Taste for seasoning. Strain into a serving jug.

serves 8

felt tips and crayons, in between putting the kids in the bath and cooking dinner. That's the kinda gal Mary is – capable, practical and adept at multi-tasking. Most of the lemons are organic and they come from her garden and the neighbour's. The manufacturing process is labour-intensive, and batches are made in 20 litre bucket lots every three months or so. Lemon cordial is de rigeur on the porch in summer with sparkling water or in a gin and tonic. It is also great added to lemon tarts too. Flushed with success, Mary now also makes lemon curd, lemon mustard, preserved lemons, lemon-herb tea and biscotti.

When I visited Mary four years ago, she said she liked the words from a Jewel song which said that maybe if we are surrounded in beauty, some day we will become what we see. 'I have a desire to try to become a fuller person and I try to encourage that in my friends and family. I think it helps if we are surrounded by beautiful things and are taught to see beauty around us. I think lemon cordial is a beautiful thing and I want the world to drink it.'

LIMES

ST ANDREWS LIMES

Is there anything cleaner or more zingy and flavoursome than lime juice? The lime has one-and-a-half times more acid than a lemon, is seedless, and is green because it's picked green. If it were left on the tree it would eventually turn yellow. Everybody knows that limes are delicious in cocktails and that they are also great in salsas and cool us in sorbets. Ant and Alison Williams had lots of Tahitian lime trees, so they took the limes to the Hawke's Bay farmers' market and they disappeared instantly. They had a feeling that limes were going to become fashionable so they thought, 'Ah ha! We have to do the value-added thing.' Instead of doing the obvious, they did the exotic; they figured that if you can preserve lemons, why not limes? Their limes preserved in salt have that unmistakable musty, sour, tangy flavour – wonderful in meat stews, salads and couscous. Only a little bit is needed to add that *je ne sais quoi* to a dish. You can't replace preserved limes with fresh limes in a recipe – they are completely different in flavour. The great thing about this product is that once opened, it lasts in the fridge for years because of all the salt. Under the pretty green and white St Andrews labels you can also find date and lime chutney, lime and saffron curd, lime cordial,

lime and vanilla-bean syrup and lime marmalade, to name a few. A recipe from Ant and Alison appears opposite (top).

LODGES
Strangely enough, New Zealand is awash with fabulous luxury lodges and private hotels. It's something we do well, and overseas visitors adore staying in them because although the service, food and general standards are impeccable, what they like most is the low-key, relaxed, not-easily-impressed nature of their hosts. New Zealanders don't grovel, we're not sycophants and we behave as if people are welcome guests in our home, which of course they are. I've stayed in many American lodges and I always get the feeling they're doing me a favour and they don't actually want me in their house. There are usually rules about where you can walk and what time you have to be in and what you can touch – in spite of the excessive politeness and fixed smiles. In New Zealand we are really happy to have you in our home, and our humour and friendliness are genuine. There are far too many lodges to list here, so I have written about my favourites.

LUDBROOK HOUSE AT OHAEAWAI, BAY OF ISLANDS
Ask any food producer from the Bay of Islands what they think about Northland and they will say that the area is under-visited and the produce underrated. Chris Ludbrook agrees with this and she is passionate about promoting the area and its products. Northland is the birthplace of our nation, so it's a very special, spiritual place to both Maori and Pakeha. The first landfall of Kupe's waka Matahourua was on the shores of the Hokianga.

Chris and her husband, Sam, have a working sheep and cattle farm called Tupe Tupe, and on that farm there is a wonderful old 1920s homestead, and in that homestead you and I can bed down in the pressed linen, perchance to dream. The garden has fig and avocado trees filtering the panoramic views of the surrounding countryside.

Chris and Sam will cook evening meals, but their farm breakfast is the big event. Cuisine choices are seasonal and driven by guests' desires and regional specialities. When I visited Chris, I got her to make me up a typical breakfast of fresh orange juice, berries, cereals, cream, yoghurt, preserves and jellies, lemon curd, stewed fruit, Sam's scrambled farm eggs, home-made Tupe Tupe sausages with spicy plum sauce, toast, muffins and coffee.

And if that isn't enough, we can buy her great produce –

L

Greek roast leg of lamb with preserved limes

1 LEG OF LAMB
4 CLOVES GARLIC
FRESH ROSEMARY OR THYME
EXTRA VIRGIN OLIVE OIL
PRESERVED LIMES, WASHED AND SLICED

1. Preheat oven to 150°C. Insert cloves of garlic into the meat and pour a little olive oil over the top. Coat the top of the joint with herbs.

2. Cover top with sliced preserved limes and also lay meat on lime slices on baking paper.

3. Wrap lamb well in baking paper so it forms a closed parcel and tie with string all over to secure.

4. Roast for 3 hours so that the meat falls off the bone.

serves 6

Limoncello

This liquid sunshine is best made with Sicilian lemons – other lemons tend not to be tart enough. To consume limoncello, find a handsome Italian, sit down under a shady tree, pour 2 frozen shot glasses and tell each other the usual lies.

6 UNWAXED LEMONS
1 X 700ML BOTTLE OF FRUIT ALCOHOL OR VODKA
200G CASTOR SUGAR
350ML WATER

1. Sterilise a large preserving jar.

2. In a bowl, pour enough boiling water over the lemons to cover them and let them stand for 1 hour.

3. Remove the lemons and coarsely zest them. Place the zest in the preserving jar and add the alcohol.

4. Meanwhile, dissolve the sugar in the water and simmer for 5 minutes until you have a clear syrup. Leave to cool.

5. Add the syrup to the alcohol mixture, close the lid and sit the jar in a cool, dark place for a month. Shake the jar every day for the first week.

6. Strain the limoncello into bottles and keep in the freezer. It is drunk straight and cold in little glasses.

makes 1 litre

Mozzarella balls baked in lemon leaves

1 FRESH BUFFALO MOZZARELLA
WEIGHING 250G
40 LARGE, SOFT LEMON LEAVES
SEA SALT AND FRESHLY GROUND
BLACK PEPPER

1. Turn oven up to the highest it
   will go.

2. Cut mozzarella into about 20 little
   chunks. Sprinkle with salt and pepper.

3. Wrap each piece of mozzarella in
   lemon leaves, securing with 2
   toothpicks.

4. Place wrapped cheese on an
   oiled oven tray and bake for about
   4 minutes. Serve immediately.

makes about 20

and it really is great. The early Northland settlers brought
so many quince, fig and citrus trees with them they are now growing wild all over
the area, so Chris takes full advantage of them, making all sorts of fig conserves,
quince jellies and pastes, marmalades, lemon curd and jellies, preserved lemons,
and orange and lime jelly. She's full of ideas as to how you can use her produce too:
melt the quince jelly into mascarpone cream to serve with quince, apple or walnut
tart; add the capsicum and chilli jelly to meat glazes; add other jellies to salsas. I
think her fig conserve would be good on top of blue cheese and lapped up with a
few slices of crusty baguette. Chris also makes jams, panforte, Christmas cakes and
fruit vinegars. All this is made in a kitchen on
the property. The website is: www.ludbrook.co.nz.
On page 30 is a Moroccan-style breakfast-bread recipe to eat with Chris's preserves.

MOLLIES HOTEL

When my Sydney family stayed at Mollies in Auckland, they said they never
thought they would ever stay in such a place, and they're still talking about it. As
with most five-star boutique accommodation in New Zealand, the staff at Mollies
make you feel that nothing is ever too much trouble. Breakfast in the theatrical
dining room is a joy, with freshly cooked fare and seasonal fruit. At the end of the
day, aperitifs are served in the bar overlooking the terrace and the harbour bridge
beyond. All this is part of the price of a room. And what a room! My parents'
spacious, two-room suite had French doors leading out on to the courtyard garden,
a grand piano, sumptuous décor, chandeliers and a lavish bathroom.

Mollies is the love-child of talented couple Frances Wilson and Stephen
Fitzgerald. Their passion for opera, design and antiques is evident in every room.
Frances teaches opera and Stephen did the interior design and wall finishings.
When you open their website it plays 'Nessun Dorma' and you are swept into
their charming world. Most of the staff are opera singers, and you can hear them
singing around the house sometimes or actually giving a concert at dinner. There
is also a health and beauty spa. And if you want dinner, they might come up with
something like snapper baked in silk paper with oysters, vegetable julienne with
herbs and a sauvignon-blanc infusion, and chateau potatoes matched with a
Seresin Estate sauvignon blanc, followed by vanillabean and rosemary crème
brulée infused with berries, almond and pistachio crisp, washed down with a sip
of Cuvée Justine Vouray Methode Traditionelle.

The salons and lounges have faux marble walls and are full of fresh flowers,
hand-painted curtains, harps, gilded mirrors, art work and eclectic damask-covered
furniture. Obviously they don't have a complaints department at Mollies – it would
be churlish to breathe, let alone permit yourself to cast aspersions. Nothing ever
goes wrong and it is impossible not to be happy there – the whole atmosphere is
one of beauty, grace and calm, and it's really depressing having to leave. The
website is: www.mollies.co.nz.

TREE TOPS LODGE

The best thing about the luxurious and enchanting Tree Tops Lodge in Rotorua are
the housekeepers, Shirley and Raewyn. Two more sterling women you would be
hard-pressed to find. At a world-class, award-winning, star-studded lodge you would

expect to find flash-Harry, grovelling, slick staff – right? Well Shirley and Raewyn are real housekeepers – grey hair, down-to-earth, friendly, Mumsy types – and I bet international visitors love leaning on the bar in the breakfast room chatting to them about ham sandwiches and hot pools. This is where John and Alma Sax are very clever – Tree Tops is faultless and everyone who works there acts like they are at home, in the politest possible way. John himself is a very approachable and affable man and committed to the concept of his eco-lodge.

Tree Tops is the only five-star lodge and estate in New Zealand fully owned by a New Zealander. It sits in the middle of more than 1000 hectares of virgin forest, native bush, waterfalls, flora and fauna, with seven streams running nearby. One stream has been diverted so that it runs under and around the lodge, and guests can see the brown and rainbow trout swimming past. There are four crystalline

lakes, 175,000 trees have been planted to enhance the habitat, and hiking and horseback trails and mountain-biking tracks have been created.

No toxic materials were used in the construction. The timber, glass and stone lodge was built three years ago from trees that were felled on the land to create the wetlands. All water comes from natural springs on the property, and air-conditioning is natural air flowing from the streams through bi-fold doors – they generate their own power from a micro hydro unit. The style is classic hunting lodge with very high ceilings, huge spaces, conservative but stylish decor, tapestries, hidden lighting, leather couches, walk-in fireplaces, stuffed game, and antler chandeliers. The overhead beams in the main room are graced by carved Maori guardians called popo. The den is fabulous – book-lined, feral, with subtle lighting that goes on when you enter the room and worn leather chairs. There are 12

Sweet fried breads with toppings

for the dough:
- 1 TABLESPOON YEAST
- 1 TEASPOON SUGAR
- 6 TABLESPOONS WARM WATER
- 450G FLOUR
- 1/2 TEASPOON SALT
- PEANUT OIL
- 1/2 CUP COARSE CORNMEAL

for topping no. one:
- LUDBROOK HOUSE FIGS, QUARTERED
- LUDBROOK HOUSE PRESERVED LEMONS, FLESH REMOVED AND SLICED FINELY
- 200G ROASTED CHOPPED ALMONDS

for topping no. two:
- LUDBROOK HOUSE QUINCE PASTE, SLICED INTO PIECES
- LUDBROOK HOUSE CAPSICUM AND CHILLI-PEPPER JELLY
- 200ML LAVENDER HONEY

1. Start the yeast proving by combining the first three ingredients in a bowl. Allow to sit for 10 minutes.

2. Sift the flour and salt into a large bowl. Make a well in the centre, then pour in the yeast liquid. Mix well, then turn out on to the bench and knead together until a smooth, elastic dough is formed. This is a wet, soft dough.

3. Divide the dough into 12 balls and place on an oiled plate. Pour some oil into a bowl. Pour the cornmeal into another bowl.

4. To make the breads, oil a large, flat bowl or plate with your fingers. Grab one of the dough balls, cover it with oil and flatten out into a long, thin oblong shape. Keeping the fingers constantly covered in oil, sprinkle on a little cornmeal and fold the dough over lengthwise. Spread more oil on and sprinkle a little cornmeal over. Roll up like a croissant and place standing up on the oiled plate. Make the other breads and leave to rise for 30 minutes.

5. To cook them, heat about 1/4 cm oil in a frying pan, flatten the breads with your fingers and cook for about 2 minutes on each side until golden and crisp. They will puff up.

6. To serve, have the toppings ready to put on the breads as they come off the pan and are still hot. Arrange the figs, preserved lemons and almonds on some of the breads and drizzle over a little of the fig liqueur. Arrange the quince paste and small dollops of capsicum and chilli jelly on the others, then drizzle honey on top.

makes 12

luxurious villas and suites around the property.

The kitchen's nice too – large, homely and anyone can go in. Guests talk to the chefs, learn to cook, hang out in the kitchen and watch. There are no rules – you eat when you want, what you want and where you want. A lot of food can be caught or harvested on the property – trout, pheasants, ducks, rabbits, wild deer, water buffalos, sheep, piko piko (fiddle-head ferns), vegetables and fruit. The entire property is organic. When I was there, chef Brian prepared a really delicious pheasant dish. He removed the legs and slow-cooked them in duck fat for a few hours. He then removed the wings from the carcass, wrapped it in bacon and roasted it in the oven for half an hour, then cut the still pink, meltingly tender breasts out and served them sliced.

In 2004 Tree Tops was chosen as one of the world's best hideaways by *Andrew Harper's Hideaway Report*, and a week's stay was offered as one of the Oscar gifts presented to every winner at the 2004 Academy Awards.

John and Alma also own and live in fabulous Florence Court in Auckland, which takes guests as well. The website is: www.treetops.co.nz.

OPOU LODGE

Opou is like no other lodge in New Zealand simply because of its exotic hosts – Robyn Bickford and Manav Garewal. When they come out of the grand house to greet you accompanied by their two whippets Tara and Begum, all Indian dress and smiles (dazzling in Robyn's case), you know you're in for something different. They must get very sick of telling people their story, because I know everyone asks. Robyn is the daughter of a country wool buyer from Gisborne and she worked with the Diplomatic Corps for 27 years, part of it in India. An astrologer told her she would go to India and meet a man from a good family. As it happens she went to India in 1984 to re-establish New Zealand's diplomatic mission. Six months later, she was at one of the 3000 parties she has either been invited to or thrown in her life and there, across a crowded room on that enchanted evening she saw Manav – tall, dark and handsome wearing a turban and dark glasses. Their eyes locked and the rest is history. Manav was in real estate and importing, having had an extraordinary education in one of the best schools in India. These two are seriously dedicated to relaxation, margaritas under the jacaranda tree, and good eating and drinking.

Because they have entertained practically all their lives, running a luxury retreat is second nature to them. They seem to have been born hospitable. You only have to blink from the swimming pool and a G&T arrives, or go up the stairs too languidly and tea arrives in a silver pot along with tiny cheese biscuits. It's only when you've inhaled six of these biscuits in thirty seconds that you think Robyn must have put mind-altering drugs in them or something. If you feel you can't possibly make it from the huge bed across the vast expanse of polished floor to the bathroom without sugar, there is homemade fudge strategically placed half way. And the bed linen! All from Jaipur, all hand-blocked in beautiful, pastel Indian designs in many-threaded cotton. The beds all wear layers of razai or hand-stitched light quilts and all the curtains are hand-blocked, specially designed and made for the long windows. The two-storeyed kauri mansion was built in 1883, has a Historic Places Trust category-one rating and is regarded as a great district taonga or treasure. It features wide, wrap-around verandas and high, airy rooms, now full of Robyn and Manav's European and ornate Asian antique furniture, paintings, Persian rugs, paisley shawls, with vases and vases of roses everywhere.

There are no rules. You can do what you want, when you want, where you want, and that includes eating and drinking. If you want breakfast at 6 p.m., nothing would seem more charming to them; in fact, the more eccentric you are, the more they like you. If a bunch of rock stars turned up in purple velvet bell bottoms and set to meditating on the front lawn they wouldn't bat an eyelid. And boy can Robyn cook! Her speciality is Indian cuisine, which she does very well, but she will do anything you ask, teaches you in her kitchen should you so request and, like Ruth Pretty, her greatest fear is that someone will die of hunger on her shift. Manav brings drinks on silver trays, is very knowledgeable about the 800 wines in his cellar and likes to slip off for a game of golf. The extensive grounds are full of jacarandas, roses, flowering cherry trees, fig and avocado trees, an orchard, and an organic vegetable and herb garden. On one of my visits Robyn cooked a wonderful aromatic goat curry, with all the accompaniments that make Indian food so visually stunning. Breakfast at the kitchen table is a tour de force – home-stewed fruit, homemade muesli, heritage tomatoes, avocados, muffins, plum friands, kedgeree, mince on toast, home-smoked salmon, fresh fish, yoghurt, toast done to order and freshly squeezed orange juice. When guests go off on a jaunt, Robyn packs them little sarnies and a bottle of Antipodes water. Quite frankly, to be in Gisborne and not go to Opou would be churlish. The website is: www.opoucountryhouse.co.nz.

L

BAY OF MANY COVES RESORT

Imagine you're sailing around in your gin palace, the cook has jumped overboard because she's sick of the frying pan sliding to aft, and you're feeling seriously peckish. Imagine then, that through the haze of gin you hallucinate and think you see, shimmering in the distance, a café just like one on Ponsonby Road. You float closer and not only is there a café in the middle of the Marlborough Sounds (Queen Charlotte Sound to be precise) but also a very good restaurant, a swimming pool, fabulous accommodation, and you can refuel at the jetty. So you get lost at the Bay of Many Coves Resort for a few days and this is what happens. You stroll into the café, sit on the sun-drenched deck and have a Ponsonby Road standard flat white, a melting moment, home-baked bread, and lime and pepper squid with warm potato salad and aïoli, and pick up some supplies from the store.

Feeling like a wee nap you walk up the hill (while slaves wheel the luggage) and settle into one of the stylish, bach-like apartments that sort of disappear into the hillside. Everything about these baches, designed by Marshall Cook and decorated by Elizabeth Wilkinson, says discreet, harmony, in tune with nature and modern. The materials are cedar weatherboards, plywood and slatted wooden decks. The colours were chosen to fit in with the changing light and shade, so there are neutral tones of greys, steely blues, biscuit and café au lait. The kitchen is fully equipped, the telly looks like a laptop, and the best part is the bedroom which has large, bi-fold windows so you can wake up to fresh air and heartbreakingly beautiful views. Not only that but the windows go right to the floor. You know that frustrating feeling when you're lying on the bed and you can't see the view? The designer has thought of everything.

Refreshed, you now stroll to the upstairs restaurant, which is so popular you have to reserve for God's sake. There's a roaring fire, a library, a bar and, of course, a deck with that million-dollar view. My idea of heaven would be staying there on a stormy night. The American guests at the table next to me when I was there had shining eyes and happiness radiating out of them. We all dined on food that was local, seasonal, fresh and zingy-modern. Obviously the menu has a lot of fish and seafood, aged beef, roasted-tomato soup with prosciutto, oxtail with risotto and one of my favourites – thin apple tart. All this is accompanied by gorgeous Marlborough wines, after which you trip back down to your bach, perchance to dream.

Bay of Many Coves is owned by ex-pats Paul and Deborah Smith and managed charmingly by Lisa Barbebes, whose partner Mark Jensen is the esteemed chef. The website is: www.bayofmanycovesresort.co.nz.

EICHARDT'S PRIVATE HOTEL

Andrew Harper's Hideaway Report said that this was the best new small hotel in the world. This historic Italianate building in Queenstown, originally a posh hotel built by Albert Eichardt in 1873, had been the object of neglect and threatened demolition until it was saved by the present owners and restored to its glorious and glamorous heyday. It is now a place you would want to stay in just for the sake of being on the premises, never mind the attraction of the mountains, alpine air and the lake right in front of you. The interiors are luxurious and gracious with a mixture of restored features and exotic collectibles from around the world, such as 18th-century leather armchairs, old railway clocks, velvet-trimmed rugs and gilt rococo mirrors. The website is: www.eichardtshotel.co.nz.

CORSTORPHINE HOUSE

Corstorphine House is the original home of the Sidey family and has been on the Dunedin social scene since 1863. It has grade-one status with the New Zealand Historic Places trust and has been brilliantly refurbished as a private hotel by its owners. New Zealand's widely respected Qualmark has awarded its accommodation five stars, and it is a member of The Charming Hotels Association. The house is surrounded by a five-hectare estate, which is in transition towards the Demeter certification in organic agriculture. This inner-city sanctuary produces flowers, vegetables, herbs, fruits, nuts and eggs for the house and locals.

I stayed in the gorgeous Art Deco room with the fairy lights around the ceiling, but the room I was most enchanted by was the small Moroccan room. The decor is in rich orange, blue and burgundy, romantically draped and with a number of fabulous carpets on the floor and walls. The window faces west so the soft evening sun warms the room and makes it glow. The bathroom features an extraordinary spiral hand-basin pedestal, which is echoed in the hand-painted motifs on the wall.

The fine-dining restaurant is in the glass conservatory and serves delicious cuisine to house guests and casual diners. With top service, occasional live music and its unique setting, the restaurant has all the ingredients for a magical evening. Where possible, chefs use produce from the hotel gardens. The wine list features many local and private wines. The website is: www.corstophine.co.nz.

Emily Schuster, Rotorua

MAORI FOOD

We all grew up eating hangi food, on those earthy, smoky occasions where you drank too much beer and irrevocably ruined someone's backyard. In my twenties someone always had the great idea to dig a big hole in the backyard with their Maori friends, heat on a fire the special stones (volcanic rocks or riverbed boulders) that you always had to go to incredible lengths to find, and buy flax baskets or construct a large wire one. Then you would do something unheard of in Pakeha culture – throw food in whole to be cooked in the ground. Whole chooks, whole cabbages, whole unpeeled kumara, and huge joints of pork with all the fat still on. In those days white city chicks like me didn't even know what a whole pig looked like. Once in the ground, the food had to be covered with damp sacks, then all the earth put back on top. This was where the excessive beer drinking came in, because you had to wait for three hours for the food to be cooked. This was also when the guitars came out and you sang every bad song you had ever heard.

EMILY SCHUSTER

My next foray into Maori food was many years later when I was shooting an episode of 'Taste New Zealand' in Rotorua. Food writers who don't know what they're talking about say there is no Maori food culture left in New Zealand. They need to get out more. The tangata whenua in Rotorua have always cooked their particular food, still do and always will, I hope. My guide Emily Schuster (God rest her soul) put kumara, kamokamo (courgette), puha (sow thistle), kotaotao shoots (thistle), koura (crayfish), lamb, eel and rotten corn or kanga piro (ghastly, but the Maori love it) in flax baskets and steamed them in the hot pools at Whakarewarewa.

Emily was gracious and sparkling, and I found the creative purity of this style of cooking rather comforting. Emily had seven children, and when she died, 19 grandchildren and six great-grandchildren. Her ancestors arrived in the area on the Te Arawa waka and her hapu was Tuhourangi-Ngati Tarawhai. Her great-grandmother was Tuhipo Waitere, a guide at Tarawera, and her aunt was the much-loved Guide Rangi. When you meet Maori they always go into their genealogy with you – where their parents came from, what river, which mountain. Emily believed that if you don't know where you come from, you don't know who you are.

Maori food, like the interior decor of early houses, is influenced by the early Pakeha settlers. Maori love steam puddings, flat bread and sweet sauces, along with wild pork, shellfish and forest herbs. They also gather fresh-water clams or kakahi, eat huhu grubs, make rewena potato bread (sort of like damper) and great fried doughnuts or fried bread called paraoa parai. The whare (house) Emily's great-grandfather built in her garden in 1927 is a perfect example of this Pakeha-Maori mix. Alongside the native architecture, carvings, traditional stitched panels and flax mats are Victorian dressers with framed photos, lace-covered tables with antique china, overstuffed armchairs and lamps. Everything had been preserved exactly the way it was, with the addition of Emily's expert craft work – piupiu (flax skirts), whariki (floor mats), tukutuku (stitched panels), korowai (cloaks) and kete (kits). She grew her own flax in the backyard and was an expert weaver.

CHARLES ROYAL

There are many impressive Maori chefs in New Zealand. One of them is Charles Royal, a softly spoken, gentle man from Rotorua who has almost single-handedly modernised and rejuvenated Maori cooking. Charles says:

'Before the arrival of Pakeha, Maori had no metal or ceramic cooking vessels. Methods of cookery were severely limited and the only containers to hold liquid were hue (gourds), wooden bowls, or vessels made from stone. Maori understood the perfection of wet steam and smoke (hangi), and could roast and bake in the open fire and bake in hot ashes. They could grill on hot stones but had no means of frying, nor did they bake or pot roast in dry heat. Their diet was light on protein and did not include any grain-food products as a carbohydrate base.

'Maori were very highly skilled in the art of hunting, fishing and cultivation, and possessed great ingenuity in creating hakari (banquets) from limited cooking resources. With the introduction of foreign foods and cooking equipment, they were quick to adapt to the ever-changing needs of everyday living, taking into consideration the wisdom to cherish and retain many foods and culinary methods of the past. Yet within these limitations their cuisine was wide-ranging, nutritious and appetising. When the Pakeha introduced different foods and equipment, Maori were quick to grasp their advantage. During the colonial era they learned to use European foods and methods, and to adapt them to their own tastes, at the same time retaining many of the favourite early methods of indigenous foodstuffs and their health qualities.'

Interestingly enough they did cook in clay in a method called manu ukui or bird in clay. Traditionally the manu, complete with entrails and feathers, was wrapped in clay and buried in hot ashes for a few hours. Once the clay was hard it would be broken, the feathers would stick to it and the lucky diners would eat the bird, insides and all. People still commonly bake in clay all over the world, and it's quite simple to do. You just buy some made-up wet clay, roll it out with a rolling pin, take a small bird like a guinea hen or poussin (defeathered and emptied obviously), maybe stick a bit of butter and some herbs inside and wrap it up in baking paper. Wrap that up in the clay like a parcel and bake in a medium oven for an hour. When you break the clay you find a meltingly soft and succulent bird.

Pre-European Maori were fantastic and sophisticated market gardeners. With the growing organic food movement there has been a real and parallel renaissance for Maori growers. There are nine regional organisations of Maori organic growers – Tai Tokerau in the North, for example, has 400-plus members and there are more than 2000 members of the national organisation. They are mostly concerned with rejuvenating the cultural heritage and building up the stock of older varieties of potatoes and kumara. Projects include setting up a seed bank, making seaweed fertiliser and establishing a pikopiko plantation.

Charles has started up a native spice and herb business with herbs and ferns he harvests from the forest. It is called Kinaki Wild Herbs. He goes deep into the forest near Pureora Forest Park (I know where but if I tell you Charles will shoot me) for days on end picking fiddle-head fern shoots or pikopiko. The unfolding fern frond or koru is, of course, the great symbol often seen in Maori art. Charles has a research site in the forest with Crop and Food Research, where they are developing techniques to cultivate pikopiko in the wild. Pikopiko are the young, curling buds of the hen and chicken fern, usually collected in the spring and summer. There are actually 312 varieties of fern shoot, only seven are edible and Charles harvests just one of them so he knows what he's doing. He goes into the forest with a bag and gumboots and looks for damp, shady areas. When I went with him I couldn't see anything at first, but after half an hour you get good at it and spy them everywhere. They are pale green with dark speckles and are tightly curled – there's no point in picking them if they've started to unravel because they are no longer tender and they taste bitter. Charles would pick about ten kilos for a week's supply, which he brings home, washes, seals the spears or heads into plastic bags or boxes, and couriers out to hotels and chefs all over New Zealand. Pikopiko will last two weeks in the fridge. You can eat them raw but they are better lightly cooked – steamed, sautéed or char-grilled. Pikopiko taste like a delicious cross between asparagus and spinach and look beautiful on a plate.

The native herbs and spices are harvested on nearly 50 hectares of family land, where the vegetation is pristine and untouched – 'beyond organic' as Charles says. He picks citric-tasting miro and tawa berries, which ripen around the first frost, and also manuka leaves which were used as a black tea substitute by Captain Cook and early settlers. Manuka has a broad-spectrum antibiotic and anti-fungal oil in its leaves and is effective as a natural treatment for yeast infection. Horopito is similar: an indigenous pepper tree found in the mountains, it is small with little green and red speckled leaves. Not only is it super-hot, but it assists with skin and tissue repair. Like saffron, it needs heat to activate; so Charles mixes the dried leaves with boiling water and then uses the paste as a rub or marinade or even an infusion into other products. For example, The Grove avocado oil makes a horopito-infused oil, certain bakeries flavour bread with it, and tourists can even buy it in a packet at the airport. Charles says it is amazing in conjunction with kelp seasoning for smoking salmon.

One of my favourites is the subtle, aromatic kawakawa leaf. Charles finds this in the bush near water in shaded conditions. The leaf is shaped like a heart, is good for the heart and assists with blood cleansing. It infuses well with oil and cream dressings, can be used with pasta, meat and seafood, and gives piquancy to fruit dressings. The kawakawa also produces sweet berries. Pandoro Panetteria is developing a range of speciality breads using karengo (seaweed), flax seed and kawakawa.

TASTING MAORI FOOD

Charles has been working with a group of businesses to promote the Great Taste New Zealand concept. Companies such as Kinaki Wild Herbs, BeesOnline, Enza Food, Pacific Harvest and others work with caterers and chefs to showcase their signature products at major events here and overseas. Great Taste New Zealand is basically a distribution company run by a very dedicated man called John Millward.

Kawakawa roasted poussin

This recipe was inspired by my friend, chef Amanda Laird.

200G FRESH CHERRIES

6 POUSSINS (BABY CHICKENS)

EXTRA VIRGIN OLIVE OIL

KAWAKAWA RUB FROM KINAKI WILD HERBS

SEA SALT AND FRESHLY GROUND BLACK PEPPER

250ML ESSENTIAL CUISINE CHICKEN JUS

BALSAMIC VINEGAR

FRESH REDCURRANTS FOR GARNISH

1. Preheat oven to 180°C. Remove the pips from the cherries and stuff the cherries into the cavity of the poussins, then truss the chickens. Rub the outside of the chickens with a little oil and sprinkle with salt, pepper and kawakawa leaves.

2. Place chickens in a roasting tray and roast for 1 hour, turning half-way through.

3. Keep the chickens warm while you make the sauce. Put the roasting tray with its juices on a hot element, scrape up the crunchy bits stuck to the bottom and add the chicken jus. Reduce a little to thicken, then throw in a jot of balsamic vinegar.

4. To serve, garnish the chickens with fresh redcurrants. This would be good with watercress salad and steamed Maori potatoes. Serve the sauce in a jug.

serves 6

All Kinaki Wild Herbs can be bought at selected shops or you can order from the website: www.maorifood.com.

Charles and John Panoho of Navigator Tours have started up a new native-food tour concept called Taste Indigenous New Zealand, where visitors get to watch and assist with harvesting native herbs as well as cook with them and eat the food. There are one- to five-day trips in three different locations, each providing a local environment from which Charles draws inspiration and resources for indigenous recipes, both traditional and modern. Visitors will also experience the wairua (spirit) of the bush, wildlife and cultural values. Locations include a private native-forest estate adjacent to Tongariro National Park, a homestay in a mud-brick house at Church Bay on Waiheke Island, and a private beach-front estate at Pakiri Beach, one hour's drive North of Auckland.

OTHER MAORI FOOD AND CULTURAL
EXPERIENCES INCLUDE:
- Kaiuku Marae in Mahia, Hawke's Bay. They welcome visitors for dinner on the second Saturday of every month.
- Long Island Tours in Havelock North take tours of Maori culture and heritage.

What Charles and other people are doing to revitalise native produce is very admirable, but fraught with difficulties. In Australia 'bush tucker' was very popular but got into trouble because of lack of supply and quality. Also, by its very nature, the collection of herbs and berries is very expensive. But Charles is no moa – like the Aussies, he's not going to stand there to get his head chopped off. Both countries realise the future lies in domesticating these plants, which is why Charles is working closely with Crop and Food Research. My prediction is that we will soon be buying these native foods in the supermarket and they will eventually become a natural part of the way we cook fusion food in New Zealand.

THE BLACK FAMILY

I was fortunate enough to be welcomed into a traditional Maori home in the Ureweras (central North Island). Well-known singer Whirimako Black introduced me to her larger-than-life brother Rapaera Black and his lovely wife, Kathy, who have 5.5 hectares on the edge of the Ureweras. Here they live with their kids, and whoever else turns up, in the large house he built and swears he'll finish one day. Because Maori are so unbelievably hospitable they always have lots

of extra beds, and when someone turns up to visit they don't say, 'Oh shoot, now I have to cook more food.' They say, 'How long are you staying, bro?' Kathy cooks two huge loaves of rewena bread in cast-iron pots every day – one for the family and one for whoever else walks in. They love eating it covered in golden syrup. This is the house of people who live close to the land and revel in it, and who all speak Maori. There are a dozen saddles hanging on one wall, half a dozen sheathed hunting knives on the wall above the kitchen table, comfy chairs everywhere and a little bright pink table and chairs in the corner where their adored three-year-old takes tea and bread with her mother. Outside there is an incongruous mix of eels hanging in a tree drying out, trestled roses, trail bikes, a huge jacaranda tree, construction tools and a pretty herb garden. Beyond the fence are the horses.

Rapaera's parents Anituatua and Stewart Black were there. They lived the way Rapaera is now living, except with a horse and cart instead of bikes and trucks, and taught him how to hunt and fish and shoot and find all the good herbs and secret food on the land. As children Ra and his nine siblings went out for puha, whereke or wild strawberries, harore or bush mushrooms, and hunted venison and pigs and fished for trout. The beautiful Anituatua had prepared something special for lunch – miiti tahu or preserved meat. She boils beef for a long time, then dries it, fries it and places it in a pot to be covered in a mixture of beef dripping and butter. It will keep like this for a long time and was utterly delicious to eat. Kathy had prepared corn on the cob, boiled pikopiko and fermented kouka or cabbage-tree heart. Later Rapaera showed me how he finds a female cabbage tree and cuts the top bit off where the heart is. You strip off the leaves and there it is – creamy white and similar to a palm heart. The tree doesn't die; it regenerates. Maori love overcooking and fermenting everything but I like the kouka either raw and sliced into a salad or grilled whole on a barbecue until just cooked.

Speaking of fermenting, Kathy gave me some raw fermented crayfish to try. This is a huge delicacy to her and I could tell she was preparing me for the gastronomic thrill of a lifetime. It was possibly the worst thing I have ever put in my mouth – and that includes the huhu grub on the West Coast and the grilled mouse in Vietnam.

Rapaera and his boys showed me where to find maraerea or large whitebait as they swim inland to fatten up for breeding. He normally dries it on the rocks or cooks it on top of Maori potatoes. If you've ever wondered how to catch tuna or eel, then they are the specialists in these parts and

M

are happy to share the experience with you. You can dive for them, catch them in net traps or catch them by hand where they hide in holes on the riverbanks. When Rapaera gets the eels home he sticks them, guts them and hangs them in a tree on hooks to dry. Then he opens them out, giving the head to Kathy who loves them, keeping the bones to cook along with the flesh. He curries them, pickles them and smokes them, and I can tell you that Rapaera and Kathy's oven-roasted eel is the best I've ever eaten – fat, juicy and flavoursome. At dinner Whirimako sang a song she had composed with her mother called 'E te Kai' about acknowledging the source of traditional foods. Whirimako, who lives in Auckland, says her body physically craves this food. Kathy roasted a huge joint of wild pork, preserved meat boiled with potatoes, eel, kamokamo or marrow from the backyard, cabbage-tree heart, bush mushrooms, fermented pikopiko and bread. Rapaera, who considers himself the boss of all he surveys, told me that when they go into the bush for a few days, the women demand that he goes out and buys wine for them.

The Black family are a tough act to follow and they know the meaning of the word love. Rapaera and Kathy take in 'bad boys', give them lots of love and attention, teach them all the skills they know – how to work hard, play hard, earn money and live off the land. At last count 400 have gone through their door. It is extremely important to them to pass the traditions on – the love of the land, the kai and respect for the culture – therein lies happiness and spiritual fulfilment.

WENDY BENNETT

Another good Maori cook is Wendy Bennett in Auckland who does upmarket catering and film-location work using indigenous produce in modern ways. For example, she says the muttonbird she is getting now seems to be salted a lot less than previously and therefore doesn't take as long to cook or need changes of water. She also makes muttonbird and moa (using ostrich) paté with anchovies; pork with miro berries on a rocket and puha salad; mussel and tuatua fritters with avocado oil aïoli; shrimp and kina on rewena bread crostini; and smoked pipi with watercress cream. How good does that sound?

PUHA

Puha is a sow thistle still gathered by Maori in country areas.

Oven Hangi

To prepare an oven hangi, you will need some muslin, string and tinfoil.

800G PORK SHOULDER OR FILLET
CUT INTO LARGE CHUNKS
250G BABY BEETROOT
250G BABY TURNIPS
250G BABY CARROTS
2 BUNCHES WATERCRESS
AVOCADO OIL AND LEMON JUICE
SEA SALT AND FRESHLY
GROUND BLACK PEPPER

to smoke the hangi:
1/2 CUP BROWN SUGAR
1 CUP RICE
1 CUP TOPSOIL

1. Preheat the oven to 200°C. Wrap the pork in muslin in two bundles and secure with string. Scrub the vegetables and wrap in muslin in two bundles.

2. To prepare the hangi for smoking, place a sheet of tinfoil in a baking tray. Mix together the sugar, rice and topsoil and sprinkle over the foil. Place on a hot element until it starts smoking. Place the bundles of meat and vegetables on top and cover tightly with tinfoil so no smoke escapes.

3. Place the tray in the oven and cook for 30 minutes.

4. Meanwhile wash the watercress. Make a dressing with 2 parts oil to 1 part lemon juice. Add salt and pepper to taste and toss through the watercress.

5. To serve, remove the food from the bundles and place on a large platter. Serve the salad on the side.

serves 4

Note: Smoking ingredients are not eaten.

M

It's really delicious if you know how to cook the famous pork and puha dish. First you catch your wild black pig, you singe the hairs off over a fire on the beach, then you cut it up and boil it with puha. The bitterness of this plant is dealt to by soaking it in water and wringing out the milky sap within – you have to sort of beat the puha. When I was a nursing student at Greenlane Hospital in the late sixties, down-country relatives of the Maori TB patients would bring in pots of this every Sunday and everyone would sit around on the floor of the ward feasting and telling stories. In those days visitors would sometimes ride their bicycles right into the ward. I doubt that would happen now.

MUTTONBIRDS OR TIITI
Technically, these fatty seabirds are sooty shearwaters or petrel, considered a great delicacy by Maori. They come and go from Siberia, hence the fat stores. Muttonbirds were an important food source for the southern Maori and one of their principal trading items. In the deed of sale of Stewart Island, the Maori and half-castes Ruapuke and Southern Mainland and their descendants were nominated as sole owners of muttonbird rights. Under 1978 regulations, 'birders' are restricted to Rakiura Maori, their spouses, widows or widowers. Only these descendants are allowed to take muttonbirds in the season from early April to the end of May, during migration. The modern Maori in the southern region are Ngai Tahu with earlier lineages of Kati Mamoe and Waitaha. The birds sought are the chicks, which nest in burrows on headlands and islands around Stewart Island.

Francie Diver of Sweet Koura Enterprises is of Ngai Tahu descent. She told me how birding happens. It's a cold and wet job and you'd really have to enjoy it. The birds mostly come out at night and in bad weather, and there ain't no glamorous facilities. The chicks are taken out of the nests and killed by quickly and firmly crushing the head between the hard part in the palm of your hands. In the old days people crushed the head with their teeth. The birding families then march off to the plucking shed, where the feathers are pulled out. I imagine a lot of storytelling and tea drinking goes on. The fluffy down that remains is waxed off, then the birds are trimmed, split, gutted and packed in salt or frozen fresh. They were traditionally preserved for sale in kelp and totara bags and this is still sometimes done for old time's sake. The cooked muttonbird is stuffed into the bag, and the rendered-down fat from the bird's stomach is then poured into the bag, sealing it and preserving it.

Muttonbirds are very greasy, which may account for the European pioneers giving them their name. My friends Wikki Oman and Wendy Bennett, very good Maori cooks, say muttonbirds are not as heavily salted as they used to be, so you just boil them for 45 minutes then put them under the grill to crisp the skin. Until recently, you first had to soak them in several changes of fresh water, then boil them for a long time, stinking the house out. If you can get hold of a fresh one, roast it stuffed with herbs and potato. Maori eat them with their fingers. They taste fishy, ducky and muttony, which sounds ghastly, but if cooked properly they are quite delicious, though an acquired taste.

To show you how desperate folk are to get their hands on muttonbirds, consider this hilarious recent subtext to the story: excluding gay and de-facto partners from the annual muttonbird harvest could breach human rights law. The Ministry of Justice, whose 'legal recognition project' team spotted the potential discriminatory criteria during a trawl through 1978 regulations governing the hunt, noted that the harvest regulations 'unjustifiably discriminate against certain persons on the basis of their marital status and possibly their sexual orientation'. They could be in breach of the Human Rights Act and the Bill of Rights Act. I'm sorry, but I have all these visions of the gay brothers and sisters turning the annual hunt into a fabulous festival with a ball, feather head-dress competitions and a marching band. A lot worse could happen.

MARIJUANA
In New Zealand we grow marijuana for medical reasons, personal enhancement, clothing and oil. Hemp-seed oil (hemp is a cousin to marijuana) is produced in Canterbury by Bruce Hill of Oil Seed Extractions. The crop, which looks alarmingly like the personal enhancement one, is grown by a farmer in Methven, an area known for its favourable soil and climate. Hemp oil is high in essential fatty acids, Omega 3 and 6, and contains gamma linolenic acid (an anti-inflammatory). If none of this means anything to you, go for the taste – it's delicious. Hemp-seed oil is cold-pressed, kept in tinted bottles and eaten fresh, not cooked. Oil Seed Extractions also produce flaxseed oil, borage-seed oil and cosmetic-seed oils. Their website is: www.osel.co.nz.

MEAT
Eating meat is not particularly necessary for either good health or survival, but humans have been eating it for centuries. So is it morally

correct and civilised to eat meat? Read *My Year of Meat* by Ruth L. Ozeki and you may never eat meat again. Read *Meat* by Hugh Fearnley-Whittingstall and you will understand why you eat meat anyway. Badly produced meat is the result of avarice, carelessness and disinterest. Well-produced meat is the result of responsibility, respect and enjoyment. There is a moral issue, but I think it revolves around the raising, treatment and killing of animals rather than whether it is right or wrong to eat meat. Animals kill other animals for food – very few die of depression or old age. We kill farmed animals for food, and it is the way we look after them while they are alive that is very important. If I were a pig, I would rather be killed by a quick bullet in the head than the fangs of a fox in my neck after a terrifying chase.

The best way you or I can exert our power to change cruel animal-rearing processes is not to buy this meat. If we continue buying it, we are condoning the stressful, uncomfortable and in some instances, painful lives of the animals whose flesh we put in our mouths. One way to eat good meat is to buy organic; another way is to shop from good butchers and specialised gourmet suppliers. Their meat is the result of good-farming practices and extensive rearing for which they don't need antibiotics, growth hormones, steroids and additive-laced feeds. If it costs more to buy and that's a problem, then buy less. Buying cheap, bad meat is a false economy. Okay, so it might be a drag to go out of your way, but you can turn it into an exciting adventure, your mouth drooling at the thought of a big, juicy, free-range chook that actually tastes like a chicken (if you know what that's like). Properly grown pork, beef, lamb and poultry tastes better than conventional meat. Friends at my dinner parties often gasp over the tastiness and texture of the meat I cook – it is not my ability as a cook but the quality of the meat.

Once the animal has been reared properly and killed quickly, the carcass must be hung in a cool place for at least a week – not put in a vacu-pack, which is the worst thing you can do (the meat sits in its own blood, which makes it soggy). This relaxes and tenderises the meat. It doesn't matter if you eat frozen meat, so long as it has been aged properly before it went into the freezer. When you get meat home from the butcher, don't cover it with plastic wrap. Meat needs to breathe so place it on a plate covered with a tea-towel.

And what about the controversial meats?

FOIE GRAS
This is the supreme fruit of gastronomy according to *Larousse Gastronomique*. Periodically I receive hate mail and horror photos of tortured geese and ducks from hysterical but well-meaning people trying to ban the production of *foie gras* (fattened goose or duck liver), a delicacy I am very fond of. You cannot buy fresh *foie gras* in New Zealand because it is illegal to force-feed, which is how the liver grows so big and tender. Ducks and geese naturally store lots of fat in their livers to provide fuel for long migration flights. When they don't go anywhere except to waddle up and down the farmyard, the livers grow fat. To help things along, they are force-fed in the last six weeks of their lives so that the livers grow to almost half a kilo. It is not true that the livers have cirrhosis or are diseased. *Foie gras* is 80 per cent fat and tastes like nothing else on this earth – buttery, sweet and vaguely livery. Once again, you have to know who the supplier is and how to read the label. The best *foie gras* comes from farms where the birds are free-range and are gently force-fed maize by the farmer with a funnel. They are not obviously distressed but run toward their feed. The worst *foie gras* comes from vile factories where the creatures live in cages, are extremely distressed and scream every time the feed comes. This you do not want to eat. Know where it comes from before you put it in your mouth.

VEAL
Again – utterly delicious. Veal is the name for young cows and calves and the meat is prized for its whiteness, tenderness and sweetness. The animals are killed at five or six months old. The good veal is free range. The calves are with their mothers so are still drinking milk plus starting on grass and cereal. These animals used to be called bobby veal and are now being sold as rosé veal because the meat is not as pale as that from the crate-confined calves that consume nothing but powdered milk.

Veal is delicious and delicately flavoured. The reality of the matter is that if all the dairy calves born were not allowed to live to become veal, the majority would be slaughtered at birth anyway. The veal you mustn't eat (which you can't buy in New Zealand anyway) is the crate-reared variety. This is an extremely cruel method of upbringing where the calf can't even turn around in its stall, never sees daylight and is fed only powdered milk. In her famous documentary on animal welfare, Brigitte Bardot let veal calves out of their stalls and they just fell over – they didn't have the strength or even know how to walk. The best New Zealand veal I have come across is produced with love and care by Organicland in Mosgiel, Otago.

M

MEN AND HOW TO FEED THEM

The expression 'the way to a man's heart is through his stomach' comes from an era when men were seen as financially interesting but culinary incompetents and women as lurking in dark corners waiting to snare a supporter and keep him dependent with cream cakes and Tui beer. Women's magazines were rampant with man-catching recipes, something that seems barely believable now. If I told my gorgeous teenage nieces they would keep their boyfriends by cooking them delicious meals, they would fall over laughing at the quaintness of it.

In her 1940 cookbook *Tui's Third Commonsense Cookery*, the wonderful Mrs Flower tells us about the meals most men prefer. They are soups (thick ones – nothing poofy like watercress consommé), a bit of fish but not much, steak and kidney pie, Irish stew (made properly, please), roast meat, mixed grill, tripe and oysters (oh boy!), rabbit and bacon, brawn, sardines on toast, apple pie and steamed puddings. It was permitted to occasionally give your man a treat if you felt he deserved it. If you were Scottish that probably meant sex; if you were English and didn't know what sex was, it probably meant Toad in the Hole with extra gravy.

Of course, men often don't get fed these days or – they feed themselves. In most modern households, the person who likes cooking, cooks. Only very unenlightened men in New Zealand can't cook, and this failing is not thought to be smart or cute. Like swimming, cooking is considered a lifesaving skill where just floating and shouting 'Help!' won't cut the mustard. New Zealand women are quite bolshy, and if the mothers haven't taught their sons to do obvious things like cook and clean, the wives will. Meals that make men happy now are simple and fresh: roast lamb rack with rosemary-sautéed potatoes and steamed bok choy; bruschetta with acid-free tomatoes on top; whole baked snapper with wasabi sauce, green salad with vinaigrette and a glass of pinot noir; a selection of New Zealand-produced prosciutto, mozzarella, tapenade, artichokes, stuffed baby peppers and pasta salad from the deli with a glass of chardonnay; New Zealand cheese with quince paste and sourdough; Kapiti cardamom and orange ice-cream with homemade preserves. There is no special treat because even though there is still no sex in New Zealand, we have our suspicions. Besides, the food is so good, the idea of special treats has become redundant. And yes, the population growth is decreasing.

Panna cotta with vincotto

Vincotto is an Italian product. It is the cooked and reduced must (the pressed juice of grapes ready for fermentation) of late-harvested negro amaro and malvasia grapes. Once the liquid has turned to syrup, it is put in oak casks with a must to mature.

1 LITRE CREAM

150G CASTOR SUGAR

VANILLA POD

3 LEAVES POWDERED GELATINE OR 2 SACHETS

1/4 CUP MILK

2 TABLESPOONS COINTREAU

SUMMER BERRIES, OR IN WINTER, DRIED FRUIT COMPOTE

VINCOTTO

1. Place the cream and sugar into a saucepan. Slit open one side of the vanilla pod and scrape the grains into the cream. Bring to the boil, then remove from the heat.

2. Soak the gelatine leaves in the cold milk for 15 minutes then heat the milk, stirring all the time to mix in the gelatine. If using powdered gelatine, pour it into hot milk and stir with a fork until incorporated.

3. Pour the gelatine mixture into the hot cream through a sieve and stir in. Stir in the Cointreau.

4. Ladle into 8 little ramekins or a bowl, making sure you stir up the grains of vanilla as you go. Allow to set in the refrigerator for 1–2 hours.

5. To serve, dip the bases of the ramekins into hot water, then invert on to dessert plates garnished with berries or fruit. The cream should not be rubbery but just gently set so that it will melt down your throat. Drizzle on some vincotto.

serves 8

MILK

New Zealand is a huge dairy-producing country. When I was a child, government-subsidised milk was delivered to your gate every morning in glass bottles. It was full-fat milk with an inch of cream on the top, which you fought your father for so you could pour it on your porridge. The cream tasted heavenly, and the milk tasted sort of thick and almost herbaceous. These days the sky's the limit when it comes to milk. You can get milk that's good for cappuccinos, milk that's good for menopausal women, milk that's good for diet neurotics and food cripples, and milk that's good for your heart. Anchor Xtra milk is 99.8 per cent fat-free with extra protein and calcium to strengthen muscles and bones. Mega Milk is 97 per cent fat-free and supercharged with calcium, with vitamins A and D added to help absorb it. Heart Wise milk is 99 per cent fat-free, low in cholesterol, high in calcium and has Omega 3 added. Apparently they all still taste like milk! The latest is A2 milk, in which the content of a natural variant of a protein, beta casein A2, has been increased. This is done by selectively milking only those cows that naturally produce milk containing A2. In this way it is believed that the health benefits of drinking milk may be increased. This milk is regarded as a premium, value-added product.

Because New Zealand produces so much milk we also produce lots of silky yoghurt, my preference being Greek-style. It is thicker and creamier because of its higher fat content. The yoghurt is strained of whey until it loses so much liquid it becomes concentrated. The unique texture prevents it from separating or curdling at high temperatures, making it ideal for use in cakes, curries and other hot dishes. My favourite is Mahoe Farmhouse. I take a spoonful of it and I am almost back on the hilltop of Santorini, gorging on yoghurt and sweet Greek honey and sipping retsina. Mahoe also make really good hard cheeses, like very old Edam, Gouda and Leidse with milk from their own organic Friesian cows. These caramely cheeses have won so many awards you would almost have to build a new house specifically to put them all in.

MUSHROOMS

Regular cultivated button, brown and portobello mushrooms bore me, but I adore freshly picked field mushrooms straight after the rain – sweet, tasty and juicy. The ones I really like are the exotic ones sometimes cultivated and sometimes hunted.

Mushrooms are surrounded by mystery, myth and magic. In my twenties I certainly found out about the magic kind – we used to pick them near the Ardmore airport in Auckland and make omelettes, which kept us entertained for days. Gods, devils, fairies, witches and sorcerers have all used mushrooms to great effect. I also think mushrooms have been considered subversive because they appear suddenly, they like dank depressing habitats and they love decay. Consider the expression 'He takes me for a mushroom,' meaning 'I'm being kept in the dark and fed bullshit'. And did you know that a mushroom-lover is called a mycophagist? Mushrooms are among the most sexually active organisms in the world, containing millions of reproductive spores. All this aside, a good mushroom is a hard act to beat in terms of taste but is not particularly nutritious, since it is about 90 per cent water. Dieters love them.

A Chinese trader called Chew Chong accidentally came across the gelatinous, greyish brown fungus known as 'wood ear' in Taranaki in 1868 and, recognising it from his homeland, started the first mushroom business in New Zealand. Wood ear was traditionally used as both food and medicine in the Chinese community and Maori also ate it occasionally, calling it hakeka. It used to be called 'Taranaki wool' because of the good livelihood it provided – huge amounts were exported to China. The main specialty mushroom grown in New Zealand now is the flavour-bomb shiitake, which is best between April and December. Shiitake caps have a soft, spongy texture and distinctive earthy, fresh flavour.

We also grow the delicate oyster or phoenix-tail mushroom in New Zealand, which look like soft, grey fans and are wonderful eaten raw because of their delicate texture and subtle seafood flavour. You can cook them in soups, stir-fries and with pasta. The honeycomb fungus looks like it should be in your shower, ready to scrub you down. It resembles a cream-coloured, frilly sea sponge, has a gelatinous texture and tastes subtly of honey. Honeycomb fungi can be used in sweet as well as savoury dishes, and they take on flavours from other ingredients and add texture to a dish, almost like a thickener. The very pretty golden needle or enokitake mushrooms are so beautiful you can hardly bring yourself to eat them. They are little with long, cream-coloured stalks and tiny umbrella caps with a delicate yet distinctly mushroomy flavour. You can eat them raw, and I would generally cook them whole so you can see the lovely shape, rather than chop them up.

Ravioli of exotic mushrooms with white asparagus

for the vinaigrette:
JUICE OF ¹/₂ A LEMON
¹/₂ TEASPOON SEA SALT
4 GOOD TURNS OF THE PEPPER MILL
1 ¹/₂ CUPS EXTRA VIRGIN OLIVE OIL
PINCH OF SAFFRON
1 TABLESPOON FRESHLY CHOPPED
CHERVIL

for the ravioli:
2 TABLESPOONS OLIVE OIL
2 LARGE SHALLOTS, FINELY CHOPPED
¹/₂ CUP FRESH BREADCRUMBS
250G CHOPPED MIXTURE OF EXOTIC
MUSHROOMS LIKE SHIITAKE,
HONEYCOMB, ENOKE, WOOD EAR
AND PHOENIX TAIL
2 LARGE CLOVES GARLIC,
FINELY CHOPPED
A GOOD SQUEEZE OF LEMON JUICE
SEA SALT AND FRESHLY GROUND
BLACK PEPPER
1 TABLESPOON CHOPPED CHIVES
1 EGG YOLK
1 PACKET EGG NOODLE RAVIOLI
ROUNDS *(from Asian food stores)*
1 EGG, BEATEN

for the asparagus:
500G FRESH WHITE ASPARAGUS

to serve:
ENOKE MUSHROOMS
CHIVES

1. To make the vinagrette, place the first 3 ingredients in a porcelain bowl, then gradually whisk in the oil. Stir in the saffron and chervil. Allow to steep for a couple of hours to develop the flavour of the saffron.

1. Heat the olive oil in a large pan. Sauté the shallots and breadcrumbs until golden and crispy, then add the mushrooms and garlic and sauté for another 2–3 minutes. Squeeze in a little lemon juice and season with salt and pepper to taste. Allow to cool, then stir in the chives and egg yolk.

2. Lay out lots of ravioli rounds and brush beaten egg around the edges. Place a heaped teaspoon of mushroom mixture in the middle of one round and top with another round, squeezing the edges together with your fingers. Keep doing this until you have used up all the mixture.

3. To cook the ravioli, bring a large saucepan of salted water to the boil, put the ravioli in 6 at a time and cook for 3 minutes. Scoop out with a slotted spoon and keep warm. Sprinkle a bit of oil over them to prevent sticking.

1. To cook the asparagus, snap the ends off ,then peel the lower two-thirds. Boil in salted water until al dente, then drain and keep warm.

1. To put the dish together, place some ravioli in the centre of the plate, top with several asparagus and garnish with some enoke mushrooms. Drizzle the vinaigrette all around and decorate with chives.

serves 6

M

FORAGING FOR MUSHROOMS

There are plenty of old mushroom hunters and plenty of bold mushroom hunters but there are no old, bold mushroom hunters, or so the saying goes. There are two types of mushrooms – those that kill and those that don't – and there is absolutely no way of telling the difference; you just have to know. In the interests of remaining conscious during research, I only tried the second kind. Everybody's terrified of eating mushrooms they find in the forest, but in reality, there are only about a dozen fungi in New Zealand that are definitely poisonous. But even though most are edible, you wouldn't want to eat them – they are too boring and tasteless.

Early Maori ate dozens of wild mushrooms they foraged from the ground, growing on dead and live trees, in scrub and among ferns. They knew which ones had to be cooked to be edible. Some of them were huge and some almost microscopic. Settlers introduced other species of mushrooms, so it is now impossible to figure out which ones are native and which introduced. Below are some of the more common and most tasty mushrooms you can hunt for all over New Zealand in autumn. Remember never to tell anyone your spot for mushrooming or they'll be having cèpe omelettes for breakfast while you weep into your baked beans. However, it is mandatory to invite them over to share your omelette once you have covered your tracks.

BOLETES

This is the crème de la crème for foragers in autumn and worth a lot of money if you collect enough and sell them to restaurants. In France they're called cèpe and in Italy porcini, and in any language they're meaty and rich and earthy. I know someone in Christchurch who makes quite a living from collecting them, and believe me, if you want them in your risotto you had better have your plastic ready. Boletes have a slimy, yellow-brown, spongy cap about 5–10cm across and a thick stem. They grow under larch, birch and pine trees. The French simply slice the cap and stalk thickly, and fry them with parsley and garlic. They can be dried and reconstituted very successfully. If you can't find any in your forest, you can buy them frozen from Sabato at what I think is a reasonable price.

FIELD MUSHROOMS

These delicious creatures are found in pastures and under pines in summer and autumn. They have a fawnish-white cap 2.5–7.5cm across with pink gills and are distinguished by their sweet, hay-like smell. I like them gently fried with a little fresh nutmeg and cream and eaten on toast. Mum used to put field mushrooms straight on the hot element then eat them with her fingers.

MOREL

This is another of the highly prized, crème de la crème mushrooms. They are found in clearings and along the edges of streams in spring and summer. They are very distinctive-looking and have a creamy, light brown, conical head with concave indentations all over it. They can grow to 18cm, have a pale stem and are hollow. In my restaurant in Paris I used to sauté them with veal pieces, shallots, butter and nutmeg, then stir in cream and pile that up on tagliatelle. I have happy memories of the sacs of dried morels being delivered to the kitchen once a month. Their refined, intense flavour is inimitable.

POPLAR

Also known as tawaka, this is a stunning New Zealand beauty isolated from poplar and plane trees. It has an unusually large veil that hangs down like a skirt.

TRUFFLE

Believe it or not you can actually find native truffles or parekoko under manuka shrubs if you are very lucky. They are hard to find as they are black and grow underground, so they usually have to be sniffed out by a pig or dog. A truffle smells and tastes like nothing in the world – musky, pungent and earthy – and you need only a few fine slices for it to perfume your potatoes, eggs or pasta. (For more information on cultivated truffles see Truffles, page 205.)

WOOD EAR

This mushroom looks like a shiny, brown, velvety ear and grows on tree-trunks in the forest. You can collect them all year round, but you have to know how to cook them as they are rather tough. The Chinese appreciate them mainly for their texture, colour and shape rather than their taste. Food writer Jenny Yee says to slice them thinly and cook lightly in stews, soups and stir-fries.

MUSSELS
Greenshell or green-lip mussels (*Perna canaliculus*) are unique to New Zealand and grow in its coastal waters. These large mussels with delicious cream or orange flesh and

Mussel & Fennel salad

2KG MUSSELS, CLEANED

1/2 CUP RIESLING

1 SMALL ONION, FINELY SLICED

1 FENNEL BULB, CORED AND FINELY SLICED

2 LEBANESE CUCUMBERS, WASHED AND CUT
INTO LITTLE BATONS

1/2 CUP CHOPPED FLAT-LEAF PARSLEY

3 TABLESPOONS EXTRA VIRGIN OLIVE OIL

JUICE OF 1 LEMON

SEA SALT AND FRESHLY GROUND BLACK PEPPER

1. Place the mussels and wine in a large saucepan, cover and
   bring to the boil. In about 5 minutes the mussels will open.
   Remove from heat.

2. When they have cooled a little, remove from shells and drop
   back into the cooking liquor. Leave to soak there while you
   prepare the rest of the salad.

3. Place remaining ingredients in a bowl, drain the mussels
   of their juice and add to the salad. Toss gently with your
   fingers and serve. You can put some of the mussels back into
   their shells for decoration if you wish.

serves 4

a distinctive jade shell are a true New Zealand delicacy.
Mussel harvesters work with other fish-quota holders, through
fisheries-management companies, to improve and monitor
fishing standards and carry out research on mussel stocks.
Nelson-based Sealord is one of the biggest mussel companies
in New Zealand. They grow organic mussels on South Island
farms with a comprehensive farm-monitoring programme
and standards developed in partnership with New Zealand
certifying agency Bio-Gro. Eight years of commitment to
healthy, sustainable seafood underpin this programme, which
is a world benchmark for organic mussel farming. Loosely
translated this means Sealord has to monitor its waters to
make sure they are free of contaminants and heavy metals.
It also has to prove the mussels are treated humanely. Who
would have thought mussels had feelings!

Marlborough is a gourmet paradise, and the district's largest
earner is mussel farming and processing. Sanford is one of the
principal companies involved. The purity of Marlborough's
waters has enabled salmon to be farmed there without the use
of antibiotics or bacteriocides.

Baby mussels, or spats, are collected from coastal waters
around New Zealand and grown on ropes until they are
30mm long. They are then stripped off and seeded on to
vertical ropes attached to the buoyed surface ropes, where
they grow to maturity. The laden ropes are then winched up
by purpose-built boats and the mussels are removed and
transported to the factory.

Although we export a huge amount of mussels, the truth
is we're not huge mussel-eaters ourselves. They have lots of
everything good in them and are a near perfect source of
protein. Analysis shows that a 100g serving of mussels will
provide one quarter of the daily protein needs for an adult.
They are low in calories, supplying only four per cent of total
daily energy needs, and contain only a little polyunsaturated
oil. Mussels are high in beneficial Omega 3 and 6 oils and
very low in cholesterol.

The best method to keep the critters in excellent condition
is to place them in a container with drainage holes in the
bottom, cover them with a thin material that will allow the
water through and place a layer of ice on top of the material.
The melting ice water will keep the mussels chilled and fresh
for up to ten days. Mussels will often be gaping or open when
you get them home. This is because they are in a very relaxed
state when held under chilled conditions. They are not dead.
If left at room temperature for 20–30 minutes and then lightly
tapped, they will close. If held under fresh running water they
will close sooner. Just steam them for a few minutes to open.

NUTS

HAZELWOOD HAZELNUTS

Ted Kempe of Hazelwood in Amberley is a self-described hazelnut fanatic who 15 years ago planted 700 trees on two hectares and in doing so established the first commercial hazelnut orchard in Canterbury – now there are more than seventy. The hazelnuts are marketed under the Southern Nuts Label. Ted emigrated to New Zealand in 1972 and worked as a travel agent before deciding to go nutty for sentimental reasons, if you'll pardon the pun. He remembered walking home from school as a kid in Hampshire and eating nuts off the trees. Hazelnut trees are very pretty and even sometimes form part of a hedgerow. The small nuts with their hard brown shells grow in clusters of one to four within a husk that looks like a little helmet. The word hazel actually comes from the Anglo-Saxon *haesil* meaning head-dress. Hazelnuts are easy to do business with – the husk splits and falls off on its own a few days after the nuts drop off the trees, and with a little roasting or blanching the skins slip off easily.

As well as keeping ten cattle and a couple of pigs, Ted also farms worms. His 'head' worm, Baldrick, was banned from a show in Hawarden after making an appearance in the food hall. Ted harvests the hazelnuts with a machine that looks and acts like a huge vacuum cleaner. When I went to visit, Ted was very keen that I do a bit of vacuuming and 'get down on my hands and knees and play with his nuts'. Then he processes them and sells them only in New Zealand at delicatessens and by mail order. When fresh they taste sharply milky, and when dried they are deliciously sweet.

Ted also makes hazelnut paste and dukkah (a mix of roasted nuts and spices). Hazelnuts can be used in both sweet and savoury cooking – cakes, pastes for pasta, sweets like nougat and Turkish delight, pastry, salads, stews and terrines. You can buy Ted's nuts from his website: www.hazelnut.co.nz.

THE HAZELNUT COMPANY

Diane and Rick Fraser grow hazelnuts in Lincoln along with quite a few other people, and they all belong to The Hazelnut Company. Hazelnuts are high in protein, polyunsaturated and monounsaturated oils and may lower cholesterol levels; they are also full of iron, copper, manganese and vitamin E. Diane says eating hazelnuts has lowered her cholesterol and blood-sugar levels, so she's all for it. They grow all sorts of varieties, the most popular being 'White Heart', which is pale with a creamy taste and texture. They sell them roasted, raw and in the shell.

KERNELZ AND WILD WALNUTS

There are walnut trees all over the South Island, their huge boughs providing shade for many a picnic. Before Jenny and Malcolm Lawrence in Christchurch started pressing their own organic walnut oil, New Zealanders had never known anything other than rancid imported oil. The taste revelation of sweet, clean, nutty oil was incredible. The couple also produce dried wild walnuts, cultivated walnuts and a beautiful paste that could put any peanut-butter hater into recovery. Look for their labels KerNelZ and Wild Walnuts. Walnut oil is very good in a vinaigrette with raspberry vinegar and the paste is de rigeur spread over a roast before cooking.

   Walnuts are also beautiful with goat's cheese – make a caramel with 40g of brown sugar and two tablespoons of water, throw in some walnuts and allow to cool. Pour this over a slice of goat's cheese and eat immediately.

KIWI CHESTNUT CO-OPERATIVE COMPANY

The Kiwi Chestnut Co-operative Company is Kiwi ingenuity in action. In the late 1990s the chestnut trees of a group of Cambridge-based orchardists were approaching maturity. The trees were a natural hybrid of Japanese and European chestnut varieties developed for New Zealand conditions, and they grew well. But there was a problem – the chestnuts they produced were particularly difficult to peel. The orchardists knew they had to make their product user-friendly, so invented a process that produces 'chestnut crumbs'. Essentially, whole chestnuts are steam-cooked and then extruded through a crushing machine, which separates the skins and the pellicles. What emerges are fine, soft morsels of pure chestnut, which are then packed in resealable bags and frozen, ready for use. With Geoff Williamson at the helm as general manager, the co-operative also produces a freeze-dried version of chestnut crumbs and has recently developed a chestnut paste in a tear-top can. The products have no added sugar, colour or preservatives and can be used in a myriad ways, sweet and savoury. To foster a taste for chestnuts, a chestnut chutney has been introduced, plus a pre-mix chestnut stuffing and chestnut-studded chocolates, all under the Castanza label – more is planned. Their website is: www.kiwichestnut.co.nz.

NUTT RANCH

David and Beverley Null produce hazelnuts in Blenheim. They make cold-pressed oil, hazelnut flour, paste, delicious dukkah, candy-coated nuts and roasted, salted ones. Their products are fresh and there is minimal processing. In the late summer and early autumn their crop is harvested by hand, quality inspected, washed, and dried to a very low moisture content. Throughout the winter they crack, process and package the products, which are then delivered as quickly as possible. Fresh hazelnuts, straight from the shell, are fantastic raw with their slightly sweet taste, creamy texture and crunch. Toasted, they develop a stronger nutty taste and crispy texture taking on more smokiness and robustness. Toasting them is a simple procedure: just spread them on to a shallow baking pan and toast them in the oven at 140°C for about 20 minutes or until the nut meat turns light golden and their skins crack.

   Hazelnut oil has a rich, golden colour and a sweet, nutty taste. Its high flashpoint makes it ideal for cooking and it has a shelf-life of about 12 months when stored in a dark cupboard. It is versitile and can be used as you would use olive oil – excellent in baking, drizzled over vegetables, in dressings or on its own with breads and dukkah. Hazelnut flour is interesting when combined with white flour in baking. Add it to biscuits, muffins and breads, replacing about a quarter of the plain flour with hazelnut flour. If using self-raising flour, add a teaspoon of baking powder to each cup of hazelnut flour. The Nutt Ranch products come with simple recipes such as hazelnut meringue, linguini with mushrooms and hazelnuts, and hazelnut oil vinaigrette. The Nulls consistently have a stand at the Marlborough farmers' market, and you can order online at: www.nuttranch.co.nz.

Walnut sauce

*This is good with pasta, grilled vegetables, polenta and roast chicken.
It would be really good as a dip for homemade chips too.*

2 SLICES WHITE BEAD
MILK
1 1/2 CUPS SHELLED FRESH WALNUTS
3 CLOVES GARLIC
1/4 CUP GRATED PARMESAN CHEESE
A HANDFUL OF FRESH BASIL LEAVES
SEA SALT AND FRESHLY GROUND BLACK
PEPPER TO TASTE
5 TABLESPOONS WALNUT OR OLIVE OIL OR A MIX
CREAM

1. Soak the bread in some milk then squeeze out. Place the
   bread in a food processor with the walnuts, garlic,
   Parmesan, basil, salt and pepper. Put the lid on and blend
   while slowly adding the oil.

2. Thin the sauce down to a thick, pourable consistency by
   blending in some cream, milk or water (cream is best).

makes 1 cup

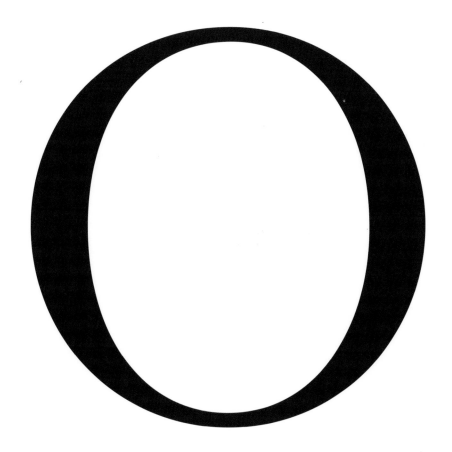

OFFAL When I was a child we ate various forms of offal – mainly pig's liver, sheep's brains, black pudding, oxtail and chicken liver. My mother knew how to cook these things because she'd been brought up on a farm, where one is always close to the life-and-death cycle. She cooked them simply, which is the best course of action because, after all, we appreciate such things for their texture and flavour. However, we all have terrifying memories of boarding-school tripe in ghastly white sauce, and shoe-leather slabs of cow liver, enough to make you vomit just to see it. I very much like sweetbreads, which I learned to cook in my restaurant in Paris, and I also learned to love tripe in Paris. When I first arrived there I ordered a dish in a bistro, not really knowing what I was ordering. When it arrived I still didn't know what it was but ate it anyway. It was utterly delicate and perfumed, and like eating tender but textured pasta ribbons. Subsequently I went on to adore *andouillettes* (tripe sausages); *andouille* (tripe salami); sweet and mild calf's liver cooked until pink in the middle; tongue and cheek, which have the most marvellous slow-cooked flavour; *fromage de tête* (head terrine); and kidneys cooked until pink in the middle.

Under my Brazilian friend's influence in Paris, I learned to use pig's ear, tail and trotter to give flavour and gelatinous consistency to black-bean dishes and *feijoada*. The sheep's brains I cooked in Paris were usually from New Zealand – creamy with a slightly sweet, clam flavour, quickly sautéed and served with a tahini lemon sauce. My farmer friend Jamie told me there is only one real delicacy in New Zealand and that is 'mountain oysters'. Next to that is lambs' tails. According to him, 'They are best eaten in the spring during docking. You cut the lambs' tails off, chuck

Sweetbreads with artichoke purée

for the purée:
2 X 390G TINS ARTICHOKE BOTTOMS OR HEARTS
EXTRA VIRGIN OLIVE OIL
2 LIME LEAVES, TORN
¼ CUP SAUVIGNON BLANC
¼ CUP COCONUT CREAM

1. Drain the artichoke bottoms.

2. Quarter and sauté artichokes in a little oil for 5 minutes with the lime leaves. Add the wine and coconut cream and simmer for another five minutes.

3. Allow to cool, discard lime leaves and blend to a smooth paste in a food processor or push through a sieve.

for the sweetbreads:
500G LAMBS' SWEETBREADS
½ CUP VEAL STOCK
SEA SALT AND FRESHLY GROUND WHITE PEPPER
EXTRA VIRGIN OLIVE OIL IN A SPRAY PUMP

1. Soak the sweetbreads in cold water for at least 2 hours. This removes the blood, producing a whiter, milder-tasting sweetbread.

2. Blanch the sweetbreads by placing them in a pot and covering them with veal stock. Bring them to the boil, then remove and plunge into iced water. Drain well.

3. To press sweetbreads, lay them in one layer on a clean tea-towel. Cover with another towel and weight down. Place in the refrigerator for at least 2 hours.

4. Remove any sinew and fat with your hands. Season sweetbreads on both sides with salt and pepper.

5. Spray some olive oil on a heated pan and sauté the sweetbreads for 2 minutes on each side. Serve immediately with artichoke purée.

serves 6 as a starter

the tails into the embers of the fire and cook them until they scream. Get hold of one, pull the skin and wool off, sprinkle a bit of salt on and eat. To get the balls (mountain oysters), you bite them out of the living animal with your teeth or you extract them with your thumb and forefinger. You fry them in butter and onions – really a great delicacy.' I have no idea what the lambs think of all this.

As for sweetbreads, they are fiddly to prepare but heavenly to eat. Sweetbread is the flowery name for the pancreas (near the heart) and the thymus glands in the throat. They come from calves and sheep. The main thing to consider when buying offal is freshness, to know where the offal has come from – it's even more important than when buying meat. Refer to the organic and free-range rule discussed under the meat and bird sections in this book. Organic and free-range offal is best. Fresh offal looks wet, shiny and of good consistency – not limpid and watery – and it shouldn't smell. Best to order straight from your butcher.

OLIVE OIL

Extra virgin olive oil (EVOO) is the most expensive fruit juice in the world. These days consumers want more and more to know exactly what they are eating and what's in it. They want it to be safe, to promote long life and health, and not to harm the environment. But most of all what people want is taste. In New Zealand we still produce food that tastes good and is good for you, and our olive oil is of very high quality, grown in a clean country. People who live among olive trees tell you their air is pure and their lives are full. They expect miracles as a matter of course.

The godfather of New Zealand olive oil is Gidon Blumenfeld, who planted his first trees in Marlborough in 1985. The cultivars he introduced and continued to propagate formed the basis of New Zealand's plantings. Other people began seriously growing olives around 1995, and now there are about 800 growers with 27,300 hectares planted the length and breadth of the country. In some areas there are co-operative marketing companies such as Nelson Olives. Some people may have 250 trees and others, like the Simonoviches, have 30,000. Currently we produce 160,000 litres a year and by 2010 should be producing over two million litres. Everyone's crazy about olive growing and we are consuming our grassy, peppery, lemony olive oil by the ton in huge quantities.

One good reason to buy New Zealand olive oil is that it's all extra virgin cold-pressed – nobody makes anything else.

Whereas with an imported olive oil, in spite of what the label might say, it's impossible to know for sure if it is extra virgin. Extra virgin oil means it comes from the first cold pressing of the olives – it has no faults and cannot be rancid.

Most New Zealand oil has less than 0.1 per cent fatty acid, which is well within the requirements for olive oils to be classified as extra virgin olive oil. 'Pure' olive oil is not pure – it is a second or third pressing and not of good quality. 'Lite' olive oil is a joke; it is not light in fat, just light in quality. The worst is pomace olive oil, which is really only fit for soap. The only olive oil that is good for you is extra virgin, fresh green oil. In New Zealand olive oil has a range of flavours, depending on where the fruit was grown and when it was harvested – butter, green apples, hay, pepper, tomato coulis, grass, tropical fruit and sometimes almonds and flowers. On its own, olive oil is a condiment; when it's combined with food it becomes a food.

Recently scientists at HortResearch, on behalf of the New Zealand Olive Association, have started training to establish a certification process for New Zealand olive oil. For oil to meet the standard it must pass chemical analysis. Then it is tasted and judged to be free of defects like sourness, muddiness, mustiness and rancidity. New Zealand oils now bear a stamp showing they have passed the test as set down by the International Olive Oil Council. To be on the testing panel, you have to have a very sensitive and well-developed palate, be mad about olive oil and train for three years. According to my friends who are on the panel, it is shocking how much imported expensive oil, which we have always considered to be perfectly good, is actually slightly rancid. Faults in oil can happen at any stage of the game – during harvesting, pressing or storage.

We make high-quality oil in New Zealand and we love winning awards. Nelson Olives Ltd's Mahana extra virgin olive oil was awarded a gold medal, and its Oriwa a silver medal at the Olive Oils of the World 2004 competition. This event, sponsored by the Los Angeles County Fair, is considered the most prestigious in the United States and attracts entries from all major olive oil-producing countries world-wide. The best show winner of the 2004 New Zealand Extra Virgin Olive Oil Association Awards was Molive Gold from Wairarapa in the boutique category. Matapiro of Hawke's Bay and Waimata of Gisborne were joint winners in the commercial category. Matapiro and Waimata were both pressed by The Village Press in Hawke's Bay, who also produce very good oil of their own.

The acknowledged guru on olive oil in New Zealand is now Margaret Edwards, who has an olive grove on Waiheke Island called Matiatia Estate. Margaret's oil is absolutely beautiful and highly award-winning, and Margaret herself is the most gracious, intelligent, lovely woman. She has attended training courses with the International Olive Oil Council in Italy and the Savantes International Professional Olive Oil Tasting programme in Australia, and judges the New Zealand Olive Oil Awards and the Los Angeles County Fair, which is the largest olive oil competition in the world. Margaret and her surgeon husband are typical of the average olive grower in New Zealand. Their olive grove started off as a retirement project and now they know so much they can't stop. I visited their home on Waiheke and immediately wanted to get out my rosary beads. The creamy-coloured purpose-built house is like a convent or monastery with its high ceilings, minimalist decor, solid antique wooden furniture and restful feel. The huge kitchen with its long, black granite bench opens up to the olive grove and a heart-stopping view of the hills. Margaret says she sees future growth in the flavoured table olives and tapenade department. Also, end-of-season and imperfect olives are being made into soaps and cosmetics. We haven't really touched on this in New Zealand yet, and there's huge scope.

VILLAGE PRESS OLIVE OIL

Wayne and Maureen Startup 'started up' their olive-growing business nine years ago as a backyard hobby. It is now one of the biggest commercial olive oil-producing businesses in New Zealand. They have a syndicate of 110 investors and 30,000 trees grown in seven groves across 45 hectares of land in the Hawke's Bay. They also buy fruit from Marlborough and have recently joined forces with Sileni Wine Estate. This was a very clever move for both of them because olive oil processing begins several weeks after the grape harvest is completed. This way the two can share reciprocal hoppers, forklifts and weighing equipment.

The Village Press has a separate processing facility, which uses two presses imported from Italy. There is the traditional hydraulic press and the spiffing new $400,000 state-of-the-art centrifugal press. Now visitors can visit the winery, eat in the restaurant, have cheese-and-wine tastings in the shop and, if it's the right time of year, can see Wayne's olive press in action. The olives are harvested by a mechanical harvester, taken to the press house and weighed, then transferred to a conveyer belt to get rid of stones, leaves, branches and other matter. The olives are then washed before going into the crusher, stones and all, where they're turned into a paste. The hydraulic presser squeezes juices from the paste and the centrifugal one spins the paste in an enclosed cylinder, sending the lighter-weight olive oil to the outside of the cylinder and thus enabling the separation of the oil from other substances like water and solids. In 2004 I asked Wayne and Maureen to press some oil under my own Peta Mathias label. We chose the leccino olive for its mildness, softness, fruitiness and floweriness.

If you want your very own little press for your very own olive grove, you can buy one from Axis Industrial. The Aquarius presses are semi-hydraulic and have separate pieces of machinery for each of the three processes of oil production. There is the mill, which smashes the olives to a paste; the malaxator, which breaks down the cells to release the oil; and the press to extract the oil. It handles 15kg batches, is easy to clean and costs about $8000. Their website is: www.axisindustrial.co.nz.

COOKING WITH AND EATING EVOO

Keep extra virgin olive oil (EVOO) in a cool, dark place as heat and light make it deteriorate rapidly. Once the oil is open, consume it quickly as it oxidises when exposed to the air. EVOO is a very sophisticated cooking companion because it will take on the flavour of the foods it accompanies to a certain extent.

HERE ARE SOME SUGGESTIONS:

- Drizzle EVOO on potatoes and sprinkle on some New Zealand Pacific sea salt and freshly ground black pepper.
- Dip a chunk of good bread in oil, then into dukkah – you could be close to heaven.
- Bake with olive oil – you can use it in muffins, biscuits, cakes, flat breads, pizzas, brownies and biscotti. EVOO's small, fat crystals yield even, finely textured, lighter baked goods. It acts as an emulsifier to produce a homogeneous batter that produces cakes with a very moist and tender crumb. A teaspoon of butter can be replaced by 3/4 teaspoon of olive oil; 100g of butter is replaced by 75ml olive oil.
- Another simple and delicious use for olive oil is on carpaccio, which can be made from duck, salmon, tuna, beef or venison. Half-freeze the raw meat, then slice it paper thin with a very sharp knife or slicer. Lay it out flat on a dinner plate, drizzle with oil and sprinkle with sea salt and freshly ground black pepper. Grate Parmesan cheese over it with a vegetable peeler and squeeze on some lemon or lime juice. In my restaurant in Paris I used to surround the carpaccio with sliced artichoke hearts and mushrooms.

OTHER USES FOR EVOO

To Muslims, Christians and Jews alike, the olive means wisdom, abundance and peace. I invariably get great feelings

Olive oil cake

5 EGGS, SEPARATED
3/4 CUP SUGAR
1/2 CUP STICKY WINE
1/3 CUP EXTRA VIRGIN OLIVE OIL
150G FLOUR
1/4 TEASPOON SALT
2 EGG WHITES, EXTRA
1/2 TEASPOON CREAM OF TARTAR
ICING SUGAR

1. Preheat the oven to 180°C. Spray the interior of a 22cm high-sided springform cake tin with oil and line it with baking paper. The paper lining the sides should stick up 5cm higher than the tin.

2. Beat the five egg yolks with half the sugar until pale and thick. Beat in the wine and oil.

3. Sift flour and salt and fold into the egg yolk mixture.

4. Beat the seven egg whites with the cream of tartar until stiff, then gradually beat in the remaining sugar. Fold this into the yolk mixture.

5. Pour the cake mixture into the lined tin and bake for 20 minutes.

6. Lower the oven temperature to 160°C and bake for another 20 minutes. Turn the oven off, cover the cake with an oiled round of baking paper and leave for another 15 minutes.

7. When cool, dust the cake with icing sugar.

of wisdom when drinking a martini, that famous cocktail which would be meaningless without an olive plopped in it. In the old days the Greek women used a big fat Kalamata olive as a method of birth control – they would put one in place instead of a diaphragm. Olive oil is also very good as a sexual lubricant because it doesn't interfere with the pH status of the skin.

On her 121st birthday, Jeanne Calment from Arles in the South of France was asked what her secret to longevity was. She said, 'Huile d'olive. I eat it in every meal and always have done. I also rub it into my skin. I have only one wrinkle and I'm sitting on it.'

You will get to heaven in better condition with EVOO.

OYSTERS

BLUFF OYSTERS

These unusual-looking oysters, *Ostrea chilensis* (tio to the Maori), are my favourites in New Zealand and some say they are the best in the world, but don't tell the Irish that. They are grown slowly in the cold, clean waters of the Foveaux Strait and in season are dredged by Bluff's oyster fleet. Bluff oysters are a national delicacy and New Zealanders eagerly anticipate the March start of the fishing season each year. They are a flat oyster that grows up to 10.5cm in length and are so expensive you have to be sitting down while you eat them. Last count was $2 each! The taste and texture is unique among oysters – meaty, sweet, fresh and slightly metallic – and they are not too big.

This delectable oyster takes five years to mature. Its shell is craggy and rock hard; its interior sweet, salty and soft. It is food for the heart (seven calories, with loads of iodine and zinc) and food for the loins also, if you get my drift. Oysters have a hugely respectable pedigree – Roman emperors ate hundreds of them at one sitting, Casanova slurped down 50 a day in his bath, gourmets in Europe wait all year for the first month ending with an 'r' to twist them open, and Viagra is an unheard-of drug in oyster communities. As soon as they come into season in New Zealand, I down a dozen of them in short order, pausing briefly to squeeze lemon and bite chunks out of brown soda bread or Vogel's.

There is an oyster festival held in April at the Bluff Events Centre where you can enjoy the succulent seafood unique to Southland, devour as many Bluff oysters as you can and drink almost as much. They ain't wimps in the south, and nothing is done by half measures. To warm the good people up and kick the festivities off, there is the Southern Seas Ball. Subsequent to that there's untold entertainment, Scottish bands, oyster eating and opening competitions, a chef cook-off and creativity awards, including the oyster-sack fashion parade, the 'inspirations of the sea' unrestricted wearable-art competition, the oyster shell sculpture competition and the Atlantis floral-art competition. You'd have a hard time finding the opportunity to suck an oyster.

There is only one thing that drives me bats about oysters in New Zealand – they are opened in advance. This is criminal behaviour, close to the criminal forced pasteurising of milk for farmhouse cheese. Will these officials please get off the grass? An oyster must be shucked to order – that way you know it is fresh and alive and the delicious liquor is not lost. It also tastes better.

It is, of course, criminal to cook a Bluff oyster but if you must, try this method. Either put the oysters in little, individual gratin dishes or arrange them in their shells on a bed of rock salt in an oven dish. Drizzle with Champagne and a little cream and top with very finely grated lemon and orange rind, sea salt and freshly ground black pepper. Grill for 30 seconds under a high heat and eat immediately.

CLEVEDON COAST OYSTERS

Coming a close second to Bluff oysters, but of course a completely different variety, are Clevedon Pacific oysters (*Ostrea gigas*) grown in the north of the North Island. Pacific oysters have flourished in New Zealand's coastal waters for millions of years.

The McCallums farm around 93 hectares and run New Zealand's third-largest oyster farm. They are the fourth generation to farm the family land on the Clevedon coast. Jan and Callum have three kids, and Jan has her own freight business. And to fill in their spare time, they have established a vineyard. Jan says that in the McCallum family all boats and children inherit family names. Even the wine is called Jasper, the original name for the McCallum chip, which is still quarried on one of the family islands off the coast.

Callum and his father put the first 24 oyster racks down in 1986, and he now has 400, producing about 8000 dozen oysters a week. They export 50 per cent of their harvest to Australia and Asia. There's nothing like going out on one of Callum's oyster barges for an oyster breakfast. And

nothing, but nothing, tastes like an oyster opened fresh from the sea – briny, clean and juicy. Callum picks you up in his arms and carries you on to the barge, cracks a few open with his knife and carries you back again, where Jan makes you coffee and biscuits. They live in a large old house in a secluded bay called Lismore Farm and when I visited they were constructing a swimming pool and tennis court. This is one of the most unimaginably beautiful stretches of coastline, and when you walk on to the land, you think these people must be multimillionaires. However, the McCallums are very practical and if the land can't pay for itself, they will be in trouble. This is why they all work so hard, because losing part of the land would be a fate worse than death. Brother John farms on Pakihi Island, which you can see from the house, and floats the cattle over on a barge when it's time to move them. The day I was there the cattle stampeded off the barge, through the flimsy barrier, through the gardens of the house and up past the vineyard. The McCallums just laughed. They are very charming, witty people, who enjoy life and make lots of jokes about the sexual powers of oysters – they had three kids in two-and-a-half years.

New Zealand has the world's safest oyster-growing waters. Clevedon oysters are grown from natural spat collection, matured in clean, pure water on racks, and are harvested daily in peak condition and processed immediately. There is no pollution, no algal biotoxins, no chemicals, no depuration (treatment to reduce bacteria) and no genetic alteration. You can buy them whole, opened and frozen in different sizes. If you are lucky enough to live in Auckland, you can order them and be eating them the same day, or can even front up to the farm gate. It's not far from central Auckland and absolutely worth the drive.

The prime eating period is in autumn and winter, and we seem to like them fat and white in New Zealand. If you buy them unopened they will last for a week in the fridge covered with a damp cloth. You shouldn't really eat a dead oyster – when you prick it, it should react.

If you can get hold of some of the McCallums' cabernet sauvignon, it wouldn't be a sad day either. They planted the two-hectare vineyard up behind the house in 1994, but it wasn't until viticulturist Craig McLeod took over that they started producing good commercial wine. And it is good – intense, well-balanced and very berry. You may not think this wine would go well with oysters, but Callum throws steaks on the barbie and tops them with oysters, which makes an inspired match.

Callum McCallum and Co., Clevedon

PAUA

Paua (abalone) is a thick, black-looking muscle about 125mm long. It attaches itself to rocks and has a colourful, flattened ovoid-shaped shell on one side, very good for using as an ashtray. Most of the paua brought up in New Zealand goes to the Asian market, where they are considered a great delicacy. In the English *Sunday Times* I read that in the Forum restaurant in Hong Kong a dish of abalone can cost you £400 or more. A good diver can bring up as many as 400 a day – 200kg!

Paua can be eaten raw or cooked. First you remove the creature from the shell, then cut off the frill around the edge and remove the stomach, which is underneath. Give it a scrub to remove the black coating, revealing pearly grey flesh, then slice it very finely with a sharp knife – it's easier to do this when it's lightly frozen. Eaten raw, it tastes slightly rubbery but very good. At this point you can marinate the paua in Asian flavours and sauté it quickly on a very high heat. Some people like to fry slices with lemon rind and garlic. Others say the way to soften a paua is to whack it twice and twice only on the foot, which is in the middle. This beaks the muscle, and the tendons are released without damaging the paua. I've seen people on Stewart Island cooking whole paua steaks on the barbecue – they just sprinkle them with salt and pepper and grill them for about 20 minutes. Cooked this way, they honestly taste and feel like butter. A fisherman told me he leaves paua out in the hot sun for two or three hours, shell side up, and it is as tender as eye fillet. If someone gives you some paua, don't be afraid – be grateful you're not in Hong Kong. A little cooking knowledge goes a long way.

I met a man on Stewart Island who gets the paua to make pearls. How does he do that? Well, very few paua will produce pearls in the wild, so he helps them along. The paua is anaesthetised to prevent rejection, then small plastic implants are carefully inserted inside each paua. If you puncture the animal it will die. Over a two-year period the paua will produce material that grows around this foreign object in the shape of a half-pearl or mabe. When fully formed the pearls are beautiful colours – green, pink and blue – and fetch big bucks. A double-A pearl should have perfect lustre, with 1mm nacre (shell) thickness covering the implant.

Only about 20 per cent of the crop actually produce a pearl of saleable quality, so it's a lot of work for small rewards.

Paua feed on a seaweed called diatoms, and the holes along the side of the shell occur naturally, allowing the water currents from which they obtain oxygen to circulate freely. The ear-shaped shell is streamlined for minimal resistance to the movements of its habitat. Paua reproduce under storm conditions, when there's extra oxygen in the water. The female releases millions of eggs and the male releases millions of sperm from cream and green sacs, and they pray and hope that some of them find each other. Paua take about seven years to reach maturity in the wild. When bred for pearls they are kept in a dark room in sea-water tanks like large aquariums, and the farmers can get very attached to them. The farmer I met loves them, and says they are intelligent and have feelings. If they are put in water that doesn't suit them they get very distressed and try to jump out. If you are sensitive please move on to the next paragraph and don't tell me I hide things from you. He says they are haemophiliac and feel pain. If cut, they bleed uncontrollably, but can heal wounds by contracting the powerful muscle around the wound. Finding out that they had feelings made it very distressing for me when I saw what they did to them at the fireman's barbecue. It didn't stop me from eating them though.

Farmed baby paua is becoming fashionable of late thanks to outfits like East Coast Aqua Culture in Napier. Obviously you can't take undersized paua from the sea, so they have to be farmed, poor little critters. Being so small they are necessarily rather tender and don't need to be bashed; in fact, you can eat them raw as is. They are hatched and grown in tanks and lovingly fed a posh diet of algae and finely ground fishmeal, which influences both the way they taste and the way they look. The flesh is paler and more delicate than wild paua and the shells are a pretty pale blue rather than green and have no rough encrustations. Managing director Brandi Dixon likes to lightly poach them

in sake or steam them and serve with mayonnaise on the side. Production is still quite small, but you can order them from the website at: www.tepania.co.nz.

OTHER PEOPLE GROWING 'COCKTAIL' PAUA:
- Rainbow Abalone and Pearls in New Plymouth
- Abalone New Zealand Ltd in Bluff
- Pendarves Abalone Farm Ltd in Ashburton
- Waipaua Aqua Farm in Coromandel

PORK

MURRELLEN PORK

I have reached the stage in life where I can only buy organic meat, or at least well-brought-up meat, not only because it has no foreign stuff in it that I don't know about, but also because I know the animal has led a good life, is not schizophrenic and has not died in terror. Once you've eaten properly raised and killed pork, it's hard to go back. Murray and Helen (hence 'Murrellen') Battersby have been pig farming for over 40 years. They know all there is to know about piggies, and have had lots of comments about their pork from friends. 'By crikey,' said these friends, 'your pork's good!' So Murray went off to talk to chefs to find out why pork was not on their menus very much, only to be told it was because they couldn't get consistent good quality. He then went and questioned MAF, who told him the reason there wasn't any consistency with pork was a condition called PSS or porcine stress syndrome. It is a condition that has arisen with the development of leaner breeds of pig because they carry a gene called halothane, which causes them to be particularly susceptible to stress. And for some reason, intelligent pigs do find it stressful to be kicked and yelled at, squashed into tiny pens and then killed in front of their friends.

Under Jeff Allen's guidance at MAF, Murray did some experiments with pig pH (acidity) levels. The world standard of acceptability in pork is a pH of 5.8. For Murrellen pork the acceptable pH level lies between 6.1 and 6.9 to get a good quality of meat. Stress makes the pH level drop and the meat is tough, pale and soft when uncooked and will exude a lot of moisture on cooking. If the pH level is low when the pig is slaughtered, the fluid in the meat will turn to lactic acid when the carcass is hung and will drip out (not a good thing). If the pH is above 5.8

the fluid doesn't turn to lactic acid but stays as glycogen, thus keeping the meat juicy, sweet and succulent. Murrellen was the first recipient of the Pork Quality Improvement Process certificate for their entire process from go to whoa – and Murray can trace back every single pig just in case someone is nutty enough not to be satisfied with their pork chop.

I'm going to bang on about this because it's really important both for the pig and for me, and I adore pork and all charcuterie. This is how Murray and Helen's pampered pigs live. The breed is the large, white Landrace Duroc crossed with a bit of Hampshire, chosen for its good mothering skills, growth rate and lean meat. Males and females are kept separate for peace, which is what should happen with humans. Why do we keep trying to live together when it is clearly not God's intention? Murray and Helen have got it right, although they seem to live together peacefully enough themselves. The pigs are handled gently; they listen to classical music, and Murray once even spent the night in his pyjamas in a pig pen, sleeping on the concrete floor to find out what it felt like. The pigs are kept in social groups of 12 or 36 in spacious pens. There is a sleeping area where the animals can stretch out, a separate dung area and ad-lib grain feeders. No drugs are used, and a consultant vet visits every two months.

Ventilation is important, too, as pigs can radiate warmth equivalent to a 1kw heater and they need a comfortable temperature of around 18–20°C. There is an electric sensor in the sheds and electric equipment including fans to monitor their temperature-controlled well-being. Because of the clean air and proper ventilation there is no pneumonia, and the pigs never have worms. Worms in animals are simply a matter of hygiene; so every time a pen is restocked after the pigs go to that big trough in the sky, they are cleaned using high-pressure hoses and strong disinfectant. In the effort to reduce stress on the ride to the trough in the sky, no dogs are used, the pigs are not crated and the conditions of transport are calm. In the truck, always driven by the same driver who knows the road, soothing music is played and there are no shock bumps or loud traffic noises. The result is that when the kill occurs, the pig is not freaked out and screaming, and the resulting pH level is high. Any pigs that don't meet Murrellen's high standard are processed and sold as regular pork. And guess what? The good stuff is not much more expensive than other pork.

Don't overcook pork. The war is over and triganosis doesn't happen any more. Quickly cooked cuts like fillets, chops, medallions and schnitzel should still be a little pink

in the middle. Allow meat to rest five minutes before eating.

For details of stockists of Murrellen Pork, see their website: www.murrellenpork.co.nz.

HAVOC PORK

Ian and Linda McCallum-Jackson are very hard-case and were put on this earth to breed beautiful piggies, there's no doubting it. They love their pigs and give them names like Doris and Nostradamus. Linda says they are intelligent and behave like humans would if they weren't socialised – selfish, jealous, moody, vain, affectionate. Ian was born to this life but Linda came to it when she married Ian. She was a human resources consultant in Auckland who met a pig farmer in the South Island and said, I'm staying down here with him. Needless to say, her JAFA friends didn't believe her, but there she is, Mrs Pig Farmer, whipping up scones and tea in the 1910 farmhouse kitchen for visitors. They are straight out of central casting: Ian in his pig farmer's outfit of gumboots, overalls, straw hat and Worcestershire accent and Linda – plump, smiling, pink lipstick and red bob. Having been on intimate terms with pigs all his life, Ian finally gave in and bought a farm in South Canterbury, which he declares perfect for pig farming – lots of grain and straw and a dry climate. His particular property has lots of stony ground, which is great for drainage – essential to outdoor farming.

Havoc Farm has about 100 pigs of the large, white Landrace breed crossed with some Durox and they process around 50 a week. Ian's philosophy is minimal intervention, so there are no antibiotics, no growth promoters and a healthy diet of grain and vegetable oil (which keeps the fat soft) with cider vinegar and garlic to keep digestion healthy. Pigs have very big litters of up to 15 or more and they can't count of course, so if they roll on a piglet, they don't realise it's missing until it is well on its way to heaven. When I was there, a sow had given birth the night before and was resting in her little A-frame bach with her gorgeous babies – all pink and clean and fragrant, and hopelessly adorable. Most piglets are weaned at three weeks, but Ian weans his at six to eight to allow them to develop strong immune systems. This is also easier on the sow as she is not forced to produce so many litters a year.

Another important member of the team at Havoc, who surely to God must contribute to the pigs' happiness, is a gentleman they call the 'gillie'. He is a farm assistant like no other. Short, dark and adorable with a treacherous sense of humour, Jock is from Clyde Bank, Scotland, and is a prize

Pork in Hay

In this recipe, the leg of pork is wrapped in muslin and cooked in wet hay. You can use an uncooked ham instead of a leg of pork.

20 PEPPERCORNS
20 JUNIPER BERRIES
1 LEG HAVOC PORK
6 BAY LEAVES
1 TEASPOON SALT

1. Roughly smash the peppercorns and juniper berries. Place the pork leg, bay leaves, peppercorns and juniper berries in a muslin bag (or wrap in a tea-towel) and tie to prevent hay getting stuck all over it.

2. Put the salt and a generous layer of hay in the bottom of a large saucepan and place the pork on top. Stuff more hay around and on top of the pork to cover it.

3. Pour 4 cups of boiling water over all and place lid on. If it doesn't fit tightly, wrap some tinfoil or a tea-towel around the edge.

4. Bake in an oven preheated to 150°C or simmer on the stove for 3 1/2 hours. Serve hot, sliced at the table with green sauce.

Green sauce

1/2 CUP ROCKET LEAVES
1/2 CUP FRESH MINT
1/4 CUP FLAT-LEAF PARSLEY
3 TABLESPOONS CHOPPED CHIVES
1 TEASPOON FRESH THYME
1 TEASPOON FRESH OREGANO
2 TABLESPOONS CAPERS
1 SHALLOT, CHOPPED
1 TABLESPOON GRATED LEMON ZEST
2 CLOVES GARLIC
3 TABLESPOONS LEMON JUICE
1/2 CUP AVOCADO OIL OR EXTRA VIRGIN OLIVE OIL
1/2 CUP WATER

1. Finely chop all the ingredients then mix everything together with a fork, or for a smoother consistency, blend all the ingredients in a food processor until thick.

serves 10

piper. He pipes at the slimmest of provocations and loves to get out the bagpipes to call the hogs to feed. He stands on the back of the truck kitted out in kilt, hat, blue Havoc T-shirt and real hobnail boots while Ian distributes the grain. The pigs have only to hear the truck in the distance and they all run towards it.

The plan for the future is eventually to grow their own grain, so as to be fully organic, and to have their own processing plant on the property. They do process some pork but want to process it all so they have full control from 'farrow to finish'. Linda loves cooking and developing new products, which she does in her farmhouse kitchen. Her latest is pickled pork cheeks; sausages; *andouille* (gut sausage); bratwurst with fresh garlic, caraway and cognac; and home-cured, properly aged bacon. She cured a leg of ham for my family for Christmas, and 20 Mathiases from Australia and New Zealand agreed it was the best ham they had ever eaten. The children shovelled it down their gobs with their hands.

The secret to Havoc's tasty pork is not only in the happy lifestyle but also the breed – in fact, Ian says most of the secret is in the breed. They are aiming for marbling, the delicious distribution of fat through the flesh, that gives it so much taste.

Ian and Linda sell the pork to a wholesaler, by mail order, to a few lucky restaurants, at the Otago farmers' market in Dunedin and from their website: www.foodlovers.co.nz. Because it is so expensive to produce pork in New Zealand, a shocking 30–40 per cent is imported, and we have no labelling on pork showing where it comes from. It could be Australian, Canadian, Chinese, Irish or American. If you want to eat New Zealand pork, look for a sticker saying '100 per cent New Zealand pork' or order it from a farm.

POTATOES

Potatoes (especially Jersey Benneys or Agrias) are my favourite vegetable, and nothing would make me happier than to eat a meal of them three times a day. They are 70–80 per cent water, 10–20 per cent starch and 10 per cent sugar, mineral and protein. The diet fascists would have us believe they are 100 per cent sugar. In terms of calories, however, eating a potato is no different from eating an apple or a banana. How can that be bad for you? The Incas worshipped potato spirits and measured time by how long it took to cook potatoes. Where have those colourful days gone?

P

Everyone else in New Zealand seems to love potatoes as much as I do, as they are our number one vegetable; we consume 450,000 tonnes of spuds every year. Varieties range from the pits – the dreaded flavourless Nadine, to the heights – the yellow, nutty, tasty Agria. If you despair of finding a delicious spud in your supermarket, why not have a go at growing them yourself. Kay Baxter of Koanga Gardens has the seeds for just about any potato you can think of and she will sell them to you and advise you on the best growing methods. Good potatoes can also often be found at the outdoor markets.

In New Zealand we have what we call Maori potatoes and what other people call heritage potatoes and what Maori chef Charles Royal calls indigenous New Zealand gourmet potatoes. They probably either came with whaling ships from South America in pre-European times or with the early settlers. French explorer de Surville planted some at Doubtless Bay in 1769, and the following year the crew of *Adventure*, the ship that accompanied Cook on his second expedition to New Zealand, made several plantings of potatoes at Queen Charlotte Sound. These ancient potato varieties are regarded as taonga or treasure, and therefore have cultural and spiritual significance. One type is called Karuparera (duck eyes) or Peruperu because Maori always believed it came from Peru. The skin is creamy-yellow splashed with purple and the floury flesh is creamy-white with yellow streaks.

There are 18 types of Maori potato identified by Graham Harris of the Open Polytechnic in Wellington. (Graham's research into Maori potatoes is described in more detail under the Heroes entry, see page 100.) All Maori potatoes are delicious and nutty tasting and my favourite is Urenika or Taewa, a long potato with dark purple skin and flesh that stays purple when cooked. There are also the Parareka, which are purple with lots of eyes and fabulously waxy and yellow within – great for potato salad. John Millward of Great Taste New Zealand describes them as having a light, buttery, popcorn flavour.

Lamb & purple potato salad

¼ CUP WATER

6 TABLESPOONS LIME JUICE

1 TABLESPOON GRATED LIME ZEST

1 TABLESPOON BROWN SUGAR

3 TABLESPOONS THAI FISH SAUCE

1 TEASPOON GRATED
FRESH GINGER

1 TEASPOON FINELY
CHOPPED GARLIC

1 TEASPOON SESAME OIL

300G PURPLE URENIKA POTATOES

200G SNOW PEAS

1KG FRESH BROAD BEANS OR 1
CUP FROZEN BEANS

24 SMALL VINE-RIPENED TOMATOES

6 HANDFULS MIXED GREENS

1 HANDFUL MINT LEAVES

SUMAC *(a red North African spice available at specialty shops)*

3 RACKS OF LAMB

1. To make the dressing, combine the first eight ingredients in a large bowl and whisk well.

2. Scrub the potatoes gently and boil in salted water until soft. Slice thickly.

3. Blanch the snow peas by plunging in boiling water for 2 minutes, then plunging in cold water. Drain.

4. Remove the broad beans from their pods and boil for 4 minutes. Drain and remove the skins. If using frozen beans, boil for 2 minutes, then remove the skins.

5. Preheat the oven to 250°C.

6. Blanch the tomatoes in boiling water for 1 minute, drain and peel.

7. Wash the greens and mint.

8. Sprinkle sumac over the lamb racks and roast in the centre of the oven for exactly 20 minutes. Remove from the oven and allow to rest while you put the salad together.

9. With your hands, gently toss the leaves, mint, beans, potatoes and snow peas in the dressing.

10. To serve, slice the racks into cutlets. Gently share out the salad mixture on to six large dinner plates, alternating with the cutlets, rearranging things if necessary to please your artistic nature. Place 4 tomatoes around the edges of each plate.

serves 6

Q GARDENS

Frances Rogers is a gentle, sparkling lady who started growing unusual varieties of vegetables over 20 years ago in her large garden in Waitara, Taranaki. She has things like artichokes, day-lily buds, daikon, loqui opo, chokos, fennel, tomatillos, okra and at least 20 different chillies including anaheim, cayenne, habanero, pasilla bajoi (so good in Mexican moles), incendiary Thai chillies and sweet, mild ancho-poblano for those summer salads. Frances also does dried spice mixes and marmalades like grapefruit and chilli, lime and mandarin, and Seville orange, lemon and ginger. She is famous for her preserves, lemon kassoundi and Kaffir lime jelly, which she concocts out the back in her professional kitchen. Need some sauce in your life? What about gumbo made from okra and tomatoes, tomatillos and coriander sauce? Or tomato oil pickle? How about feta in oil and curry leaves, coffee jam, date chutney with garlic, or blackberry vinegar? Frances can always be relied upon to do something inventive and sexy – something to give your taste-buds a rev up. Shoppers from all over New Zealand come to her little roadside store next to her house, and you can also order from her website at: www.qgardens.net.nz.

The following pickle won an award for Q Gardens at the Chilli Festival in Sydney.

one hundred & seventy-three

Green-chilli pickle

1KG LONG GREEN CHILLIES
1 TABLESPOON SALT
1 TABLESPOON TURMERIC POWDER
1 TABLESPOON BLACK MUSTARD SEEDS
1/4 CUP VINEGAR
2 TABLESPOONS CHOPPED GARLIC
2 TABLESPOONS CHOPPED GINGER
1 CUP OIL
1 TEASPOON FENUGREEK SEED
2 TEASPOONS CUMIN SEED
1 CUP CHOPPED CORIANDER OR PARSLEY

1. Wear protective gloves for this. Cut the stalks off the chillies and dice. Sprinkle with salt and turmeric and leave overnight.

2. In a blender, purée the mustard seeds, vinegar, garlic and ginger.

3. Heat the oil in a large frying pan and add the fenugreek and cumin seeds. Add the blended mixture and chilli together with the liquid that comes from them. Cook and stir occasionally until the oil rises and the chillies are cooked. Add coriander or parsley and heat thoroughly.

4. Pack into sterilised jars and seal. Refrigerate after opening.

makes about 2 cups

Q Gardens
Interesting vegetables and interesting things in o...

GHERKINS

EGG PLANT

BASIL

COURGETTES

BEANS

CHUTNEYS

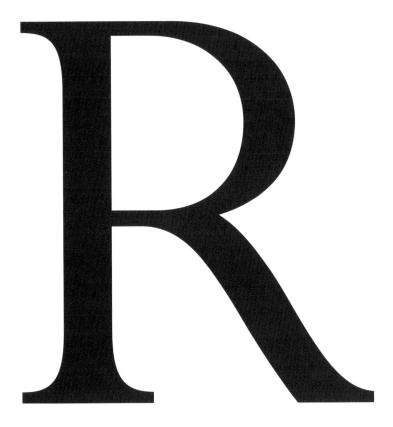

ROSES

According to Moroccan Berber women, who have the most lucid, pale skin, you should splash your face in rose water morning and night. Not only does it refresh and moisturise the skin but like lavender, is a tranquilliser and antidepressant. If you sleep with a bag of dried rosebuds under your pillow, you will have sweet dreams forever, and if you add a drop to mint tea you will never be sad. You can also add rose water to your final hair rinse to prevent hair loss. Most of the great perfumes are made of roses. Decoratively, the rose has been used in furniture design, in tapestries and other textiles such as lace, silks, wall coverings, illuminated vellums and painted fans. It is lovely seen on glass and jewellery, metalwork, carving, enamels and ceramics.

We're great rose growers in New Zealand, and lots of us make rose-petal jam. One day I got caught in a kitchen with rose aficionado Keith Stewart, who informed me that roses mean sex. Did you know that? I asked him why men, particularly, seemed to be keen rose growers.

'Female sexual organs,' said he.

'What?' said I.

'Roses resemble female sexual organs.' He said, nodding enthusiastically.

'Gosh. All those ordinary-looking, middle-aged men. I wouldn't have thought they had it in them. But I suppose it keeps them off the streets.'

'The rose is an ancient symbol of sensuality, fertility and womanhood. It stands for the universal woman who, as the great goddess, is mother of the world. Mother's Day . . .'

'Don't tell me you going to try to make dear old Mother's Day into a sex symbol?' I gasped.

'Mother's Day is a fertility rite, Peta, a celebration of fecund

Gazelles' Horns

for the almond paste:

250G BLANCHED ALMONDS

125G CASTOR SUGAR

1 SMALL EGG

1/4 TEASPOON CINNAMON

3 TABLESPOONS MELTED BUTTER
OR VEGETABLE OIL

2 TABLESPOONS ROSE WATER

1/2 TEASPOON ALMOND EXTRACT

for the pastry:

300G WHITE FLOUR

1/2 TEASPOON SALT

3 TABLESPOONS MELTED BUTTER
OR VEGETABLE OIL

90ML ROSE WATER

90ML COLD WATER

for the gazelle's horns:

FLOUR FOR ROLLING THE PASTRY

OIL IN A LITTLE BOWL FOR
ROLLING THE PASTRY

ICING SUGAR FOR DUSTING

1. To make the almond paste, place the almonds in a food processor and process until powdered. Add other ingredients and blend until it forms a sticky paste.

2. Roll heaped teaspoons of the almond paste into little sausages, fat in the middle and tapered at each end. Chill in the fridge while making the pastry.

1. To make the pastry, place all the ingredients except the oil and icing sugar in a food processor and blend until a ball forms.

2. Knead by hand or with a dough hook in the mixer for 10 minutes. The pastry will be elastic and soft.

3. Divide pastry into 4, rub in oil and leave on a plate.

to make the gazelles' horns:

This is an unusual pastry in that it has a lot of water and very little fat, so requires a particular way of rolling.

1. Sprinkle a little flour on the bench. Take some oil from the bowl with your fingers and rub on to the rolling pin.

2. Roll out one of the quarters of pastry, pushing with the rolling pin to stretch it. Sprinkle with a little flour if necessary, flip and keep rolling and stretching until the pastry is thin like cardboard.

3. Preheat the oven to 200°C and grease a baking sheet. Press rounds out with an 8cm pastry cutter. Brush the outer edges with water, place a sausage of almond paste on the top half, fold pastry over and pinch edges together with fingertips.

4. Shape the pastries into a horn or crescent with your fingers and place on the baking sheet. Prick each horn with a fork to prevent them expanding and splitting. Keep going until you have used up the rest of the pastry.

5. Bake for 10–15 minutes or until pale gold. Don't allow the pastries to brown or they will harden.

6. Dust immediately with lots of icing sugar and serve piled up on an ornate tray.

makes approximately 40 pastries

R

women. It has been held annually through 2000 years of Christianity, and as far back as Roman times or even further. They worshipped Flora, the goddess of fruit trees, vineyards and flowers. You gave women roses on this day. The original rose has five petals only, symbolising the five appendages of the body – legs, arms and head, which capture the essentials of life – sex, birth, life and death.'

'But Keith, the rose has other significance too. What about church? What about funerals?'

'Yes, of course. Eventually the rose became a religious symbol associated with the Virgin Mary, and also there were secret rose gardens in monasteries containing magical plants. The Apothecary rose had medicinal properties.'

'I'll never be able to look my neighbour in the eye again.'

'Hell, yes,' said Keith, brimming over with passion, 'there's nothing like a steamy, full frontal, powerful rose …'

'Stop! I can't bear it. I only came in here for a cup of tea.'

The Arabs invented the distilling process centuries ago and their alambic or quettara stills are basically the same as a modern still – it takes seven pounds (3 1/2 kg) of rosebuds or orange blossoms to make one gallon of fragrant water.

The ancient Persians made wine from rose petals. Rose-petal water is used to flavour cakes, pastries, desserts, meat stews, salads, ice-creams and sorbets. A spray of it will make a busload of hot tourists smell wonderful and it is widely used in beauty preparations. All roses are edible. You can add rosewater to poached apples, sprinkle it over grated apples and add a dash to a cherry clafoutis. Eating rose-flavoured sweets like Turkish delight and rosewater and cardamon ice-cream is like eating summer, romance and longing, somehow. Dried roses are part of the aromatic spice mixture called *ras-al-hanout*, used in tagines, meatballs and couscous. Rather than being overwhelmed by the powerful spices like turmeric, nutmeg, paprika and cumin in this mixture, the roses add a musky, haunting flavour.

In North Africa, where they eat with their hands, a jug of rose or orange blossom-scented water is poured over the hands before and after the meal. Quite often the first thing served at a meal is a glass of cool, rose-perfumed almond milk. Scatter crimson rose petals over the dinner table, in fountains and down the driveway so that when the person of your dreams comes home, they will have soft petals underfoot.

SAFFRON

The word saffron comes from the Arabic *zahafarn*, meaning yellow thread. Saffron comes from the stigmas of the mauve flowers of the *Crocus sativus* and can be used in both savoury and sweet cooking. The harvest finishes late in April and collecting the crocuses is a romantic or back-breaking task depending on how you look at it for the little, ground level, purple flowers have to be picked at dawn, leaving the field bare. As if by magic, when you get up the next morning at dawn, the field is purple again and you start all over. Then you have to pick the orange stigmas out of the crocuses one by one and dry them. When cooking with saffron, you have to make sure it's the real thing. The safest way of knowing is to buy it in thread form, not powder. It's the most expensive spice in the world, because 70,000 stigmas are needed to produce 500g of saffron. But it goes a long way and has the most exotic, earthy, musky smell. The taste can border on bitter if you use too much. Its glorious reddish orange colour is considered to be holy in Tibet. It not only dyes food, but is also used to dye cloth in Asia, and will dye you and your clothes if you get it on yourself.

People who grow saffron are romantic lovers of nutty food, like the olive growers and, to a certain extent, grape growers. They love doing it, but the global economic reality is that it can only ever be a luxury product. The saffron yields from established crops at Clyde are estimated to reach 24.3kg per hectare, up to twice that obtained in traditional saffron-producing countries, but high labour costs in New Zealand appear to limit the opportunities for competitive production.

New Zealand saffron is of exceptionally high quality and is the most beautiful I have ever seen – long, plump strings of red-gold perfume. The more intense the colour of saffron,

Roasted pork hock with preserved lemons & saffron

for the pork:

3 GENEROUS PINCHES SAFFRON

1 PRESERVED LEMON

MURRELLEN PORK HOCK

1/2 TEASPOON SEA SALT

FRESHLY GROUND BLACK PEPPER

2 TEASPOONS FRESH CHOPPED GINGER

1 CINNAMON STICK

4 CLOVES GARLIC, SMASHED

1/2 CUP DRY WHITE WINE

1 1/2 CUPS CHICKEN STOCK

2 TABLESPOONS MANUKA HONEY

for the vegetables:

SMALL TOMATOES ON THE VINE

LEMON-INFUSED OLIVE OIL

SEA SALT AND FRESHLY GROUND BLACK PEPPER

300G COOKED HARICOT BEANS

2 CLOVES GARLIC, CHOPPED

1/2 RED ONION, CHOPPED

2 TABLESPOONS FRESH CORIANDER, CHOPPED

2 TABLESPOONS LEMON OIL

1. Prepare the saffron by soaking the stamens in 2 tablespoons of hot water for 30 minutes.

2. Remove the flesh from the preserved lemon and discard it, rinse the peel and cut it into thick strips.

3. Preheat the oven to the highest it will go. Rub oil and salt into the skin of the hock and place in an oven-proof dish. Around the meat put the salt, pepper, ginger, cinnamon stick, garlic, saffron with its juice, preserved lemon strips, wine and stock.

4. Roast the hock for 15 minutes on high or even under the grill to harden the crackle, then lower the temperature to 170°C. Pour honey over the pork and cook for a further 1 hour and 45 minutes.

5. Meanwhile prepare the vegetables – roasted vine tomatoes and white bean salad.

1. To roast the tomatoes, preheat the oven to 220°C. Place the vines of tomatoes on a baking sheet, brush with lemon oil and sprinkle with salt and pepper. Roast for about 15 minutes. Turn the oven off and leave them there until you are ready for serving.

2. To make the white bean salad, gently toss the beans with the other ingredients.

serves 4

the more intense the aroma and flavour of this exotic spice.

One of the first people to grow saffron commercially in New Zealand was Errol Hitt of Eight Moon Saffron in Rangiora, North Canterbury. He started in 1994, and since then others have followed, notably TerrazaSaffron in Hawke's Bay, Gourmet Gold in Marlborough and Premium NZ Saffron in Rangiora, who grow it organically. Errol and Rosemary Hitt have thirty 40 metre long beds with four rows of crocuses in every bed. The Hitts also run deer and keep bees, which is typical of saffron growers all over the world – you would never try to make a living from saffron alone. Errol reckons Canterbury is the perfect place to grow saffron, as it is exact antipodes of one of the biggest saffron-growing countries in the world, Spain. 'If you draw a line straight through the earth, bar a few Chinamen, you'd hit a Spaniard.' Eight Moon Saffron is of extremely high quality – it is deep orange-red and has a beautiful pungent aroma. You can buy it at delicatessens and direct from Errol.

Wonderfully, there is even a saffron association, a festival and a saffron queen. It happens in Hawke's Bay and is run by Rochelle and Ian Schofield of TerrazaSaffron. There are about 40 members of the association, mostly from Hawke's Bay but some also from the South Island.

The Schofields began growing saffron in 1994 and for those first years, despite many requests to do so, they made a conscious choice not to sell saffron corms until they had built up their own stock to a viable level. Their original corms were from the Crop & Food Site at Redbank Central Otago – now Sam Neil's vineyard. Rochelle says:

'Four years ago we realised the true potential for the industry was for Hawke's Bay to become a significant producer of quality saffron. Our soil and climate offered the perfect conditions for growing world-class quality saffron. At that time we were receiving enquiries for quantities of 50–100kg from Italy when our production was a mere 5–6kg per harvest. The most practical solution seemed to be to see if there were reasonable numbers of others prepared to become growers. Initially we sold a small number of corms to four or five locals. In early 2003 together with those locals we held a field day to test the water. One hundred and twenty people registered (we had thought we would be lucky to attract 20 or 30). Dreams turned into reality when we staged the first saffron conference, which aimed to provide information and assistance to established, new and potential growers.'

The aims of the association are simple: to provide a forum to

share knowledge, ideas and concepts related to saffron; to promote Hawke's Bay saffron nationally and internationally; to foster the highest standards and to develop and maintain a reputation for quality saffron; and to encourage camaraderie among growers. In her opening speech at the saffron conference Rochelle said that living with saffron was like living with a demanding, seductive mistress. 'At times you curse her but you can't leave her, for she has no substitute.' Just one day is envisaged as an initial event, staged for growers, chefs and foodies who have assisted or been involved on some level. The harvest festival is centred around a daytime meal with a saffron theme. There is a saffron queen, a few saffron challenges and plenty of good humour and anticipation. Rochelle says, 'Funny how in our complex and technological world something as simple as the celebration of a harvest appeals to so many. It's great!'

SALMON
Akaroa Salmon in Akaroa Harbour near Christchurch is my favourite farmed salmon in New Zealand, and it has been around for a while. Father and son team Tom and Duncan Bates started the business 20 years ago and now produce about 150 tonnes a year. It is currently the only sea water salmon farm that is 100 per cent New Zealand-owned and is still a family business. Tom and Duncan are salt of the earth, wonderful people with a lot of integrity – grafters – not

Salmon poached in olive oil & vanilla

1 LITRE EXTRA VIRGIN OLIVE OIL

1/2 VANILLA POD, SPLIT OPEN

GOOD SPRIG OF FRESH TARRAGON

4 PEELED SHALLOTS

600G CARROTS, PEELED
AND CHOPPED

SEA SALT AND FRESHLY GROUND
BLACK PEPPER

PINCH FRESHLY GRATED NUTMEG

1 TABLESPOON FRESH
TARRAGON LEAVES

1 TEASPOON EXTRA VIRGIN
OLIVE OIL

SPLASH OF MILK

16 SHALLOTS, PEELED

400G BABY PEAS

BUTTER

4 X 200G SALMON FILETS

LEMON OIL FOR DRIZZLING

TARRAGON LEAVES FOR GARNISH

1. The day before you wish to cook this dish, heat the litre of olive oil, vanilla, tarragon and 4 peeled shallots to tepid in a braising pan. Turn the heat off, cover and leave to marinate overnight.

2. Boil the carrots in salted water until very soft. Drain and purée in the food processor with salt, pepper, nutmeg, tarragon leaves, teaspoon of olive oil and milk. Keep warm.

3. Sauté the 16 shallots in a little olive oil until just soft. Keep warm.

4. Boil the peas in salted water for five minutes. Drain, toss in a little butter and keep warm.

5. Dry the salmon on paper towels and gently place it in the oil marinade. If the oil doesn't cover it, add some more. Using a frying thermometer, bring the temperature up to 100°C (no more but it can be less) and poach for 15 minutes.

6. Remove fish with a slotted spoon and drain on a cake rack over paper towels. This prevents the oil from soaking back into the fish.

7. To serve, make a circle of peas around the edge of the plate. In the middle place a hillock of puréed carrot and lay the fish on top. Arrange the shallots around and give the lot a few good twists of the pepper mill. With your thumb half over the bottle neck, drizzle the dish lightly with lemon oil. Garnish with a sprig of tarragon.

serves 4

Note: The marinade that the salmon is cooked in can be used again to cook the fish. Strain the marinade through a coffee filter, add a slice of lemon rind and store, covered, in a dark place.

growing the most but the best. Their salmon is a gourmet, glamorous product, and once you start eating their cold-smoked salmon, you can't stop. It's really good with fresh dill or mint, sour cream, freshly ground black pepper and lime juice, and a glass of chardonnay. The Bates have a really sophisticated sales pitch. It goes like this: they walk into a restaurant with a fresh salmon, put it on the counter and say, 'This is what I grow, it's the best, I'm really proud of it and I want you to eat it.'

They do fresh salmon, and also hot- and cold-smoked Chinook salmon. And when I say fresh I mean six to 24 hours from ocean to plate, harvested five times a week. The fish are gutted and processed within two hours of being killed; a bigger operation just can't do that. For salmon to taste good it has to come from very cold water, and have lots of room to move and develop muscle. The clean, unpolluted water of Akaroa harbour provides an excellent environment – the ideal water temperature and good current flows ensure maximum oxygen levels at all times. In terms of taste, texture and consistency, sea-reared salmon is superior to its freshwater cousins. It is less fatty and firmer, with a gorgeous red colour. Recently there have been concerns about farmed salmon not being healthy; but at Akaroa the fish are in great condition, thanks to being hand-fed in closely monitored, low-stocked cages. No antibiotics are used. The farm is right in the middle of a wild salmon run so there are lots of feral salmon swimming outside the pens. And if they like the area, Tom figures, his will too. The top chefs in New Zealand rave about this wild salmon, comparing it to Scottish and Alaskan salmon.

Salmon is one of nature's healthiest foods, packed with Omega 3, calcium, potassium and essential vitamins, and you should eat it at least once a week. Scientists credit the Omega 3 unsaturated oil with the ability to lower cholesterol levels and reduce the risk of cardiac arrest.

Akaroa Salmon is a niche producer at the top end of the market. Their salmon is not available in supermarkets, but they will courier it to any destination in the country, however professional or private. In June 2002, Akaroa Salmon moved into their new purpose-built factory in Riccarton, Christchurch, where they have a factory shop. You can also find Akaroa Salmon at certain top-end delicatessens and good food shops like Sabato in Auckland. Their website is: www.akaroasalmon.co.nz.

SALT

The human body needs salt (sodium chloride) to help digest foods and turn them into living tissues, as well as to help transmit the nerve impulses that contract the muscles. Our bodies contain almost 450g of salt and, to maintain normal health and vigour, each day we need to replenish the salt used by the body. Where do we get our table salt from in New Zealand? Marlborough has everything necessary to extract salt from sea water – lots of sunshine, lots of wind, lots of land, lots of sea and not much rain. Almost every grain of salt in New Zealand – 65,000 tonnes of it – starts at Dominion Solar Salt Works at Grassmere in Marlborough. It's a fascinating place to visit. Everything at the site is bleached out – there are huge salt mountains and dry wastelands of pink, blue, turquoise and white ponds as far as the eye can see. Even the huge machinery is eerily bleached, and by the end of a visit you have the taste of salt in your throat just from breathing. Sea water is pumped through more than a dozen lakes that slowly evaporate the water. Three years after entering the first lake the sea water ends up at the colourful crystallising ponds (the colour is caused by micro-organisms that produce different colours at different levels of salinity), where it is ten times more concentrated than when it started out. The water is so saturated with salt, that the salt simply drops to form a bed at the bottom of the pond, and you just have to drain the pond and harvest your salt. On a hot day 40 tonnes of sea water are pumped into the lakes every minute, and that doesn't even equal the amount of water lost to evaporation in that very same minute. So you've got all these salt lakes and salt mountains, but what if it rains? It's like adding water to whisky. Why would you when it takes them ten years to get the water out? The answer is that rain is lighter than brine, so it stays on the top and is decantered off.

We're all in love with designer sea-salt crystals like Maldon, which make you think you're eating fairy food. The pretty flakes cling to food better than standard salt because of their larger surface area, so you get this delicious crunchiness. Why eat the flakes instead of prosaic old iodised table salt? Common table salt is boiled to remove impurities, has things added to it to make it pour, has more than 99 per cent sodium chloride and has added iodine, which our betters have convinced us we need for healthy bodies. Flaky sea salt is simply evaporated sea water and retains the natural minerals and trace elements our bodies need. Strangely enough, flaky sea salt tastes less salty and has a softer, more rounded, non-chemical flavour, which is due to the fact that it is only about 83 per cent sodium chloride. Good sea salt takes on the flavour of food, never overpowering it and always enhancing it.

In answer to the world's fashionable salt flakes, Dominion

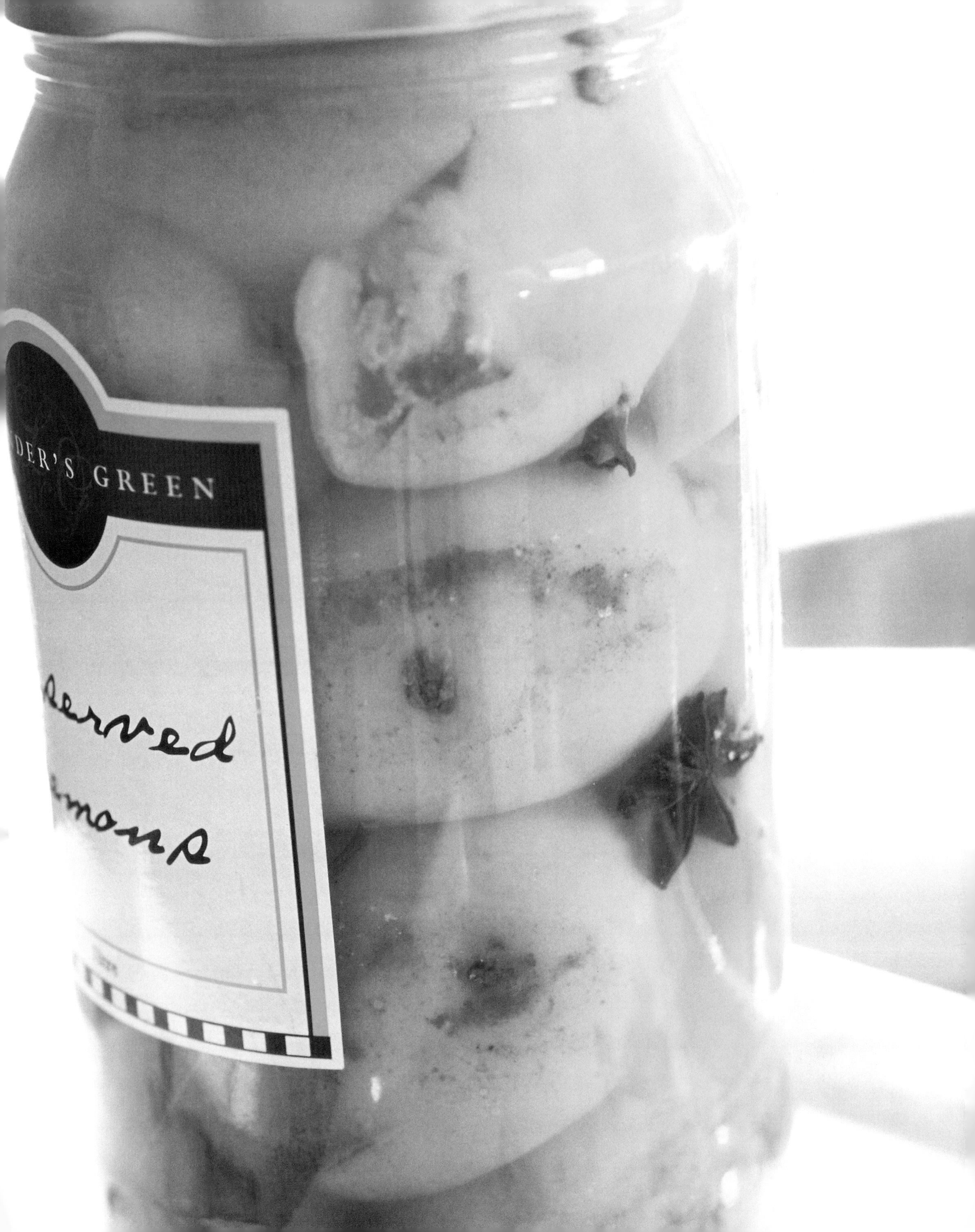
DER'S GREEN

Salt came up with their own method of creating them and their product is called Marlborough Flaky Sea Salt. The technique is desperately secret, but I have been into the room where it is made. Of course I will die if I tell, so I'll just say it is a marvellous sight seeing the warm crystals rolling out of the machine like snow flakes. Basically, after harvest, the brine is slowly heated to the point where delicate pyramid-shaped crystals of salt appear. These are initially allowed to drip dry and finally they are dried using warm air at low temperatures prior to packaging. The finished product is light, flaky, pyramid-shaped sea-salt crystals.

However, because the evaporation takes place in an open pan it does not produce crystals of uniform size. As there is no further processing carried out after drying, the resulting product will contain salt crystals varying in size and shape. This adds to the feel and taste sensations of the salt. The minerals have not been washed out and you can see by its creamy crystals that it doesn't have anything added to it. Marlborough Flaky Sea Salt has BioGro certification but doesn't claim to be strictly organic, as it is a mineral. The processing is organic though, which means they have an organic quality system and treat the product in all respects as though it is organic. There are also monitoring systems set up to analyse the incoming sea water on a regular basis. In a blind tasting of international flaky sea salts carried out by *Cuisine* magazine, Marlborough Flaky Salt came out on top in terms of taste and texture. You can buy it everywhere in its pretty blue and white packets.

SAUSAGES
New Zealand is a nation of sausage lovers, with 31.5 per cent of us indulging at least once a week. Aucklanders alone eat an estimated 50.8 million sausages a year, but according to our very own sausage expert Glynn Christian, South Islanders make the best ones. We even have a Great New Zealand Sausage Competition organised by Retail Meat. We cook and eat bangers on golden beaches and in sunny backyards. In my opinion, sausages should be coarsely (not finely) minced, should contain a bit of fat, some onions or shallots, maybe some spices and herbs, and they should have crispy skins made from gut. They should have no preservatives, additives or breadcrumbs (or not too many) and they can be made from anything you like – chicken, seafood, vegetables, offal, pork, beef, lamb or venison. There are many good sausage-makers in New Zealand, some of them making organic sausages. Or you can make your own. If you can't be

Salt-preserved lemons

Preserved lemons are now as fashionable as sun-dried tomatoes were and just as delicious. Here's how you find them in your cupboard.

2KG THICK-SKINNED LEMONS
300G SALT
1 BAY LEAF
A STICK OF CINNAMON
3 CLOVES
6 BLACK PEPPERCORNS
FRESH LEMON JUICE

1. Scrub the lemons with a hard brush.

2. With a sharp knife, cut each lemon lengthwise, stopping 1.5cm before the end to keep the halves attached. Cut each one lengthwise again, as if you are cutting them into quarters, again stopping 1.5cm before the bottom so that the quarters are still attached.

3. Sterilise the jars in boiling water or in the oven for 10 minutes.

4. Hold the lemons open by squeezing gently and stuff both ends with salt. Close them with your hand and pack them in the jars, squeezing them in and poking in the spices as you go.

5. When the jars are full, press the lemons down well and sprinkle with a tablespoon of salt. Fill the jar right to the top with lemon juice. Leave some air space before sealing the jars.

6. Leave the jars of lemons in a cool place to steep for at least a month. Don't mind if a white film forms on top – it's natural and is easily washed off. The lemons will release their juice, which mingles with the salt, producing a honey-thick, unctuous syrup. Don't discard it – use it in salad dressings and to flavour tagines and other stews.

7. To use a preserved lemon, remove it from the jar, rinse well in running water, ease the pulp out with your thumb and discard it. Cut the peel into thick strips and use with fish, chicken, duck or lamb. It can also be added to salads or relishes. The jar of lemons must be refrigerated once opened.

enough for 2 x 1-litre preserving jars

White bean & sausage stew

300G DRIED WHITE HARICOT BEANS
1 SAVOY CABBAGE
1KG PICKLED PORK
2 CARROTS, PEELED AND QUARTERED
2 SWEDES, PEELED AND QUARTERED
1 ONION STUDDED WITH FOUR CLOVES
4 CLOVES GARLIC
SEA SALT AND FRESHLY GROUND BLACK PEPPER
BOUQUET GARNI *(bay leaf, thyme, parsley)*
500G SPICY SAUSAGES
500G WAXY POTATOES LIKE DESIRÉE, PEELED
AND QUARTERED
DIJON MUSTARD TO SERVE

1. Soak the beans overnight and drain.

2. Remove the outer leaves of the cabbage and quarter. Put the cabbage quarters into salted boiling water for 10 minutes. Drain, run under cold water and core. Set aside.

3. In a large, heavy-based saucepan put the beans, pork, carrots, swedes, onion, garlic, salt, pepper and bouquet garni. Cover with water, bring to the boil and simmer for 1½ hours.

4. Add the sausages, cabbage and potatoes. Return to the boil, then lower to a simmer for 30 minutes. Taste the broth for seasoning.

5. To serve, remove the meat from the pot and drain the vegetables, discarding the bouquet garni and reserving the broth. Reduce the broth by boiling if you think it needs more flavour. Cut up the pork and sausages. You can then either eat the broth, vegetables and meat together in a large, shallow soup bowl, or eat the broth first, then serve the meat and vegetables as a second course. You should eat this *potée* or stew with lots of Dijon mustard.

serves 6

bothered fussing with gut and a stuffing machine, just shape them and roll them in breadcrumbs.

Glynn's favourite sausage of the snarler type is the long, peppery Cumberland sausage – usually curled and baked, and served with mashed potatoes and gravy. Otherwise it is the slightly pink, roughly textured, Italian pork and fennel. The pink colour comes from the addition of nitrite, which makes them much safer to eat, as well as being nicer to look at. A combination of these two types of sausage – or more – on a large platter in the middle of the table is the best thing to happen to any group of people. My personal favourite is also the Italian-style fennel and pork sausages and Salumeria Fontana in Henderson make a delectable *cotechino*. *Cotechino* is made from pork and pork rind, giving it a gelatinous texture. It is flavoured with cloves and cinnamon and needs to be simmered for at least two hours but it is absolutely worth the trouble.

Jeremy Schmid of Little Boys Sausages won the supreme award at the 2004 Great New Zealand Sausage Competition for a duck and porcini sausage. Although I like coarse but tender snarlers, Jeremy's duck and porcini was very finely ground and emulsified with red wine. I found it very good. This guy is a pro. He was an outstanding cooking student at Auckland Unitech, worked in Switzerland, won awards at top Auckland restaurants, won a scholarship to the Culinary Institute of America in Napa Valley to study charcuterie and co-owned Palazzo Roma in Drury. He's a guy to watch, as I'm 100 per cent sure he ain't finished tickling our taste-buds yet. Jeremy also makes inspired snarlers like venison, juniper and garlic; chicken, fennel and apple; beef, paprika and caramelised onion; and *merguez* (spicy lamb).

THESE ARE THE BEST SAUSAGE-MAKERS I KNOW:
- Swiss Deli in East Tamaki, specialising in European-style sausages like krakauer, kabbanos and weisswurst
- Salumeria Fontana in Henderson, specialising in Italian style sausages like cotechino, fennel and pork, and luganega di monza (coarse-cut pork with wine, pepper and garlic)
- Globus Hungarian Smallgoods in Manurewa, specialising in salami, black pudding, debrechni (hot-smoked pork sausage with Hungarian paprika) and Hunter's sausage (hot-smoked veal and venison)
- Little Boys in Te Aroha
- Blackforest Gourmet Butchery in Tauranga, specialising in German-style sausages like veal bratwurst, smoked kranksy and a coiled pork bratwurst

Stuffed peppers with grilled chorizo & salmrejo sauce

for the peppers:

220G TIN GOOD-QUALITY TUNA IN OIL

1 SMALL TIN ANCHOVY-STUFFED GREEN OLIVES, CHOPPED

1 HARD-BOILED EGG, CHOPPED

SEA SALT

1 JAR NAVARRICO PIQUILLO PEPPERS

1. Loosely mix the tuna and its oil, olives, egg and salt together with a fork. Gently stuff it into the peppers.

Salmorejo sauce:

1 CUP CUBED WHITE BREAD, CRUSTS REMOVED

500G SWEET, RIPE TOMATOES, SKINNED, DESEEDED AND CHOPPED

1 CLOVE GARLIC

$1/2$ TEASPOON SEA SALT

$1/2$ TEASPOON SWEET NEW ZEALAND ORCONA SMOKED PAPRIKA

$1/4$ CUP EXTRA VIRGIN OLIVE OIL

2 TABLESPOONS PRENZEL SAUVIGNON BLANC VINEGAR

1. Soak the bread in water and squeeze dry. Place the chopped tomatoes, garlic, salt and paprika in a food processor and purée.

2. With the motor running, gradually add the bread, then drizzle in the olive oil and finally the vinegar. Serve chilled or at room temperature.

for the chorizo:

3 CHORIZO SAUSAGES, SLICED INTO THICK ROUNDS

1. Thread the chorizo slices on to skewers and grill for about 10 minutes.

to serve:

1. Place a stuffed pepper on a plate and arrange the chorizo on one side and the sauce on the other.

serves 6

- Blackball Salami Co. on the West Coast specialising in low-fat salami, black pudding and Continental-style sausages

SALAMI

Sheila and Alan Climpson, sterling people from Kent with backgrounds in farming and food technology, make the best salami I have tasted in New Zealand. A salami has to have a minimum of ten per cent fat in it – it is by its nature a dry product so it needs fat for taste and moisture. The Climpsons not only make their five kinds of salami (with 20 per cent pork fat) on the property, but the meat comes from their own organic Sussex cattle. Once made, the salami are fermented, dried and wood-smoked with manuka, then hung for two months to cure properly. The 'factory' is in a series of small sheds in the lee of a huge layered mound of rock, with a karaka tree shading the cool store and the sound of water trickling down the rock face.

  The family business was started by Alan and Sheila on the farm at Clifton in Golden Bay, at the top of the South Island. Golden Bay has many attractions, stunning scenery, and a reputation for the arts and crafts and fine hospitality. Initially, while the couple were perfecting recipes and the technique of curing the salami, it was produced only for family and friends. The product became popular, with a demand for 'the healthy salami' from people who wanted to avoid nitrites, artificial preservatives and colourings. In 1998 the Climpsons started with a small processing plant on the farm, selling the salami from their pottery showroom. The demand for it keeps growing and they are expanding their production capacity. In 2002 Sheila and Alan's son Robert and his wife BJ joined the business. These two have a farm at Dovedale which produces most of the beef for the salami and they are now involved in the production. Golden Salami is sold all over New Zealand in high-end delicatessens. You can find out where by visiting their website: www.goldensalami.co.nz.

SCALLOPS

When I first saw queen-scallop shells in a basket in Dunedin, I thought they had been painted, but no, the bright orange, pink, yellow and white shells are as nature intended them. Queen scallops are unique to the deep, cold, brilliantly clear waters about 16km beyond Dunedin's harbour mouth. They are small – about the size of a little clam – with both shells curved. They are difficult to catch because they can avoid trawling nets, swimming quickly by

Queen scallops with cream & whisky

1 LARGE HANDFUL PER PERSON OF SCALLOPS IN THEIR SHELLS, CLEANED
LOTS OF CHOPPED GARLIC
BUNCH OF FRESH DILL, CHOPPED
CREAM
SEA SALT AND FRESHLY GROUND BLACK PEPPER
WHISKY

1. Heat a deep, heavy-based pan over a high heat then put in scallops. Cover and cook on a high heat until they are just open, shaking occasionally.

2. Remove the lid and add the garlic, dill, cream, salt and pepper. Toss for a minute to heat the sauce, then throw in a good tipple of whisky, tipping the pan a little to ensure a very hot surface for the whisky to catch flame.

3. When the flame has subsided, eat the scallops with some steamed Jersey Benney potatoes.

Note: When cooking this meal always invite a blue-eyed fisherman around to share it, otherwise it will stick in your throat and taste salty from your lonely tears.

clapping their shells together and jetting along with the force of the expelled water. It was a cold day in Dunedin when I cooked my first queen scallops but the fisherman who caught them only started to feel the chill when icicles began forming on his Speights. Queen scallops are sweet and tender but really need to be cooked fresh; the frozen ones are less successful.

SCONES

Scones come from Scotland, the name being derived from the word 'sconbrot' meaning fine white bread, but they mostly became popular in England and thence New Zealand. A scone must have baking powder, a flour such as barley, oat or wheat, and some sour liquid like buttermilk, yoghurt or sour milk. They must be made quickly, cooked fast on a high heat and eaten warm immediately with butter. Irish bannock and soda bread and Yorkshire fat rascal bread are very similar, and in the old days all these soda breads were cooked on a griddle over the fire. In 1879, a New Zealand shopkeeper called Thomas Edmonds started making his own baking powder. His catch phrase was that your scones were 'sure to rise' if you used his powder made from cream of tartar, soda and flour. The Edmonds products are now produced by Bluebird Foods, are still selling like mad, and the *Edmonds Cookbook* is the best-selling cookbook in New Zealand.

Scones are normally eaten for morning or afternoon tea and can be sweet or savoury, or even made with mashed potato. When I was a child my father used to leave Mass early to rush home and whip up a batch of scones so they would be just coming out of the oven as we came down the driveway. By the time we got into the kitchen they would be wrapped up in a tea-towel, smelling like the faith, hope and charity we still had in our hearts from Mass. They sometimes had dates or cheese in them and were eaten with thick slabs of butter. At afternoon tea, scones are commonly seen wearing jam and whipped cream, and they will be hanging out at A&P shows, your nana's parlour and bridge games.

SEAWEED

VALERE SEAWEED

It's hard not to notice that there's lots of seaweed in New Zealand. Roger and Nicki Beattie own and manage paua quota, farm paua and pearls, manufacture marine farming technology and provide fisheries consultancy services. Nicki is a doctor and she had the brainwave to turning some of their seaweed into a treat not only for paua, but also – because it is so good for us – for the other small beings in her life, her children. Seaweed is rich in iodine and has a powerful effect on the thyroid gland, on the metabolism in general, and in the mobilisation of fats in particular. It can act as a diuretic and help reduce fluid retention. The stuff that was clogging up their paua lines has now become the entirely delicious kelp pepper, which they process and call Valere which is Latin for good health.

The current seaweed harvest in New Zealand is 16 tonnes dry weight and is used for the manufacture of kelp powder and kelp salt for the health-food market. It is

Basic scone recipe

This scone recipe is very simple and shouldn't be mucked around with. The flour must be sifted as lightness is everything. The amount of butter is small and is rubbed or cut in with two knives. The sour milk is mixed in with knives or hands. The finished dough is wet, and the cut dough must be at least 3cm thick. Don't put the scones in the oven until you hear visitors coming down the driveway. Like cheese-making, if you can make a good scone, it means you are a real woman or man.

2 CUPS FLOUR
2 HEAPED TEASPOONS BAKING POWDER
1/4 TEASPOON SALT
2 TABLESPOONS BUTTER
1 CUP BUTTERMILK

1. Preheat the oven to 220ºC and grease a baking tray, or use a non-stick baking sheet.

2. Sift the dry ingredients into a bowl.

3. Rub or cut in the butter, then mix in the buttermilk with your hands or a knife.

4. Turn the wet dough out on to the bench and knead lightly for a few seconds. Press or roll out to 3cm thick, then cut into squares about 5 x 5cm.

5. Whip them into the hot oven for 10 minutes.

also used as fertiliser and a food stabiliser, thickener and emulsifier. The kelp the Beatties use is called *Macrocystis pyrifera* or butterfish kelp and it is the fastest-growing kelp in the world; it grows half a metre a day and can reach 35 metres in only three months. It grows in 'forests' from Stewart Island up to the Wairarapa, off the north Otago coast, and in Foveaux Strait and around the sub-Antarctic islands. The mature blades have a corrugated surface, are golden-brown in colour and have a pliable texture. Historically, seaweeds have been harvested commercially in New Zealand since the 1940s, but there is a much longer history of traditional use by Maori.

Valere seaweed is grown on lines in Wainui Bay in the Akaroa harbour, and the Beatties handpick it for the best-looking product. It is transported in special bins, then slowly air-dried on racks at a temperature below 30°C over a few days. It is then put in sealed bins, milled to three different grades and bottled into 25g shakers or refill packs. It is brown when harvested, but turns green as it dries. They call it kelp pepper, but it tastes salty and zingy and … well … seaweedy. It's very good with meat, egg, fish, shellfish and as a dip with Canterbury olive oil.

PACIFIC HARVEST

Finally, New Zealanders are starting to eat the delicious seaweed called karengo that has been all around us forever. The Maori have always used karengo, which is like Japanese nori. They throw it in the hangi, steam it like any other green vegetable and sauté it with butter. Pacific Harvest in Auckland processes seaweed so you and I can have it in our salad. Doug and Louise Fawcett gather seaweed in Kaikoura over the winter months. The lettuce-like fronds are pulled off the rocks at low tide, washed in the sea and sun-dried. They are then sent up to the factory in Auckland, where they are processed for selling. The fronds are passed through a mill to remove impurities and break them up, then they are separated into soft flakes and little fronds for packaging. Karengo is softer and milder than kelp, so it can be used for different purposes. Seaweed is terrifically good for you. It is loaded with amino acids, minerals and vitamins, and I find it really moreish with that slight saltiness and clean taste of the sea. I like sprinkling it on food, and the Fawcetts recommend using it as a garnish in salads and soups. It is obviously fab with fish and seafood and is good to use as part of a smoking mix.

The Fawcetts also produce exotic delicacies like smoked kelp, flavoured kelps, flavoured salt crystals and agar gelatine. You can buy their products at health-food shops and delicatessens, and you can find them in restaurants all over the North Island. If you go to their website: www.pacificharvest.co.nz, you can access lots of groovy ways to cook with seaweed.

SLOW FOOD
Slow Food followers love a bit of dirt with their veg and plenty of bacteria in their cheese. They adore calories. But there is one thing the Slow Food movement won't tolerate and that is being rushed. I discovered Slow Food when I was in Dublin in 1999, eating duck liver parfait and black pudding in a small restaurant. When I read the brochure it immediately struck a deep chord in my breast. I thought, what a good idea, what an obvious idea, what intelligent and whimsical people the Italians are!

Slow Food was started in Italy in 1986 by journalist Carlo Petrini who was so incensed that a foul McDonalds had opened up on the beautiful Spanish Steps in Rome that he put his foot down and said, 'Right, that's it, I will be provoked no longer.' He saw the prospect of the golden arches upstaging the splendour of the Spanish Steps as a perfect metaphor for everything that was wrong with modern eating – the triumph of efficiency over taste, standardisation over diversity and acceleration over appreciation.

Thus Slow Food was born – a non-profit organisation that champions traditional artisan methods of producing good food and the simple slow pleasure of eating it. Good food and the preparation of it with love is a perishable art to be protected at all costs. There are 700 Slow Food convivia in over 50 countries rediscovering the flavours and savours of regional cooking and banishing the degrading effects of fast food. This is called ecogastronomy – linking ethics with pleasure. I am a member and international judge of Slow Food, so I know intimately what goes on at Slow Food dos. We organise evenings or outings around a theme – for example, a Vietnamese night where we eat Vietnamese food, have guest speakers, drink good wine, laugh our heads off and stay up too late. Or it might be a visit to an olive grove, where all the workings are explained, oil is tasted with beautiful food, and we sit quietly and slow down.

Slow Food have a cultural agenda and a passionate manifesto promoting a philosophy of pleasure, safeguarding our food and wine heritage and educating young people into a proper relationship with food. They have taken as their symbol the wise slowness of the snail, because they believe we have been enslaved by speed and a fast life and the only way to oppose this folly of mistaking frenzy for activity is to eat flavourful food. They also have a scientific research and documentation project called the Ark of Taste, aimed at safeguarding and benefiting small-scale agricultural and food production. Thousands of different kinds of charcuterie, cheeses, animal breeds and plants are in danger of disappearing forever. The ironing out of tastes, the excessive power of industrial companies, distribution difficulties and misinformation are the causes of a process that could lead to the loss of an irreplaceable heritage of traditional recipes, knowledge and tastes. And they put their money where their mouths are – for example, by giving monetary prizes to winners of the Slow Food Awards, repairing a vineyard's dry stone walls, building a local abattoir, or bringing a struggling cheese-maker to everyone's notice, thus saving his business. This is called the defence of biodiversity.

Slow Food is about taste – not globalised taste where every hamburger tastes exactly the same in every country, but the real taste of real food, which is different from every soil in which it is grown. They organise huge food events, most notably the Salone del Gusto (gastronomic fair) in Turin, Slow Cheese in Bra, Italy, Slow Fish in Genoa, Westward Slow in Denver, Aux Origines du Gout (the origins of taste) in Montpellier, France and the German Cheese market in Neiheim. There is a classy Slow Food magazine, *Slow*, written in six languages and published four times a year. The standard of writing is very high, it is printed on recycled paper and is full of exciting stories with titles like 'From Socialism to the EU', 'Defending Raw Milk Cheese', 'Food for Men' and 'US Women, Fat and Sex'. I look forward to every issue with baited breath and beating heart. They also occasionally put out issues of *SloWine* magazine, all about wine, spirits and beer, vineyards, artisan workshops, people, history and culture.

The most recent and most fabulous project of all has been the opening of a Slow Food University of Gastronomic Sciences, housed at two sites – Pollenzo near the headquarters in Bra and Colorno near Bologna in Parma, both in Northern Italy. Pollenzo is housed in a neo-Gothic complex built in 1833 and contains not only the university but also a hotel, a restaurant and a wine bank. It is set in large grounds surrounded by cultivated fields and woods. I have toured the university and stayed in the hotel – the rooms are charming and the breakfasts to die for, with cheeses, mostardos, quince paste, artisan jams and thick yoghurt. Colorno is housed in the stunning 18th-century Ducal Palace with period gardens. The aim is to create an international research and training centre, working to renew farming methods, protect biodiversity and maintain an organic relationship between gastronomy and agricultural science. Go and look at the website right now: www.unisg.it.

TO FIND OUT MORE ABOUT A SLOW FOOD CONVIVIUM IN YOUR AREA:

- For Auckland, go to: www.aldente.co.nz for Slow Food events, or email Raffaela and Paolo Delmonte at: slowfood@ihug.co.nz.
- For Manawatu, email Barry Pemberton at: yerpapem@infogen.net.nz.
- For Otaki, email Jean Harton at: slowfoodkapiti@xtra.co.nz.
- For Wellington, email Richard Klein at: slowinfo@mariapias.com.
- For Christchurch, email Bill Bryce at: bilbo@clear.net.nz.

At the writing of this book Slow Foodies all over the world were meeting for apple day to celebrate apples and orchards and their place in our landscape and lives. How wonderful is that? But wait – there's more! There is a global movement afoot called Slow Activism, which wants to slow the world down. Life is so fast, we work so much and things are changing so quickly that we are suffering stress and depression as a result – so much so that doctors are increasingly prescribing a holiday rather than medication. To be overworked is admirable; to be a happy slacker is derided. We have lost the balance of work, family and activity, in other words, a quality of life. Here's how to get started in your new sane, slow, idler's life: drink tea instead of coffee, get up late instead of early, meditate, eat long lunches, throw away the television and talk to your family, become a writer instead of a chef (much easier), go for long walks and have long conversations with strangers that are leading absolutely nowhere. It is now official – laziness is the ticket to old age. Scientists in Germany have found that too much exercise is bad for you and that doing less could lengthen your life. I knew that.

INTERESTING READING MATERIAL:

- In Praise of Slow: How a Worldwide Movement is Challenging the Cult of Speed by Carl Honoré.
- Willing Slaves: How the Overwork Culture is Ruining Our Lives by Madeleine Bunting. She says that the past two decades have seen work elevated to a different level

and in the process helped create a culture of overwork. In the 1960s we decided that it was through work we found ourselves.

- Bonjour Paresse (Hello Laziness) by Corrine Maier.
- How to be Idle by Tom Hodgkinson. He also edits a magazine called The Idler, which celebrates laziness and attacks the work culture of the Western world. He says that long periods of languor, indolence and staring at the ceiling are needed by any creative person in order to develop ideas.
- The Joy of Laziness: How to Slow Down and Live Longer by Drs Peter and Michaela Axt. They say that pounding the treadmill, exercising excessively and leading a fast, stressful life leads to high blood pressure, heart and artery damage and the production of more free radicals (those pesky molecules which speed ageing). Laughing is healthier than running (I could have told you that) and people who would rather laze in a hammock than run a marathon have a better chance of living to a ripe old age.

MATAKANA SLOW TOWN

Matakana is a cute little town just north of Auckland and the people of Matakana have had the brilliant idea of making themselves an official Slow Town as set down by Slow Food. All over the world there are Slow Cities and Towns that require their members to preserve rural and small-town identity and to support production based on local cultural traditions and community hospitality. There are 70 Slow Towns in Italy, one in Britain and some up and coming ones in the United States. Matakana is crawling with vineyards, orchards, potteries, markets, olive groves and very expensive seaside homes. If you wanted to be happy forever, you would probably go and live there.

The two gals at the helm of Slow Town are Sally Meiklejohn and Dorothy Andersen. There are two farmers' markets, bike paths by the river, and a Matakana Village shopping and leisure centre is being built as we speak. Banish from your mind what you know of the words 'shopping and leisure centre' and think sympathetic architecture, good design and very good food. Do not think polyester leisure suits, low-rent drongoes and pinball machines. Slow Towns are not nostalgic backward places; they just want to reclaim what it used to mean to live in a small town – sharing food, firewood, stories, companionship, entertainment and work. They want to give the inhabitants a feeling of pride in where they live. And it's okay if you wear designer clothes and lipstick, because if Slow Food is

SUGAR Some people think that sugar is white death, the consumption of which will result in mental and physical morbidity or worse. Some parents think sugar makes their children hyperactive and aggressive. It is the parents who are driving the children nuts, not the sugar. Sweets make you happy and stop you from fainting in church. We don't call our lovers 'honey', 'sugar' and 'sweetie' for nothing – we do it because they are the dulcet decadence in our lives. They are our emotional seratonin.

In our culture we not only blame horrible children on sugar, we make it responsible for murders, heart disease, obesity, diabetes and anaemia. Nobody says, 'We are born loving sugar – how can it be bad for us? Is God trying to kill us?' No. They say, 'Get thee behind me Satan sugar. Stop making me delirious with pleasure.' If it were true that sugar is bad for you, the entire population of Brazil would be in prison for crimes of hyperactivity, because if they don't have a kilo of sugar in every dessert they can't function. I blame it on the samba. The truth is that any carbohydrate taken in excess will cause these problems, not just sugar. Now watch my lips when I say this: you can't trick sugar into not being sugar – honey from the buzzy bees, molasses from the Bayou, black unrefined sugar from the swamps of Thailand and coloured coffee crystals from Paris are still sugar. Brown sugar is not better than white sugar – the only difference is the colour and texture. A gram of sugar is a gram of sugar and it has four calories. Sorry.

How I know all this is because I went to the famous pink Chelsea Sugar Refinery in Auckland. It's great in there – all you have to do is lick the walls and you've got your hit for

S

the day. Chelsea is the only sugar refinery in New Zealand and, frankly, those folk deserve a medal. Until 1882 all New Zealand sugar was imported from Australia. Then, in 1884, the Birkenhead refinery was built on 65 hectares of prime land called Duck Creek. Working there was pretty miserable and very labour-intensive. Even as late as 1969, James K. Baxter wrote, 'Along those slippery floors a man might break a leg, and the foul stink of diesel fumes flows from the packing shed, and men in clouds of char dust move like animated dead.' (Char is the ash produced from burned cow bones, originally used for clarifying the sugar liquor. These days they use carbon dioxide and milk of lime.) The old part of the refinery is still like that – black and sticky, but the main part is so automated and clean the machines almost look human.

This is how sugar turns from that cane stuff growing in hot fields in Australia into the fine white grains in your tea. Every six weeks 28,000 tonnes of it arrives on the boat from Queensland in the form of raw unrefined sugar, not sugar cane. It is poured into a huge warehouse and sits there like blond sand dunes, waiting to be transferred by a medieval-looking conveyor belt into a mixer where the crystals are combined with a sugar syrup called 'sweetwater'. This process softens the outside coating of the sugar and turns it into a swirling, brown gloopy mass, which is then spun in a huge washing machine of hot water to clean it. It then becomes an amber liquid, and passes through a screen to remove more impurities and some colour. This liquid is pumped into carbonated tanks to be clarified by the chalk formed by lime and carbon dioxide. The amber liquid is then decoloured to become clear and is pumped into airtight vacuum pans, where water is evaporated off by boiling to leave sugar crystals. The crystals are dried and conditioned with dehumidified air to keep the product free flowing. That's how you make white sugar. Silky, soft icing sugar, indispensable in making shortbread, is also produced like that with the addition of tapioca starch.

If you want to make demerara sugar you harvest it in the cane fields of Mauritius. Demerara is derived from the initial pressing of the sugar cane, which allows some of the molasses syrup to remain in the crystal. What you are left with is a clear, golden colour and distinctive crunch, very good served in coffee. Golden syrup and treacle are by-products of the refining process and valued for their rich, chewy, slightly bitter qualities. Dark cane or muscovado sugar has a full-bodied, intense, exotic flavour, excellent in chocolate cakes and Indian and Asian recipes. It is made from natural molasses cane syrup and dissolves easily.

Christmas cake

2KG MIXED FRUIT, SUCH AS CURRANTS, RAISINS AND SULTANAS
6 TABLESPOONS SHERRY, COGNAC OR RUM
500G BUTTER
500G DARK CANE SUGAR
1 TABLESPOON GOLDEN SYRUP OR TREACLE
6 LARGE EGGS
1/2 PRESERVED LEMON, FINELY CHOPPED
500G FLOUR
2 TEASPOONS BAKING SODA
1/2 TEASPOON SALT
1 TEASPOON MIXED SPICE
1 TEASPOON GROUND CINNAMON
1 TEASPOON CURRY POWDER
200G WHOLE BLANCHED ALMONDS

1. Soak the dried fruit in the alcohol overnight.

2. The next morning, preheat the oven to 160°C. Cream the butter, sugar and golden syrup or treacle until soft and light. Beat in the eggs one by one.

3. Stir in the preserved lemon, then add the sifted flour, baking soda, salt and spices.

4. Stir in the alcohol-soaked fruit and almonds.

5. Line a large, tall cake tin with baking paper and pour in the mixture.

6. Place the cake on the lower rung of the oven and bake for 1 hour, then lower the heat to 120°C and bake for another 3 hours.

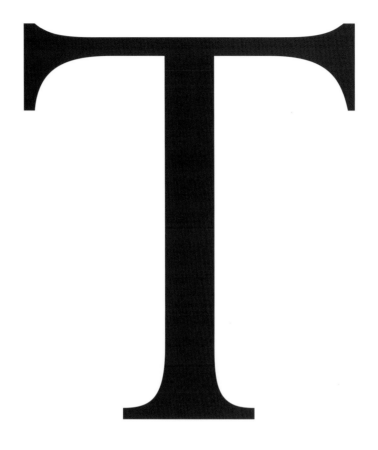

TAMARILLOS

This fruit is an icon in New Zealand, though it is originally from Central and South America. Ruby red or yellow, subtropical tamarillos or tree tomatoes are delicious eaten fresh as they come, make fantastic chutney, and are also good heated in the microwave so you can peel them easily, then plopped warm on vanilla ice-cream. They are sweet, zingy and tart, and New Zealanders are mad about them. When tree tomatoes began to be exported in the late sixties, the New Zealand marketing people decided to come up with a more distinctive name. They combined the Maori word tama meaning leader with *rillo* from *amarillo*, the Spanish word for yellow. The name has now become accepted worldwide.

TOMATOES

After potatoes, there is only one other vegetable that raises passion in my breast and that is the tomato, which strictly speaking is a fruit. The tomato of today is a complex item. No longer the love apple of days gone by, it is rather a crimson sphere carrying the genes of economic demands and social values. It seems to be the representative of food globalism. People never say in cafés and fashionable restaurants, 'Onions and turnips don't taste the way they did in the past.' No. They say, 'Look at this disgusting tomato! Not like the ones my father used to grow.' Part of the problem is that we no longer eat seasonally – we expect to have tomatoes all year round. The other part is that we have caught the 'beautiful' disease. We think

Honey-poached tomatoes

This recipe was inspired by the Moroccans, who make marvellous jam from tomatoes and honey.

1 CUP MANUKA HONEY

1 CUP WATER

½ TEASPOON GROUND CINNAMON OR 1 STICK

2 TABLESPOONS HOT PEPPER VINCOTTO

1½ TEASPOONS ORANGE-FLOWER WATER

6 LARGE TOMATOES INCLUDING STALKS

2 TEASPOONS SESAME SEEDS

POWDERED DRIED ROSEBUDS

KAPITI FIG AND HONEY ICE-CREAM

1. Place honey, water, cinnamon, vincotto and orange-flower water in a saucepan and dissolve together on a low heat.

2. Add tomatoes and poach very gently for 45 minutes.

3. Carefully remove tomatoes.

4. To serve, spoon some juice over the tomatoes, sprinkle with sesame seeds and powdered rosebuds. And have a glass bowl of ice-cream ready on the side.

serves 6

tomatoes have to look perfect, round and red. Well, they don't. Tomatoes can be green, red, pink, yellow, orange and almost black. They are best eaten in late summer. Some of the tastiest ones are the Roma Italian tomatoes. Quite often the vine-ripened ones are good too. But think about 'vine-ripened' – now we have to pay more to go back to nature's method. Doesn't anybody remember that all tomatoes grow on a vine?

The best tomatoes I ever ate in New Zealand (the very best were in Greece) were grown by Sue Sue. (Would you believe she married a guy called Mr Sue?) I will never forget the day I was teaching at Ruth Pretty's Cooking School in Te Horo and wasn't happy with the tomatoes. 'Never fear,' said Ruth, 'I'll call Sue Sue and she'll save the day.' Sure enough, an hour later a box arrived bursting with edible rubies of all sizes and shapes. Sue grows tomatoes that taste the way we imagined tomatoes tasted in our reinvented pasts – juicy, sweet, acidic and full of sunshine. Her tomatoes tasted almost as if they were still warm from the vine. If there's one thing you should grow, even if you have the tiniest windowsill, it's tomatoes.

I like making tomato sauce for spaghetti with fresh basil and garlic, eating ripe tomatoes with fresh mozzarella, olive oil, pepper and sea salt, and slow roasting acid-free ones with a sprinkling of olive oil, sugar and thyme for two hours.

There is such a thing as good hothouse tomatoes and they're grown by New Zealand Hothouse in Drury. One day, Brett Wharfe thought that there must be something easier than farming, a job where you can swan around indoors and maybe sit behind a poncy desk. He hit on hothouse tomatoes, but I doubt he even sees his desk these days. He bought his first four hectares in Ramarama and planted tomatoes under 1860 square metres of glass. Brett foresaw a growing need for greater professionalism in production and presentation of product, and was one of the first rebels to break away from the auction system. He went straight to Tom Ah Chee of Progressive Enterprises and got a contract to supply direct to Foodtown, Countdown and Three Guys supermarkets. New Zealand Hothouse now has nine hectares of state-of-the-art glasshouses on three sites growing tomatoes, as well as a core group of independent growers delivering their superior produce. The award-winning facility is one of the largest and most technologically advanced in the southern hemisphere. Brett now co-owns New Zealand Hothouse with David Levene (formerly of Levenes paints and homeware), a charming and interesting man, well-known in business circles for his innovative marketing and retail strategies.

It is absolutely fascinating walking through this giant world of glasshouses where all sorts of secret things are going on. Computers monitor the respiration of individual plants, and are able to tell when plants need more heat and when to open and shut the vents. Carbon dioxide levels are also monitored to ensure the plants get exactly what they need in the photosynthesis process. Water and nutrients are supplied to each plant through computer-controlled individual drippers. There are no weeds and therefore no herbicides in this world of glass, because the plants grow in pumice and sand. But there are pests, and they have a cute way of controlling them. When I mentioned the word 'organic' it made Brett a bit tetchy, as it does lots of growers in New Zealand. 'Actually,' he said, 'we have a better system, which is our answer to organic; it's called biotechnology. Instead of spraying we use predatory insects for pest control, and bumble bees are introduced to naturally pollinate the flowers.' Sure enough, when I looked closely at the posts

T

at the end of rows, there were little bee hives with very busy bees buzzing around. The fruit is left on the vine then hand-picked when flavour and taste are at their best. You can buy the delicious, sweet tomatoes as acid-free, cherry, truss (on the vine) and loose. The lines are called Summerhouse, Vintage Harvest and Super Sweet.

TOURISIM

TUI INN ADVENTURES AND ACCOMMODATION

Grant and Tangi Davan live in a remote settlement on the west coast of the North Island, south of Kaitaia in Northland. The tip of Northland is sacred to Maori, who believe this is where the spirits of the dead leave Aotearoa to make the voyage to Hawaiki, the ancestral homeland. Grant is actually Pakeha, but thinks he is a Maori – he talks the talk and walks the walk. A day with Grant might go like this: start by travelling on horseback through the Herekino harbour to a large, isolated, perfect West Coast beach; there you would collect and eat raw mussels, dive for kina and paua, and fish for mullet using nets; then you'd find a rusty old bit of tin, lay it over an open driftwood fire and sit on the beach to watch the sunset; when the tin got hot, you'd throw mussels, seafood and fish on, then eat. Then you'd feed the horses and let them find their own way home. At the end of the day you'd get the 4WD home, stopping off at the pub for a cold one.

Grant nets the fish either in the sea or the harbour. Netting in the sea is a two-person job. The fish are located by looking for brown-coloured areas caused by plankton, which attracts the fish that feed on it. One person carefully wades in, without spooking the fish, and unrolls the net, with the other person staying closer to the beach. Then the two people converge, trapping the fish. In the harbour Grant uses his leaky old tinny and rows to where the fish are jumping. The net is rolled out and set, left for half an hour and then drawn in, hopefully with mullet in it.

You can also do day or night hunting tours for possum, wild boar and goat, either on horseback or in the 4WD. Accommodation is backpackers' quarters and a campsite. A day with Grant and his family is a hilarious and beautiful thing, and will cost you the grand sum of $60. For more information go to the Taitokerau website: www.taitokerau.co.nz/tui_inn.htm.

GRAEME AVERY

Graeme is a highly successful entrepreneur, international businessman and athletics administrator, the former owner of Vinotica – the specialist gourmet food outlet – and chairman of Sileni Estates vineyard. He is the holder of all manner of voluntary sporting positions and founder and chairman of the Hawke's Bay Food Group and Hawke's Bay Wine Country Tourism Association. He made his fortune in medical publishing and then in 1996 decided to do something completely different focusing on the area of food and wine, thus Vinotica and Sileni Estates were born. Sileni is a winery, restaurant, culinary school, gourmet food store, and wine club with events, tours and tastings. When Graeme got to Hawke's Bay he discovered great produce and great vineyards but no co-ordination. He saw that the wholesale and supermarket structure worked against the small artisan producers, so he established the Hawke's Bay Food Group to develop the potential of both in terms of selling outlets and tourism. Why not put everyone under a common banner and draw support from each other, at the same time creating a direct market for the produce?

This led in 2000 to the Hawke's Bay Farmers' Market and a regional food trail, a tourism co-ordinated self-drive trail to 'farm gate' sales and producers. But the hook still wasn't big enough, so Graeme went on to develop the Hawke's Bay Wine Country brand. Graeme is a strong believer in regionalism. 'If you get the regions organised and strong, the country follows – this is where New Zealand needs to be,' he says. Graeme is a fervent believer of added-value exports and has spent much recent time establishing more than 20 international markets for Sileni. He also helped establish the very successful New Zealand food, wine and tourism restaurant, the 'Kiwi Grill' in Newburyport, Boston, in the USA.

A recent development at Sileni has been the creation of a new home for The Village Press olive oil company, who now press their olives in two presses on the property. Also there have been major renovations to extend the size of the restaurant and the cellar-door shop areas, along with function rooms. Graeme was awarded 'New Zealander of the Year 2003' by *North & South* magazine for his contribution to business, tourism and sport.

The website is: www.sileni.co.nz.

HAWKE'S BAY WINE COUNTRY FOOD TRAIL

The Wine Country Food Trail goes from strength to strength, and the participants can be recognised by the brilliant sunshine logo in blue, yellow and red on their farm posts, winery doors, orchard gates and restaurant portals. The latest innovation is the terrific and extremely well put together *Complete Guide to Hawke's Bay Wine Country*, edited by Jeanette Kelly. Jeanette is a very clued-up woman who came down from corporate Auckland to Hawke's Bay with her husband Ian Hawthorne – Ian owns the best café and grinds the best coffee in Hawke's Bay. She took one look at Hawke's Bay and efficiently organised the food guide, doing the practical work to implement Graeme Avery's ideas. The classy guide book has sections on wine, dining and food, arts, tours, attractions and lodgings. There are fold-out maps, colour photos, history, events – in short everything a person needs to be happy in Hawke's Bay. In February there is Harvest Hawke's Bay, a huge wine, food and music festival. The Mission Concert at Mission winery also happens in February, attracting 25,000 punters to hear an international performer. In March there is the Edible Arts Festival, which kicks off with Napier's Great Long Lunch. In June there's the Hawke's Bay Winemakers Charity Wine Auction. In October there's the Hawke's Bay A&P Show and the A&P Mercedes Wine Awards. As you can see Hawke's Bay is a party province and they spend their lives lurching from one celebration to the next.

The other really great thing about Hawke's Bay is that they have the longest place name in the world – Taumata whakatangi hangakoauau o tamatea turi pukakapiki maunga horo nuku pokai whenua kitanatahu, which means: the hilltop where Tamatea with big knees, conqueror of mountains, eater of land, traveller over land and sea, played his koauau to his beloved. The Taumata walk is near Porangahau, Central Hawke's Bay. Maori chief, Tamatea, composed this lament to name the prominent hill as a tribute to his brother, who was killed in battle there. Hundreds of years later, the 250-hectare farm is still owned by Tamatea's descendants, the Scott family.

CREATIVE TOURISM

The originators of these workshops for visitors are Crispin Raymond and Greg Richards. They define Creative Tourism as 'learning a skill on holiday that is part of the culture of the country or community being visited'. They say that 'creative tourists develop their creative potential and get closer to local people, through informal participation in interactive workshops and learning experiences that draw on the culture of their holiday destinations'. In other words, don't just stand there passively watching, get in there and do

it. Creative tourists become actively involved in the culture of the countries and communities they visit. While the cultural tourist enjoys visiting a pottery studio or sampling a range of local foods for example, the creative tourist takes part in a pottery course or learns to cook local dishes. The creative tourist is always a participant, someone who learns by doing, someone who finds enjoyment and fulfilment in developing new abilities, someone who wants to interact with local people. As a result, creative tourists get closer to the cultures of the countries they visit.

You can do workshops on Maori culture, on taste and on art. The taste workshops include olive oil, organic brewing, winemaking, seafood preparation and cooking, and making pavlova. (See 'Loaves and Fishes' entry under Cooking Schools, page 59.) They will also recommend accommodation. All this can be perused on their website at: www.creativetourism.co.nz.

THE BIG PICTURE

This is such a good name, with its layers of meaning, and the ingenious Phil Parker is such a perfect host for a gig like this. The Big Picture in Cromwell, Central Otago, is a one-stop promotion/education centre for the wine industry. Phil is famous for making his own methode champenoise, and First Light Red wine, and for his Smash Palace wine bar in Gisborne with the DC3 perched above it. He met his beautiful wife Cath in 1987 and between them they have six children. They came to Central Otago for a holiday, and the rest is history. Now you can find Phil enthusing to the punters in the aroma room, the auditorium, the café and the wine shop. His vision was to create a user-friendly wine experience for the time-constrained visitor who doesn't know a lot about wine but would like to. Wine tourism in Central is big, but Phil feels a lot of travellers appreciate a bit more information before hitting the vineyards. The Big Picture gives you enough information to get the most out of your wine-trail experience by teaching you a few basics.

The Big Picture is also a food experience, because you get to eat stylish food in the café. Phil and his chef Paul are also developing wine- and food-tasting plates, which are really for the enthusiast because they're quite complicated. For example, he will give you a glass of pinot noir along with unusual food concoctions to illustrate the flavour notes found in the wine. The high note is flowers, violets, spice and honey; the middle note is berries; and the base note is earthy flavours like thyme, kumara and mushrooms. This is a clever and sophisticated idea. It reminds me of the gardens

T

at Copia, the wine institute in Napa Valley in California, where they have enclosed gardens for different types of wine. For example, you have a cabernet sauvignon garden with flavours and smells growing in it that remind you of those flavours in the wine – mint, cherry trees, blackberry bushes, sage. Also in the garden are vegetables that would go well with the wine, such as artichokes and beetroot.

The first part of The Big Picture experience is the aroma room, where you can let loose your senses and discover the smells that are used to describe wine varieties and styles. There are over 200 aromas, including 20 perfumes to instruct an 'aroma memory'. Then you move into the flight room or auditorium, seating 45, for an 18-minute 'virtual flight' in a helicopter across the spectacular landscape and vineyards of Central Otago. As you visit each vineyard, you see the winemakers talking about their wines, and at the same time you taste their wine, which is sitting in front of you. Moana Jackson sings on the flight and talks about the whakapapa of Central Otago. You also get a good view of the lay of the land. After your flight, you can have something to eat in the courtyard and choose from the selection of 45 local wines.

This is such a good idea that I'm hoping Phil will do The Big Picture all over New Zealand. The website is: www.wineadventure.co.nz.

TRUFFLES

The black Périgord truffle (*Tuber melanosporum*) is a fungus that produces its fruit under the surface of the soil. Truffles are black, roughly spherical and covered with small diamond-shaped projections, which make them look a little like deformed avocados. The Périgord truffle prefers a limestone-rich alkaline soil and a climate similar to that found in the hills to the south of the Massif Central in France. Such sites can be found in North Canterbury, Hawke's Bay, North Otago and Poverty Bay. *Truffières* (truffle plantations) have also been established elsewhere, on naturally acidic soils that have been dressed with large amounts of lime. Most of the *truffières* have been established well away from trees that might harbour fungi and compete for space on the roots of the host trees. An adequate amount of moisture in the soil (but not an excess) is also known to improve truffle yields. All the New Zealand truffle plantations have some form of irrigation.

In 1987 Alan Hall and his wife Lynley planted half a hectare of English oaks and hazels, impregnated (please pay attention) with the spores of black truffles. The Froggies said it couldn't be done, and even if it could, the fungus would taste like some impoverished bush pig mushroom, bearing no relationship to the noble black Périgord truffle, one of the most expensive foods in the world along with caviar and *foie gras*. But this is New Zealand folks, and what we can't do with some No. 8 wire doesn't really bear scrutiny. So when Dr Ian Hall of the Crop and Food Research Institute at Mosgiel and his brother Alan Hall decided that they wanted truffles in their very own backyard, they went forth and planted some.

Since Alan's *truffière* was established, a further 20 have been planted between Ohiwa in the Bay of Plenty and Alexandra in Central Otago. And wouldn't you know it – in the Uzés area of the Languedoc in France, they are now successfully growing truffles from inoculated trees.

According to recent information from France, fruiting normally begins nine to ten years after planting, although occasionally it can begin earlier. Truffles are normally harvested during midwinter with the aid of specially trained dogs. In France it is now illegal to use pigs to sniff out the truffles because after the season, some irresponsible truffle hunters were turning the pigs out into the wild where they were unable to look after themselves. Demand exceeds supply. Bobby the truffle hound at Alan's place has found many truffles – the first weighing 250g and the largest a huge 475g.

The good news is that Ian Hall, Gordon Brown and James Byars wrote a book called *The Black Truffle*, touted as a world first – the only book about truffles written in English – and covering such topics as truffle history, cooking with truffles, establishing a *truffière* and notes about harvesting truffles and marketing. The bad news is the book is out of print.

The latest news with Alan and Lynley is that they don't have time any more to grow the truffles for restaurants, so busy are they using the fungi to inoculate baby trees for sale to other truffle growers. There are nine growers in Gisborne alone. The world cannot have too many truffles – it is hugely undersupplied. So desperate are Asians for them that one day a Korean businessman turned up on their doorstep with a suitcase full of money, demanding to be supplied with 100kg a day! They still have Bobby, the ex-customs and excise dog, to sniff the truffles out of the warm ground. So if you still want a truffle, you can go to their gate in the season and they'll probably sell you some. A 20g truffle costs $60. Their website is: www.oakland-truffles.com. The best way to eat truffles is finely sliced on to creamy pasta, scrambled eggs or potatoes.

VEGEMITE

Vegemite is a spread made from yeast extract and is one of the clearest markers of cultural identity of any food in the world. If you say you love Vegemite, people don't say, 'Oh, you must be from Bolivia.' No. They say, 'Oooh yuk, you must be a New Zealander or Australian.' It is thick and black, and tastes salty, caramely and sharp, and every New Zealander is addicted to it spread on their morning toast, which is then cut into soldiers. It is also very good on sandwiches that have been slathered with butter, and a small dollop of it has improved many an insipid gravy. It was invented over 80 years ago in Australia and contains yeast extract, malt extract, caramel, vegetable flavours and vitamins. Any human who is not a New Zealander or an Australian loathes it – everyone else still eats truckloads of it. We are born with only one taste preference and that is for sweetness, so we had to learn to like strong-tasting Vegemite just as we had to learn to like other harsh tastes such as coffee, alcohol and pepper. In my babyhood in the 1950s I was privileged to listen to a wee song that went like this:

We're happy little Vegemites, as bright as bright can be.
We all enjoy our Vegemite for breakfast, lunch and tea.
Our mummies say we're growing stronger every single week
Because we love our Vegemite,
We all adore our Vegemite,
It puts a rose in every cheek.

Okay, so it's a little repetitive but when you're five you don't notice because you're too busy smearing the delicious stuff all over yourself.

Then there is Marmite, which was invented by the

English. The word comes from the French *marmite* meaning stock pot. It is sweeter than Vegemite (which is a copy of Marmite), but basically the same thing, and contains yeast, wheatgerm, caramel, sugar, herbs, spices and vitamins. Most people think it has meat extract in it, but it doesn't. Maybe it used to, but it doesn't anymore. We in New Zealand eat about equal amounts of Marmite and Vegemite.

VENISON

The first deer (red deer and fallow deer) to be imported into New Zealand landed in Nelson in 1861. By 1917 a hundred deer had been imported and up until 1930 their descendants were protected. Protection was lifted because the deer were causing over-grazing of forest canopies and erosion. The deer were then hunted – sometimes by helicopter, sometimes on foot – to keep them under control, until our European cousins thought it would be a good idea to eat our excellent venison.

In 1968 over 150,000 carcasses were recovered in the South Island alone. The demand for deer meat from overseas was so great that in 1969 it became legal to farm deer in New Zealand in a system called fanning. There was some concern about the ability of deer to adapt to life in captivity, but deer had already shown how smart and versatile they were by feeding at night to avoid the helicopter shooters. As it turns out, farming has worked well, and now most deer are farmed on mixed livestock farms, that is, with sheep and beef. Because deer were classified as game, the processing of feral deer carcasses that had been shot had to be kept separate from other meats. Farmed deer also required separate slaughtering plants, so special abattoirs were built alongside feral processing facilities. In 1990 the Game Industry Board had the brilliant idea of marketing New Zealand venison under the name cervena, however, nobody in New Zealand ever got used to this name, and it seems to be less used now.

There are 1.8 million deer in New Zealand on 4000 farms and the South Island has 64 per cent of the national herd. New Zealand now has the most advanced deer farming in the world, and no steroids or growth hormones are used. Those woolly southerners love wild meat. Venison is sold as medallions, stir-fry venison, and minced and diced venison in the New World and Pak 'n Save supermarkets in the South Island. There are also other suppliers throughout New Zealand. For export, venison is increasingly sold as chilled, high-quality cuts, rather than frozen. Our farmed venison is much more melt in your mouth than wild deer. However, as venison has almost no fat, care has to be taken when cooking it so that it remains tender. Small cuts should be cooked until still pink in the middle. Roasts, contrary to popular opinion, do not benefit from marinating – the wine just leaches moisture out of the meat. I have found the gentle art of poaching to be an excellent solution.

Poached venison

You will need a table napkin and some kitchen string for this recipe.

900G (MORE OR LESS) DENVER LEG OF VENISON, BONED OUT

NEW ZEALAND SEA SALT AND FRESHLY GROUND BLACK PEPPER

HANDFUL OF FRESH MINT LEAVES

3 SPRIGS OF FRESH DILL

WHOLE NUTMEG

1 LITRE VENISON OR BEEF STOCK

BOUQUET GARNI
(thyme, bay leaf, parsley)

1. Lay the venison leg out flat, sprinkle generously with salt and pepper, lay on the mint and dill leaves and grate about $^1/_2$ teaspoon of nutmeg all over. Roll up in a napkin and secure with kitchen string.

2. Bring the stock to the boil in a large saucepan and throw in some pepper, salt and the bouquet garni. Place the venison in the saucepan, add water to cover, turn down to a simmer, cover with a lid and poach for 20 minutes for medium-rare and 30 minutes for well-done.

3. Remove the meat from the saucepan and rest for 15 minutes still rolled in the napkin. If you're going to eat the venison at room temperature, just leave it in the napkin until you need it. If you're eating it hot, take the napkin off and carve thick slices at the table. This is very good eaten with ratatouille.

serves 6

Verjuice roasted leg of lamb with fennel

This lamb is covered in an almond and hazelnut paste, then roasted in verjuice and served with sautéed fennel bulb wrapped in vine leaves. It would be good with slow-roasted tomatoes and pasta.

for the paste:
1 CUP BLANCHED ALMONDS
1 CUP HAZELNUTS
¼ CUP FRESH SAGE
2 CUPS PARSLEY HEADS
(keep stalks for roasting liquid)
4 CLOVES GARLIC
SEA SALT AND FRESHLY GROUND
BLACK PEPPER
¾ CUP EXTRA VIRGIN OLIVE OIL
¼ CUP WHITE VERJUICE

for the lamb:
¼ CUP EXTRA VIRGIN OLIVE OIL
1 CUP VERJUICE
1 CUP WATER
1 LEMON, QUARTERED
1 BUNCH FRESH SAGE
1.8KG LEG OF LAMB

for the fennel:
1KG FENNEL BULBS
1 CUP VERJUICE
24 FRESH, TENDER, MEDIUM-SIZED
VINE LEAVES
EXTRA VIRGIN OLIVE OIL IN
SPRAY CAN

1. Preheat the oven to 200°C.

2. To make the paste, roast the almonds for about 5 minutes or until starting to colour and release their essential oils. Then roast the hazelnuts and rub off the skins with a tea-towel.

3. In a food processor, blend the nuts with the herbs, cloves, salt and pepper until fairly smooth but still a little chunky, adding the olive oil as you go.

4. Finally blend in the verjuice and taste for seasoning. The paste should be quite thick.

1. To roast the lamb, lower oven temperature to 175°C. Put the olive oil, verjuice, water, lemon wedges and sage into the roasting pan and place the lamb on top. Make superficial slashes in the skin of the leg and spread the paste all over, pushing it into the cuts.

2. Roast in a fan oven for 50 minutes for pink at the bone, and just over 1 hour for well done. Cover with tinfoil if the crust appears to be burning.

3. Remove the lamb from the oven, cover with tinfoil and let rest for at least 15 minutes. Meanwhile remove the herbs and lemons from the sauce, taste for seasoning and keep warm.

1. While the lamb is roasting, prepare the fennel. Chop off the stalks, cut in half lengthwise, remove the woody heart in a V-shaped cut and discard. Wash fennel and plunge into boiling, salted water for 5 minutes, drain, rinse in cold water to refresh colour and pat dry.

2. Heat the verjuice. Blanch the vine leaves by dipping them for 1 minute in the very hot verjuice. Pat dry, then spray with olive oil.

3. Gather the fennel into bundles, wrap the bundles in the vine leaves and attach the edges of the leaves with toothpicks. Sauté the fennel bundles in a little olive oil in a frying pan for about 5 minutes on each side until golden.

4. To serve, slice the lamb from top to bottom (not across) to get the best of every slice. Eat up the fennel bundles, vine leaves and all.

serves 6

two hundred & nine

VERJUICE

Verjuice or verjus is the liquid extracted from unripened grapes. It is unfermented and tastes like apples that have been marinating in lemon juice. Maggie Beer had already made it famous in Australia, and a wonderful woman in Hawke's Bay called Alison McKee was the first person to start making it in New Zealand in 1999. Her company is called thevineco, and from her own vineyard Alison handpicks midsummer riesling and cabernet sauvignon grapes which have a high acid and low sugar content.

Verjuice dates back to the Middle Ages, when it was mixed with lemon juice, sorrel and other herbs and spices for use in sauces, condiments and in deglazing. It is excellent for deglazing pans, and in vinaigrettes and sauces, red meats and poultry. Because like many under-ripe fruits the early-picked grapes are high in pectin – the substance that causes jam to set – verjuice also has an emulsifying action, giving a silky texture to sauces. It must be refrigerated after opening, and I think it's gorgeous as a summer drink with a slice of lemon and an ice-cube. Alison also makes verjuice and vanilla-bean syrup, which received fantastic reviews at the London Food Show, and verjuice mustard.

VINEGAR

Anyone can make vinegar and still more anyones can make flavoured vinegars, but only one outfit in New Zealand can make proper aged vinegar according to the French 'Orléans' method. Most modern vinegars are manufactured over a few days in stainless-steel vessels. These have built-in oxygen delivery and temperature-controlled systems. This is the fastest and cheapest way to make vinegar. Prenzel, however, do things the slow way, producing an infinitely better product. They fill some oak barrels with Marlborough sauvignon blanc wine and some with cabernet sauvignon wine, then seed them with an acetobacter or vinegar 'mother'. The barrels are put in an insulated shed – which contains up to five barrels kept at 30°C. The idea is to increase oxygen supply, so that the barrels lie on their side and each one is only half full. A hole is left in the barrel so that the air can flow over the surface. After three or four years all the alcohol has gone, then the liquid is diluted with water to bring the acetic acid level down from around seven per cent to five per cent. The vinegar is then filtered to get rid of the mother, but not pasteurised as this changes the flavour. This is the Orléans method. It is wasteful, as some of the wine is lost through evaporation – 'the angel's share'. It is also expensive, as a considerable amount of storage and labour is involved.

But the result is incomparable to the forcing tanks of industrial vinegars. Prenzel vinegar tastes as it did to the medieval palate, with a wide range of layered flavours and subtleties. No attempt is made to sugar or otherwise soften the product – it is just pure vinegar with no chemical additives of any kind.

Prenzel's website is: www.prenzel.com.

Beetroot carpaccio with sauvignon-blanc vinegar

4 MEDIUM-SIZED BEETROOT (ABOUT 700G)

3 TABLESPOONS EXTRA VIRGIN OLIVE OIL

SEA SALT AND FRESHLY GROUND BLACK PEPPER

2 TABLESPOONS PRENZEL SAUVIGNON BLANC VINEGAR

2 CUPS ROCKET GREENS

2 TABLESPOONS FRESH FETA CHEESE

2 TABLESPOONS CHOPPED FRESH MINT OR VIETNAMESE MINT

1. Preheat the oven to 200°C. Trim beetroot and place in a roasting pan. Brush with one tablespoon of oil and sprinkle with salt and pepper. Roast for one hour or until very tender.

2. Remove beetroot, cool and peel. Slice very thinly on a mandolin grater or with a sharp knife.

3. Arrange beetroot in a petal pattern on four dinner plates. Drizzle with one tablespoon of oil and one tablespoon of vinegar. Sprinkle with salt and pepper.

4. Toss rocket in a bowl with the other tablespoon of oil, the other tablespoon of vinegar, salt, pepper and crumbled feta. Arrange in a small pile in the middle of the beetroot and sprinkle with mint.

serves 4

WASABI

Wasabi is a rhizome of the *Cruciferae* family. There are two varieties of wasabi grown in the world – one in clean, cold streams and one in soil. Wasabi can be difficult to grow, preferring cold winter to hot summer and taking 18 months to two years to mature before harvest. It has a very clean, refined heat – unlike the copycat stuff found in tubes, which is a combination of horseradish, mustard and green dye with a little true wasabi added. If this paste were real, it would be very expensive. The best way to eat wasabi is to grate some of the root directly on to your plate, keeping the rest of the root fresh in a glass of water in the fridge. The heat dissipates very quickly, as it is so volatile; and the big problem for producers has always been how to preserve it. One of the secrets is oil. Once you've figured out how to capture it in oil, you have a valuable product on your hands.

Hi Tech Foods in Christchurch have managed to do this.

And of course, once you've tasted fresh, real wasabi, it's very hard to go back. We discovered wasabi in New Zealand via Japanese cuisine and now we use it in all sorts of ways – it's wonderful in mayonnaise, mashed potatoes, butter, on sandwiches and with fish, seafood and meat. Some chefs put it in ice-cream and chocolate desserts.

A number of studies have shown that the active ingredients in *Wasabia japonica* are able to kill a number of different types of cancer cells, reduce the possibility of getting blood clots, encourage the body's own defences to discard cells that have started to mutate, and act as an antibacterial and antifungal agent against food poisons.

Coppersfolly in Christchurch make a pure wasabi paste that tastes of the real thing and doesn't have any horseradish, artificial additives or fillers – it's called Pure

Wasabi and it's grown in soil with no sprays. The paste is mixed with oil, lemon juice and citric acid. You can buy it in good food shops or order it from the website at: www.coppersfolly.co.nz.

New Zealand Wasabi Ltd in Warkworth make Namida Paste. No pesticides, herbicides or non-organic sprays are used on this water-grown wasabi. All inputs are certified organic. The wasabi is hand-picked, sorted and washed prior to grading. You can buy it from their website at: www.wasabi.co.nz.

Unfortunately nobody in New Zealand will sell you fresh wasabi, but you could make friends with a grower …

WATER

Water resources and aquatic ecosystems are essential to New Zealand's economy. They are also a significant part of our natural heritage and our recreational activities, and of particular practical and spiritual value for Maori. Water quality in New Zealand, although generally high by world standards, varies considerably. Substantial rainfall feeds an extensive lake and river system, but fresh water is distributed very unevenly across the country. In some places water is plentiful, but in other areas demands sometimes cannot be met.

The best sites for hydroelectric power schemes have already been used, and to develop most of the remaining sites would conflict with other uses. The quality of our coastal marine environment is highly variable too, with less than 0.1 per cent of our marine environment currently protected, compared with 30 per cent of our land area. Land use intensification is placing even greater pressure on both the marine and freshwater environments, and these support some of New Zealand's most important ecosystems and much of the country's biodiversity. Plentiful, clean water is part of New Zealand's heritage. Managing our waters to make sure they stay that way – or are restored to this state – is a task for all of us.

One day about 20 years ago, the developed world mysteriously stopped drinking tap water. There is absolutely nothing wrong with New Zealand tap water, in fact in some areas, it is delicious, pure spring water. Suddenly we had to drink bottled water and now we're addicted to it. They say we have to drink lots of water because we lose three litres of the stuff a day from breathing, perspiration and elimination.

We bottle lots of spring water in New Zealand, and the one I like the best is Simon Woolley's Antipodes water, not only for the soft, crisp, clean taste but also for the design of the bottle. I love the taste of the mineral silicate in water, which is good for the breakdown of aluminium in the body, and Antipodes has lots of it. Silica is picked up by water as it runs through clay. I think that's why I also like swimming in rivers; I like the muddy, minerally taste and smell of river water.

Simon got the idea for the shape of the bottle from the old half-gallon sherry bottle New Zealanders used to be so fond of. The glass bottle, which comes in 500ml and 1000ml sizes, is so chic you can put it on the table. I prefer sparkling water, but you can also get it still. You can use sparkling spring water in cooking. It's good to mix it into the batter for tempura, the French cook carrots in it, the Serbs make bread with it, and some people make sorbet with it.

On the Antipodes bottle it says, 'To be at your table today this water has been brought to the surface from the deepest water reservoirs in New Zealand. It has spent decades under enormous pressure in vast underground canyons more than 200 metres below the surface. This pressure from within the reservoirs creates a natural filtration process that has led to Antipodes being scientifically categorised as the deepest, highest-quality mineral water in New Zealand. It has then been bottled at source providing a purity, clarity and taste that can only be found deep down at the end of the earth. Gently carbonated with the finest bead, Antipodes is the perfect partner for fine foods. Drink chilled, drink often and live well.'

This water is primarily for the trade, but Simon delivers on order to your home and his website is: www.antipodeswater.co.nz.

WHITEBAIT

When I was a child, whitebait (inanga in Maori) were plentiful and cost almost nothing. You could even get them in fish-and-chip shops. Now they cost a fortune. Be careful not to buy the inferior, tasteless, frozen Chinese variety. The West Coast region of the South Island is one of the few places in New Zealand where whitebait still run. During the season, September to November normally, people flock to the mouths of rivers and streams with their nets, or erect their stands to scoop up this delicacy, which has an almost mythical status on the West Coast. Whitebait nets can be purchased at any sports shop or hardware store in town along with all the strict rules and regulations.

All whitebait spend part of their life cycle in fresh water and the other part in the sea. Tiny fish hatch in late autumn and are carried along rivers out to sea, where they live and grow over the winter. In the late winter and early spring, whitebait migrate back up rivers and streams, finally settling and growing in bush-covered streams and swamps. The start of the migration is thought to be influenced by river flows and phases of the moon. Mature inanga adults migrate downstream to lower river sections and estuaries to spawn in grasses that are covered by water during spring tides. The eggs remain in the grass until the next spring tide covers them again, when the young hatch and are carried out to sea.

On the East Coast of the South Island, whitebait are something of a secret and folk from these parts talk little about them. Each spring when the water warms and the moon is full, whitebait run the mighty Waiau River. They are found near the river mouth, and access is tricky, so they use jet boats to get at them. I got the following recipe from a gentleman down there who drank whisky and water in equal measure. It's a rich recipe but the creamy sauce, delicate whitebait and soothing pasta seem made to go together.

WILD FOOD
Wild food is what people in Asia, South America, Africa and current war zones eat for breakfast, either because they don't have anything else to eat or they don't believe in waste. In New Zealand we think it's desperately reckless and intrepid to eat worms, possums, scorpions and anything caught threshing about in the bush. Game is of course another thing and an entirely honourable source of meat. There is a Wild Food Festival in the West Coast region of the South Island every year, and the best thing about it is the genre of people who attend and the stall that sells spit-roasted wild pig. The Wild Food Festival is unlike any other food or wine festival in New Zealand in its complete lack of pretension and in the friendliness and warmth of the West Coast people. They make visitors to the festival and to the West Coast feel like a million dollars, which must be why people keep coming back year after year. It certainly ain't for the sautéed huhu grubs, bulls' penises, grasshoppers and mountain oysters (sheep's testicles). This festival, which started off humbly in 1990, has grown hugely. How many food festivals do you know of that have a traditional band and end with a hooley in the form of a barn dance? You can get some good beer there, too, and wild mountain moonshine served by drench gun. And you can also meet wild mountain men, if that's what your taste runs to.

Whitebait with tagliolini

for the sauce:
2 SHALLOTS, FINELY CHOPPED
2 TABLESPOONS BUTTER
2 CLOVES GARLIC, FINELY CHOPPED
1½ CUPS CHARDONNAY
300ML CREAM
SEA SALT
FRESHLY GRATED NUTMEG
FRESHLY GROUND GREEN PEPPERCORNS

1. In a medium-sized saucepan gently cook the shallots in the butter.

2. Add the garlic and wine, and reduce by boiling to half the amount.

3. Add the cream and peppercorns and reduce again for a few minutes.

4. Add salt and nutmeg to taste and keep warm.

for the rest:
200G FRESH TAGLIOLINI
(VERY NARROW STRIPS OF PASTA)
400G WHITEBAIT
FRESHLY GRATED PARMESAN CHEESE
FINELY CHOPPED PARSLEY OR CHERVIL

1. Cook the pasta until and drain.

2. Cook the whitebait in the hot sauce for 1 minute.

3. Twirl the pasta into the centre of 4 warm plates, pile whitebait on top, spoon on some sauce and top with Parmesan and chopped parsley or chervil.

serves 4 as a starter

RRECTWEIG

NO SPRINGS

546 / 49

HUTCHINSON'S
Auto-Beam

index

VIKING

Published by the Penguin Group

Penguin Group (NZ), cnr Airborne and Rosedale Roads, Albany,
Auckland 1310, New Zealand (a division of Pearson New Zealand Ltd)
Penguin Group (USA) Inc., 375 Hudson Street,
New York, New York 10014, USA
Penguin Group (Canada), 10 Alcorn Avenue, Toronto,
Ontario, Canada M4V 3B2 (a division of Pearson Penguin Canada Inc.)
Penguin Books Ltd, 80 Strand, London, WC2R 0RL, England
Penguin Ireland, 25 St Stephen's Green,
Dublin 2, Ireland (a division of Penguin Books Ltd)
Penguin Group (Australia), 250 Camberwell Road, Camberwell,
Victoria 3124, Australia (a division of Pearson Australia Group Pty Ltd)
Penguin Books India Pvt Ltd, 11, Community Centre,
Panchsheel Park, New Delhi 110 017, India
Penguin Books (South Africa) (Pty) Ltd, 24 Sturdee Avenue,
Rosebank, Johannesburg 2196, South Africa

Penguin Books Ltd, Registered Offices: 80 Strand, London, WC2R 0RL, England

First published in 2005
1 3 5 7 9 10 8 6 4 2

Designed and typeset by Athena Sommerfeld
Text editor Cook Publishing Services
Prepress by microdot
Printed by Everbest Printing Co. Ltd, China

ISBN 0 67 004560 8
A catalogue record for this book is available
from the National Library of New Zealand.

www.penguin.co.nz